THE
CHINESE-AMERICAN METHOD

RAISING OUR CHILDREN WITH THE BEST OF BOTH WORLDS

Linda Hu and John X. Wang

Translated by
Fanny Wang and Kathy Wang

Order this book online at www.trafford.com
or email orders@trafford.com

Most Trafford titles are also available at major online book retailers.

Printed in the United States of America.

ISBN: 978-1-4669-7366-4 (sc)
ISBN: 978-1-4669-7365-7 (hc)
ISBN: 978-1-4669-6843-1 (e)

Library of Congress Control Number: 2012923924

Trafford rev. 01/17/2013

www.trafford.com

North America & international
toll-free: 1 888 232 4444 (USA & Canada)
phone: 250 383 6864 ♦ fax: 812 355 4082

Contents

This book is narrated by Linda Hu

CHAPTER 1

News of Victory

Initial Victory

December 14, 2007. After school, Fanny rushed home without staying in school for an extra moment.

The air was filled with tension when she arrived. The invisible pressure made it impossible for us to breathe. My entire family was extremely anxious as we hovered in front of Fanny's computer. We had been waiting for this moment for the whole day because today, Yale would announce its Early Action decisions. For so many years, we, along with our children, put in so much effort to obtain a good education for them, so you can imagine how much we wanted Fanny to receive good news!

Fanny's eyes were fixated on the computer screen. From her fingers constantly typing on the keyboard, we could sense her nervous energy, but we could not read her restlessness or expectations from her facial expressions. Bill stood off to the side, as usual, chattering about his *Pokémon* hero, Reshiram.

"Bill, can you be quiet?" Fanny had finally had enough and called him out.

"If this is America, don't I have the freedom of speech?" Bill snapped back. As we were about to interrupt their argument, Kathy joined the fray as she held our family's pet cat, Blacky.

"Bill, shut up!" she ordered firmly.

Facing the alliance of his two sisters, Bill had to surrender, but his mouth still could not stop.

"Yes, I'm sorry, my two queens!" he sullenly retorted, always wanting to get the last word in any conversation.

Yale University is among the world's best colleges. In its long history, many outstanding students have been rejected by its admissions office. We all wondered if the same result awaited Fanny.

At 5:00 PM, it was time for Yale to release its decisions. However, when we checked its Web site, we only saw an error message informing us that the server was down because the traffic at the moment was too heavy. There were countless students and parents just like us, waiting for this moment, and we envied those who had already seen their results. After what seemed like an eternity, we successfully accessed the Yale Web site and logged into Fanny's account.

"Woof, woof!" The picture of Yale's bulldog mascot was barking at us loudly from the top right corner of the Web page. Under the mascot, "Welcome to Yale!" flashed in large letters.

"Fanny has been admitted!" we all cried out. My eyes began to tear up with joy. We cheered loudly, giving each other high fives in celebration.

Yale's admissions letter to Fanny said,

> *Congratulations on your admission to Yale College, Class of 2012! It gives me great pleasure to send you a letter that honors your accomplishments and marks such an important moment in your life. You have every reason to feel proud of both your work and your aspirations.*

On December 23, 2007, our family boarded a flight to the Florida State Resort in Fort Lauderdale. I joked with Fanny before we left, "This holiday season was depending on you. If you were not accepted into Yale, you would never hear the end of it from us."

This made Kathy and Bill roar with laughter. On the side, Fanny turned to John and shyly pleaded, "Daddy, you have to help me!"

With John on her side, Fanny was freed from our teasing. We were all happy to be together and on our way to sunny Fort Lauderdale to have a great vacation as a family.

Christmas with the Family

As the airplane gently flew through the clouds, Kathy and Bill chattered nonstop in the front seat. However, Fanny was surprisingly quiet.

"Look! Apparitions of the Virgin Mary! Doesn't that cloud look just like your face, Fanny?" Kathy pretended to be surprised, pointed to a piece of cloud, and shook Fanny. Fanny, curious, turned to look out the window.

"Who says it looks like me? It looks nothing like me!" Fanny exclaimed.

"It looks just like you!" Bill chimed in with Kathy. I touched John's shoulder, and we smiled at each other. We knew that Fanny was still thinking about the applications she had sent to Harvard University and Princeton University.

We had a great time in Florida with our children as we relaxed with the sun, sand, and waves. The sky was so blue, and the sun was so bright. At the same time, we also looked forward to more and even better news from other colleges!

News of Victory

Fanny applied for eleven universities in the United States: Harvard, Yale, Princeton, MIT, Columbia, University of California—Berkeley, University of Pennsylvania, Johns Hopkins University, Caltech, Cornell, and New York University. These are all elite U.S. colleges with highly competitive admissions processes. Although we were confident that Fanny would have a good chance of gaining admission into some of these universities, we were not going to relax anytime soon.

When applying to U.S. universities, a student's high school performance plays a large role. Universities not only examine the student's ninth to eleventh grade high school performance but also base their decisions on the first half of twelfth grade and the student's midterm grades and test scores. At the end of the student's senior year, the high school sends the student's complete transcript to the university the student is going to attend. If the student's grades fall, the university can withdraw its offer of admission. This expectation was clearly pointed out in the Princeton University acceptance letter:

> *Let me remind you that your admission to Princeton is contingent upon the successful completion of your senior year. We expect that you will keep up the high academic standards and good conduct you have maintained throughout high school.*

Therefore, Fanny needed to maintain her "high academic standards," though nobody doubted that she would.

One afternoon in March 2008, our doorbell rang.
Ding-dong!
We rushed to the door.
"Congratulations!" the postman said with a smile as he handed Fanny a large heavy envelope. Our eyes grew as wide as saucers when we

saw that it had been sent by the Massachusetts Institute of Technology. At that moment, we were all thinking the same thing.

Super! Fanny captured another school! Without even opening it, we knew that a big thick envelope from a university meant another acceptance.

From April 6 to April 14, 2008, Fanny received admissions letters and packages from a number of colleges, including New York University, Johns Hopkins University, UC Berkeley, and the California Institute of Technology. The CalTech admission letter stated,

> *The staff, faculty, and students on the Admissions Committee see in you, not only an accomplished student, but also a person with the passion and creativity to pursue study in mathematics, science, and engineering at the highest level. You have an opportunity to take your place amongst a community of scholars with an extraordinary record of accomplishment and a shared commitment to become leaders in the scientific community . . .*

We waited patiently for the arrival of April 15, because this was the day that all the Ivy League schools would release their admissions decisions. At 5:00 PM, Columbia University gave us the first reason to celebrate. Then there came acceptances from Cornell University, the University of Pennsylvania, and Princeton University:

> *Congratulations! I am delighted to offer you admission to Princeton's Class of 2012. Your academic accomplishments, extracurricular achievements, and personal qualities stood out in a record pool of more than 21,000 applications this year. We know from reading your file that you will take advantage of all Princeton has to offer and that the University will benefit from your many talents.*

The good news kept rolling in, but we still hadn't received anything from Harvard. Since it used e-mail notifications, it took more time to send out all the results, keeping us on tenterhooks. From 5:00 PM onward, some students began posting their admissions results on the

Internet, and we anxiously checked Fanny's e-mail constantly. Finally, at 7:00 PM, Fanny received the e-mail from Harvard, and the first words were the words we had been dreaming of:

I am delighted to inform you . . .

"Fanny has been admitted to Harvard!" Everyone shouted the words over and over again until they echoed throughout the house. The entire family was deeply immersed in the joy of success.

After the cheers, we carefully read the acceptance letter from Mr. William Fitzsimmons, Dean of Admissions and Financial Aid at Harvard:

> *I am delighted to inform you that the Committee on Admissions and Financial Aid has voted to offer you a place in the Harvard Class of 2012. Following an old Harvard tradition, a certificate of admission is enclosed. Please accept my personal congratulations for your outstanding achievements.*
>
> *This year over twenty-seven thousand students, a record number, applied for admission to the entering class. Faced with many more talented and highly qualified candidates than it had room to admit, the Admissions Committee took great care to choose individuals with exceptional character as well as unusual academic and extracurricular strengths. The Committee is convinced that you will make important contributions during your college years and beyond . . .*

At the bottom of the letter, there was a handwritten note: "Hope you will join us!"

It seemed like we could see his welcoming eyes staring at Fanny, looking forward to seeing her on the prestigious campus. My heart was difficult to restrain; it felt like it was trying to jump out of my chest.

Two sisters with their parents at Harvard

The deluge of good news brought our family happiness, laughter, and confidence; but the news also elicited some subtle changes in the children's behavior. Kathy's sense of humor was filled with more confidence, and Bill was more respectful to his sister Fanny. Although Fanny was still very humble, we saw that her face beamed with joy and excitement.

I used to say that if Fanny was admitted to Harvard, I would be so happy and feel like I was living in a dream. Harvard has always been an outstanding school known for its excellent education, not only in the United States, but also worldwide. Fanny was a very fortunate girl!

Fanny had been successfully admitted to many top universities, which convinced John and me that we had raised our children correctly. We had not been born and raised in the United States; so initially, we did not understand the U.S. education system, college admissions standards, or culture. The road to Fanny's good education and her proper cultivation was not straight and smooth, but full of twists and turns and scattered with sticks and stones. In the continuous process of understanding and exploration, we had to change our methods, paths, and directions multiple times. On the road to success, Fanny was our family's pioneer in the United States. Her complex, winding path was filled with much effort and many struggles. In the process, we also gained a significant amount of experience, which guided our efforts to develop Kathy.

Two years later, in 2010, thanks to our joint efforts, we once again experienced the thrill of receiving admissions letters bearing good news, one after the other. This time, though, they were for Kathy. Kathy was also admitted to Harvard, Yale, Princeton, Columbia, Brown, and the other prestigious Ivy League schools to which she had applied.

At that time, the two Wang sisters became front-page news in the community. Their story was the center of much discussion at school, between friends, and throughout the community. When people passed along this incredible news, they also inquired as to how it happened.

Behind this one story, there are simply too many other stories and anecdotes to share. The following stories record the laughter of our joy and the difficult journey we took to guide our children to where they are today.

CHAPTER 2

The American Dream

In 1980, Professor T. D. Lee of Columbia University, winner of the Nobel Prize in Physics, launched the well-known China-U.S. Physics Examination and Application (CUSPEA) program. Every year until the program ended, approximately one hundred promising undergraduate students from Chinese universities were invited to the United States in order to study and obtain their PhDs. In 1982, John had the honor of being selected as one of those students.

While studying at New York University, John witnessed Professor Lee's elegant style at the podium and was occasionally given the honor of listening to Professor Lee discuss social issues related to education in an individual setting. In laymen's language, Professor Lee explained the current problems of physics; and through these conversations, John discovered that Professor Lee not only had remarkable academic accomplishments, but also discussed ideology at a high level. In the past few decades, Professor Lee has been supportive of China's reform efforts and has made tremendous contributions to help China make the transition to a modern society. To commemorate his wife, Mrs. Huijun Qin, and to promote education in China, he used their savings to set up the "Jun Zheng Fund" in order help a new generation of Chinese students. Professor Lee is not only a master of contemporary science, but also a shining example of a humanitarian.

His Story

John's life has been full of hardship. When he was a child, most of his time was spent in poor rural counties. He lived through ten years of chaos during the Great Cultural Revolution in China and struggled for five years during middle and high school (three years in junior high, two years in high school). He had to attend four different schools for political and family reasons, making him miss a lot of basic education, but he never stopped chasing his dreams. When he fell behind in his classes, he borrowed his brother's textbooks and caught up in that vulnerable time. He had nowhere to go after middle school for political reasons, so his father advised him to learn a workman's trade to survive. He resolutely refused and declared, "No matter what, I want a higher education!"

Facing his strong determination, his father had no choice. In order to make John's dream of studying come true, his father had to ask everyone for help. Finally, a high school in the desolate countryside, more than ten miles away from home, generously accepted him; but he was not allowed to officially register as a student. Often, he walked more than twenty miles on harsh mountain roads in order to attend school; the opportunity to learn was that precious to him. During that time, he studied very hard, enjoyed helping others, and was highly praised by his teachers and classmates.

In 1975, he graduated from high school. The prevailing regulations stated that only one graduated child per family could stay in town with his or her parents. The other children, after their high school graduation, had to go to the countryside to become farmers. Because his two brothers had been sent to the countryside already, John could have stayed in town with his parents and become a substitute teacher. Under the same circumstances, most young graduates would have considered it a very attractive opportunity. However, he gave up the chance to stay in town and instead chose to go to the farms in order to witness the real life most young people were experiencing. During his time in the countryside, it was hard to find food, so the other youth from the city often went back to their parents' homes to eat meals. He rarely did so because, at that time, everyone in the city had been issued limited food supplies by the government. He knew if he ate more at home, then his parents would have to eat less, and he could not bear to divide his parents' rations. Therefore, he often went to the fields to do heavy farm work, dizzy with hunger. Although the difficult rural life and near-constant hunger left him with chronic stomach problems, this harsh experience made him even more strong and determined.

John with Professor T. D. Lee

In 1977, he passed the first national examination held after the ten years of chaos in China, was accepted by the University of Science and Technology of China (USTC), and entered the Department of Physics. Because he had never learned English, he raced against the clock to do so after entering college, starting with the alphabet. He made flash cards and carried them everywhere; even during lunchtime, while he was standing in line, he would concentrate on memorizing a few words. He had no basic grammar background in either English or Chinese, so learning English grammar was particularly difficult for him. To solve this problem, he repeatedly read and memorized English textbook articles. Memorizing the articles had three advantages: remembering words, familiarizing himself with syntax, and learning common idioms. The best time for him to memorize English articles was during the middle of the night, when everyone else was asleep. Even in the freezing winter, when the wind knifed against his face, he wrapped himself up in a cotton-padded jacket and resolutely stood outside, loudly reading and memorizing English articles. Finally, he began to reach the level of the students with a strong English background. At the University of

Science and Technology of China, he established a new goal: to go to the United States or Europe for further education in order to broaden his horizons.

In 1982, Professor T. D. Lee of Columbia University made his dream come true. At New York University, John studied under Professor Lowenstein—a very generous man who he came to regard not only as a respected professor, but also as a good friend—and received a doctorate degree in physics. During the later part of his time at New York University, he formulated a new concept which had market value, which was affirmed by Professor Lowenstein. In his spare time, he taught himself computer languages and struggled to write computer software. He hoped to one day have his own business.

My Story

In 1984, I graduated from the Department of Chemistry at Anhui Normal University in China and was assigned to Tunxi First Schools as a high school teacher. In 1985, I met John when he came back to China from the United States He was very frank.

"I'm just a poor student, and we would have to struggle for success. Are you afraid of that?" he asked.

Without any hesitation, I replied, "No, I am not afraid!"

I thought that since Professor Lee had accepted him into his program, it certainly showed that he was a very smart person. He demonstrated his honesty by telling me the truth about being a poor student, which many young people cannot do. Since he was the perfect fit for me, I had no reason to hesitate.

John and I share the same belief: our lives should be built on the basis of our own ability. We used the same philosophy to educate our children.

Following John's footsteps, I came to the United States in 1986. Together, we started a new life that was, at times, both sweet and bitter. In the beginning, our life together in America was very difficult. John studied hard in college to learn and explore his options while he worked as a teaching assistant in order to support his family. When I first arrived in America, my poor English made me hesitant to speak to people. Every time we went out, I always pushed him in front of me, and he always spoke.

A few days after arriving in the United States, John had to go to school. I became bored staying at home, so I called John to let him know that I was going to go on an adventure: I was going to take the subway alone and come to his school to see him. This made him very nervous because I had only been on the subway once, and that time, he had been with me. The New York Metro was very complicated, and since I couldn't speak English very well, he worried about whether I would be able to arrive at his school. He strongly advised me not to take risks, but I pushed his concerns aside and headed to the subway to have my adventure.

Based on my memory, I boarded on the subway in the direction of New York University. When I stepped off the subway, I was tense, excited, worried, and scared. I looked around the unfamiliar station and broke into an anxious cold sweat. A cacophony of questions suddenly filled my head.

"Did I go in the wrong direction?" "Did I take the wrong train?" "Should I go back?"

My mind was a mess because I did not have money to buy another subway ticket, and I did not even have the money to make a phone call. *What could I do?*

For a long time, I lingered in the subway station before I finally calmed down and figured out that I gotten off the subway one stop early. Luckily, I had not left the station. I reboarded the subway and soon arrived at my destination.

When I got off the subway again, I hummed songs as I happily walked toward John's office. I had not gotten far before I saw John walking quickly toward me. When he saw me, he grabbed me and declared, "You scared me. Why did it take you so long?"

After I described what had happened, he looked at my proud face and did not know whether to laugh or to cry. I was very glad I had taken this step by myself and decided to find a job. For several years, I worked in various industries including garment factories, laundromats, dry cleaners, and restaurants. Not every experience was comfortable, and sometimes they were very harsh, but they did help me learn how to communicate in English.

Our American Dream

The year 1990 was a turning point in our lives. John graduated from New York University, and Fanny was born. At the time, John had two offers: one in New York and another in Salt Lake City, Utah. Because he planned to set up his own business eventually, we made a comparison of living expenses in Salt Lake City and New York City. We discovered that the cost of groceries, housing, and utilities were relatively low in Salt Lake City, and that Salt Lake City was a good place to start a business. After weighing our options, we decided to move. When we arrived in Utah, we realized that the transportation system was not as convenient as that of New York City, so we used our little savings to buy an old car for commuting.

While in Salt Lake City, John played multiple roles. He worked hard at work and developed his own software during the evening and on weekends. Since the barrier to starting a software business was relatively low, he decided to start a software company as a first step before moving on to a larger goal.

After two years of effort, John completed the fundamental work for a new software product. Technically and intellectually, he was well-prepared to set up a computer software business, so he quit his job to start his own company.

Starting a company requires money; since we did not have enough savings, we had to borrow money from our friends. We are very grateful to those friends who helped us financially because we would not have been able to start our business otherwise.

Since we started from scratch, we had to do everything on our own, from writing the software, marketing our product, and shipping the packages to our customers. This was very risky, but we believed we would succeed, so we worked day and night. Each of us had clear responsibility: John led the company's direction and wrote the software, his partner also wrote the software and was in charge of marketing, and I answered the phones, processed the mail, and rocked Kathy's stroller. In the beginning, we could not afford to hire any employees, so we were all unpaid labor. I would fold tens of thousands of marketing letters by hand and put them into envelopes. The envelopes' paper edges were like sharp knives, often cutting my skin and making my fingers bleed. Whenever that happened, I would just put a bandage on my cuts and keep working. Every evening, John would work past midnight in the office. The next morning, we would load the heavy boxes of letters that I had prepared during the evening at home onto vehicles.

The partner in charge of marketing was unsuccessful, and we quickly ran out of borrowed money. John expressed his concern about the situation, so the partner agreed to let John try marketing instead. After taking over this additional job, John performed a significant amount of market research and analyzed the market data before beginning a wide range of market testing. At the last moment, he found that directly mailing the letters to potential customers was a practical and useful advertising technique. He also decided to set different prices for the product depending on the customer's needs. Then, John made the bold decision to put all the available money into marketing. When we were all alarmed, John confidently told us, "Let's see the miracles roll in after a month."

A month later, he successfully restarted our marketing efforts, and the company began to make a profit. We were all impressed with John's insightful predictions and his strong initiative. The business began to flourish, and we were able to hire new employees.

In 1993, I felt that my menstrual cycles were off; but because I was too busy, I did not see a doctor. I believed that my exhaustion was the cause of the discrepancy. Day by day, as my stomach grew larger and larger, I began to wonder, *Do I have cancer?*

To avoid distracting John, I chose to ignore it. One day, my stomach had a slight fluttery movement, and I wondered, *Am I pregnant again?*

This made me rush to the doctor. The doctor scolded me, "You are five months pregnant! You have given birth to two children, so how could you have not known?"

The company was still very busy, so I had no way to care for the pregnancy. I still had to work day and night. During the day, I answered the phone, packaged our software, and kneeled by the file cabinet to pull customer information. At night, I did the housework and kneeled on the ground to help the children take their baths.

In September 1993, our third child, Bill, was born. Perhaps it was because I had not rested well or paid attention to my nutritional intake during the pregnancy that Bill was born seriously ill and required near-constant hospital care. During that time, I was both physically and mentally exhausted. Thankfully, my mother stood behind me and supported us during that difficult time. John held Bill and told him, "I'll do whatever I can to save your life."

Even in such a difficult situation, we overcame the hardship together.

During the period when we expanded our business, we did not have any days off, and we often worked until midnight. Every weekend, we took our children to the office so we could keep an eye on them while we worked. Fanny was often willing to help fold the boxes we used for shipping. When the children were tired, we put our clothes on the floor and let them rest there. Although they were still little, they could feel the hardship and our struggles, and they came to understand that success is not easy.

Through our continuous efforts and hard work, our first scientific software was warmly received by the market, and orders came in from all over the world: from universities, research institutes, scientific consultants, chemical companies, and more. Later, we developed two other scientific software products. Our specialized products and bold initiative won people's respect and established our success.

In 2001, due to his contributions to science and technology, John's biographical data appeared in the Marquis *Who's Who in America.* Page 5520 contained the following entry:

> *Wang, John Xiaowu, software company executive: b. Hefei, Anhui, China, July 6, 1958; came to US, 1982; s. Zhi Dao Wang and Xian Zhen Fang; m. Lin Hu, Aug 24, 1985; children: Fanny, Kathy, Bill . . .*

Linda and John

In 2002, John was selected for the Marquis *Who's Who in the World*, where his entry was recorded on page 2302. His accomplishments made us all proud, and because of them, our entire family was listed beside him.

We believe that our efforts also affected our children's decisions and philosophy later in life. Our determination and creative mind-set definitely had a significant impact on them. We often tell them, "Your future is in your hands. You should work tirelessly to build your own future."

CHAPTER 3

Educational Differences

It is an indisputable fact that there are cultural differences between the Chinese and American philosophies of childhood education. When we have gatherings with our Chinese friends, we often lament how mainstream Americans seem to misunderstand the role of Chinese-American families in their children's education. We have tried to explore what leads to these misunderstandings and have come to the conclusion that each culture's educational methods have both positive and negative aspects. For decades, we put much effort into studying and understanding the differences so that when we started guiding our children's educations, we could integrate the better parts of both cultures.

Standing in front of Widener Library at Harvard

In Chinese culture, parents have attached great importance to their children's education for thousands of years. Parents always selflessly dedicate themselves to their child's growth and future and promote typical Chinese family values: strong bonds and caring relationships between every member. In recent years, the rise of homeschooling in the United States is evidence of the recognition of strong parental involvement in their children's education. Without a doubt, both the development of a country and the progress of a culture are inseparable from education. We should not only adhere to these traditions, but also help them to flourish.

Many methods commonly used by Chinese parents have merit. Chinese parents ask their children to strive for excellence. There is no doubt that this type of practice helps children unleash their potential. The Chinese mentality of encouraging children to study hard is one that would be worth further development in the U.S. culture. As Thomas Edison once noted, "Genius is one percent inspiration and ninety-nine percent perspiration."

Therefore, in order to educate our children, we used the Chinese educational philosophy as a base, yet we also actively searched for and applied other effective learning methods. For instance, the American educational system emphasizes the flexible use of knowledge. The U.S. culture emphasizes teamwork, leadership, creative ability, and dedication to community service. These traits make the U.S. proud to be a world leader in almost every aspect. These values have been embedded in the traditional Chinese culture as well, as evident in proverbs like: "Be the first to worry about people's concern and be the last to share people's joy."

Another Chinese quotation, "After hearing the truth, I have no regret to die," recalls the famous statement by the American revolutionary, Patrick Henry: "Give me liberty, or give me death!" The regression of these values in Chinese culture is not due to a flaw in the culture itself, but rather the result of long dictatorships ruling China that have diminished its former glory.

In America, we have inherited these new ideals of creativity and teamwork and incorporated them with the values of Chinese culture. By combining the best of both Chinese and American educational philosophy, we were able to craft a specialized guide for our children's education. We actively encouraged our children to participate in social activities to contribute to the community and strove to inspire their creativity. We poured in endless efforts to develop their leadership skills while maintaining their team spirit, in addition to ensuring that they reached their full academic potential. We worked toward developing them to be well-rounded people, with an understanding of the two cultures they had inherited.

Intuitive Learning

In U.S. schools, teachers try to find new or different ways to explain and solve problems in order to teach their students flexibility in problem solving. Let's consider a simple math problem: 32 x 12 = 384.

Normally, Chinese teachers will only teach the student one method and use it constantly:

$$
\begin{array}{r}
32 \\
\times\ 12 \\
\hline
64 \\
+\ 32 \\
\hline
384
\end{array}
$$

While teaching the same skills as the Chinese teacher, an American teacher may also explore the problem in another way:

32 x 12 = 32 x (10 + 2) = 32 x 10 + 32 x 2 = 384.

The Chinese approach is a rigorous repetition of logical operations, while the American approach is more flexible. The American approach of splitting the number into its components and simplifying the problem helps students gain a deeper understanding of numbers.

American schools focus on training the children's interest in learning, beginning with conceptual knowledge. For example: How do you solve 40 + 3?

In elementary schools in the U.S., teachers start by teaching grouping with physical objects like beans. By organizing groups of 10 beans, the student can create a total of 4 groups with 3 beans left over. Four groups of 10 make 40 beans, and the extra 3 make 43.

Chinese parents might laugh and say that this method is slow and a waste of time, but this is part of America's educational philosophy.

This interactive style of teaching makes the learning process more interesting to children and helps them develop the habit of connecting their knowledge with their environment. It also encourages children to look at problems from a different perspective in order to solve them, laying down the foundation for their future development. It is like the Chinese saying, "Preparation may decrease the time required."

Small children often lack patience and concentration, so we should discover interesting ways to guide them. In order to teach young children to count, start counting things that they care about so it is fun for them. For example, counting pieces of breakfast cereal can keep a child's interest, since cereals come in a large variety of shapes, tastes, and colors. While children count the cereal, they can also play other games such as grouping them by color or by shape. Compared to counting on your fingers or scribbling figures on paper, the U.S. approach makes teaching children easier and more enjoyable.

After we learned this method of counting beans at school, we practiced it at home and taught it to other children as well. We played a game of counting the fish in our fish tank to see who could count the fastest. Since the fish moved constantly, in order to win the game, the children needed to be focused and patient.

Soon, though, they finished counting. To make the game more interesting and longer-lasting, we eventually asked Kathy and Fanny to play a game together, each offering a criterion for the other to count, such as "How many have a red tail?" or "How many have large upper eyelids?" By designing their own games, they learned to pay attention to the different characteristics of each fish. Sometimes they came up with two different answers for one criterion and clamored for us to be the referees. This then became an exercise of our patience and made us feel like we were shooting ourselves in the foot!

I still remember when Fanny was a toddler. Since she loved pizza, we visited Pizza Hut quite often. At the time, she could only say disjointed syllables; so each time we drove by a Pizza Hut and she saw its sign, she would raise her little hands and cheerfully say, "Zza, zza." We brought our children outside often and noticed that they enjoyed the experiences and learned fast in the natural environment.

When Fanny was learning about fractional numbers, she was confused by the concept of fractions. I tried to explain them to her repeatedly, but she still looked up at me without comprehension. Then,

John suddenly had an idea; he took an apple and cut it into pieces to illustrate concept of fractions. After a few iterations, she understood them completely. Working with an interactive object proved to be easier than simply working out arbitrary numbers on paper.

There is a popular card game in the Chinese community called "24." The game is played with two or more people. Every hand, four cards are displayed, and the players can use any mathematical operations to produce the number 24. We played this game very often. At first, we gave them handicaps since their mathematical ability was still developing, but when they became more skilled, we played the game on even ground.

Through these entertaining methods, we were able to inspire and develop our children's intelligence. They had fun and were happy, but they also learned many things, giving them the best of both worlds.

Chinese schools enforce rigorous teaching methods, which have the advantage of strengthening a child's logical thinking and problem-solving accuracy. This enhances the child's ability to achieve high scores on standard exams. American schools encourage children to view problems from different angles and emphasize the practical use of knowledge. Over time, Chinese students are without equal in academic exams and competitions, but American students' creativity is unrivaled in the world.

When we educated our children, we tried to incorporate the beneficial aspects of both cultures. We wanted them to fully understand the concepts and grasp their applications as proficiently as possible.

Team Spirit

From elementary school to college, American education stresses the strength of the team. In American schools, teachers often devise group projects in which the students' overall performance depends on their teamwork in order to foster their spirit of solidarity. American children and parents are particularly keen on sports; at school or on college campuses, sports teams are always popular.

We believe that teamwork is another positive aspect of American education. Teamwork is not reflected only in sports; it can be manifested in many ways. A variety of different activities including research and even nonathletic games can also promote teamwork. Since our children were not good at sports, we encouraged them to develop this spirit through alternative methods. We often participate in fun family activities in order to promote solidarity within our own family.

When our children were young, they worked together with other children in the neighborhood to sell lemonade in the summer. They would set up their lemonade stand near an intersection, each child with his or her own responsibility. Some children worked as salespeople, some as cashiers, and some as suppliers. When they were short on hands, we were pleased to offer our help to keep their stand running. To support their business, we and our neighbors also bought their drinks and became their customers. By doing this, the children worked together while having fun. After a happy business day, they shared their profits, the reward of their hard work. This experience taught the children about the benefits of working together as a team to reap the fruits of their labor.

When they were young, our children liked to play Running Bases with the other children. Two predetermined areas on the ground served as the bases, and one child stayed between the two bases and tried to capture the other children as they ran back and forth between the bases. I noticed that one child looked left out, so I proposed that they change the rules of the game. In the new rules, they chose two children instead of just one to stand between the bases. This way, they could play together on a team and devise a strategy to capture the children running between the bases. With these changes, the game became more complex and fun to play.

On one occasion, Kathy did not receive a good score for a project she and a classmate did at school because her partner did not finish her work. Kathy felt very bad and angrily told me, "Mom, next time I do not want to do a project with partners. I will do it all by myself."

This was a great opportunity to talk about the power of teamwork. I gave her a pair of chopsticks, and I asked her, "Can you break this pair of chopsticks?"

"Of course, it's easy!" With a smile, she easily broke it.

Then I gave her a bunch of chopsticks and asked again, "Can you break all these chopsticks together?"

She looked at me puzzled. I urged her, "Give it a try!"

She blushed and tried and tried, but she had no way of breaking all the chopsticks at the same time.

"This is the power of teamwork," I told her. "You can easily break down each pair of chopsticks, but you cannot break an alliance of chopsticks."

Then, I gave her a pair of wooden chopsticks and a pair of bamboo chopsticks and asked her to try again.

"Which was easier to break?" I asked. She stated that the wooden chopsticks were more easily broken. Now she understands that she needs not only the power of a team, but also the ability to choose quality teammates.

"Furthermore, when team members encounter difficulties, they need to support each other. Only by doing this will your team be invincible," John added. To take further advantage of this learning opportunity, John described one of his experiences many years ago when he was in elementary school.

In one of his camp activities, two teams had to compete against each other to see which team could reach the top of a mountain first. Other than two strong big boys, most of his team members were relatively weaker than the other team's. At first glance, his team had no way to win the game because the rules required that everybody on the team reach the top of the mountain in order to win. In the end, though, his team won.

"But how?" Kathy asked curiously.

To reach the top of the mountain, everyone had to pass through a narrow mountain ridge. When the competition started, the two larger boys on John's team first occupied the pass: one above and one below. They stayed there to help their whole team pass the ridge. The boy on the lower end of the pass helped raise his teammates while the boy at the top pulled them up one by one. By working together, John's team smoothly crossed the ridge. In contrast, on the other team, each member tried to reach the top by themselves so they all became stuck in that narrow pass.

"This is the strength of teamwork! This is the spirit of teamwork!" John summed up strongly.

Columbus on Trial

American education pays more attention to each child's individuality and encourages children to think independently. In our school district, the school requires students to do a social survey and write up a report summarizing their results when they are still in third grade. The children at that age were expected to comfortably write a two-page article. Kathy finished her community survey, but when she completed her writing, it ended up being only a half page long. When she showed her work to me, I was very surprised by her ability to write. Later, though, I discovered that her report was the shortest of her class.

Kathy once wrote an article with the title "Is Success Accidental or Inevitable?" Fanny also wrote an article with the title "Is Being Deaf Good or Bad?" According to the Chinese perspective, their choice of topic was wrong and undebatable, but they believed that their views could be justified. They argued, "We can provide strong enough evidence to prove our point is correct."

I simply replied, "Well, let's wait and see."

Surprisingly, they both actually received high scores. Of course, we sometimes worried about them thinking about things incorrectly, so we had in-depth discussions with them to correct their misunderstandings. The following is an essay that Kathy wrote in middle school, recording an interaction between her and John:

> One of the things we share is one of a few inside jokes, which makes it particularly valuable. My family is a stereotypical Chinese family, so we don't have many laughable stories to really tell. They support my academics, set the rules, and strongly advise not participating in activities which they think I will fail at. It is not that they are brutal tyrants. I love them as they are, but most talk is centered on school or news. I wouldn't really wish for them any other way, even if we only have one real inside joke.
>
> The joke starts on the day when I was taking the SAT. After the long test, I detailed to my dad what I wrote for an essay. My point was that you don't have to work hard to make discoveries. One of my examples was of John Sutter and all that he did, in my words, was "dig a hole and find a gold nugget." For my

whole life, my parents have preached hard and smart work; so when my father hear this, he was astonished, but laughed it off. The whole car ride was spent while he lectured me about hard work and good ethics. Now when my siblings and I want something without a good reason, or if we haven't earned it, my parents will ask, "Are you trying to dig a hole and find a gold nugget?" My answer is always: yes.

Americans are very open to ideas. The courage to think outside the box marks the uniqueness of America's outstanding educational system. Kathy often participated in high school mock trial activities. Their cases were usually based on historical figures and events so that students could judge the merits and demerits of history. On one occasion, they put Christopher Columbus on trial and charged him with murder. In the mock court, students were appointed as judges, witnesses, prosecutors, defense lawyers, and members of the jury, much like an actual court. The prosecution and the defense expressed their views and passionately exchanged arguments as they examined and cross-examined the witnesses. The jury calmly sat and watched the drama, carefully considering the arguments. Finally, the mock court ruled that Columbus, the man who "discovered" America, was guilty of murdering Native Americans. This was surprising because of his well-known position in American history and the perception of him as a great adventurer, even a hero. However, the school educates its students in a diplomatic way so that the students retain their own independent perspective of the law and can formulate and express their own opinions.

American education promotes childhood exploration and innovation. American education trains independent thinking, the courage to venture outside societal conventions, and the daring to challenge authority. Perhaps it is because of this that America has the world's best political system and leads the world in scientific research. Maybe this is why the United States hosts the most Nobel Prize winners and has been a world leader for the last few decades.

The innovation process comes with a lot of risks. Fanny looks frail, but she in fact likes adventure and excitement. Every time we go to an amusement park, such as Disney World or Disneyland, she always rides the highest and most dangerous roller coasters. When riding on a swing, she always challenges herself to swing as high as possible. Since she was small, we have continuously provided constructive criticisms to promote her spirit of adventure. We have taught her to not be afraid of risk and to always try to push forward. Given her personality and characteristics, we encouraged her to push herself further in high school; but we never expected that she would eventually dare to challenge the teacher's authority, even in a respectful way.

American Parenting

When we first arrived in America, John and I falsely stereotyped mainstream Americans as white people who did not care about their children's education and passed on their laissez-faire attitude to their children. As a matter of fact, that is not the case at all.

We have now lived in this country for almost three decades. During this period, we have moved from the East Coast to the Midwest and then back to the East Coast. We have lived in several different regions and witnessed many white American families paying a great deal of attention to their children's education.

According to families' financial capabilities, the degree to which families can financially invest in their children's education varies. For families struggling under the poverty line, the parents have to work hard to make a living so they may be unable to look after their children's education. For middle-class families, their children's education receives more attention. The wealthy families simply do not hesitate to send their children to expensive private schools for a better education. Recently, there was a report in the news that a private elementary school in New York City has an even lower acceptance rate than Harvard University.

In recent years, homeschooling has become more appealing to many parents. To meet this new educational endeavor, the common application forms now have a specific section for homeschooled children. For the families that choose homeschooling, one of the parents must give up their job and teach their children full-time. He or she is responsible for teaching English, math, physics, social studies, the sciences, and a variety of other subjects. What a commitment! What a selfless dedication! At a meeting with other parents whose children had applied for Harvard, I met a mother from Massachusetts who was homeschooling her children. For her children's education and future, she gave up her high-paying job. After years of homeschooling, in order to balance the development of her children, she sent her children to a public school to train and develop the children's social skills.

Overall, in the U.S., children in elementary school through junior high school have plenty of time to play and enjoy their childhood. As long as the children complete their homework and have decent grades, parents generally may not give them extra homework. During this time, children spend a lot of time participating in sports and other school activities. However, once the children enter high school, parents will usually support their children by helping them with their homework, studying for exams, and applying to colleges.

For example, in the neighborhood where we live now, there are six middle-class white families. Of these, only one mother is working full-time, while the other mothers stay at home to take care of the children. When their children need help in academics, most parents will try their best to explain the concepts. For the parents who can coach their children, they will often offer their help and supervise their children when they do their homework. For the parents who cannot offer help themselves, they usually hire a private tutor for their children. When their children need extra help, parents send their children to summer school.

Many times, when the children played together outside, I would hear the calls of mothers and the whistles of fathers telling the children that it was time to go home and do their homework. After children enter high school, their academic performance becomes the first priority because colleges only want to see high school transcripts and are not interested in elementary or junior high school transcripts. A college education in America is very expensive, especially at private universities. Most families cannot meet the cost of the education on their own, but many parents take out loans to pay for their children's college expenses.

Generally speaking, typical American parents do not push their children in an almost endless pursuit of top grades like some Chinese-American families. American parents are more focused on the child's balanced development, emphasizing the child's autonomy and interests. But for Chinese-American students to succeed in the United States, they face more challenges than Caucasian, Hispanic, or African-American students. Statistics show that in most colleges, admitted Asian-American students' average SAT scores are more than

100 points higher than their counterparts in other ethnic groups. In reality, Chinese-American students have to work harder to be successful.

Another thing we appreciate about American schools is that they expose children to many different occupations from an early age. This helps develop the children's independent thinking and decision-making skills. In elementary school, schools usually invite parents to visit and teach the students about their job. Alternatively, the school may also allow the students to miss a day of school so that they can visit their parents' workplace in order to observe their work. Later, the students write a report about their day at work and may present it to their class.

To further introduce students to the possibilities that await them after they have completed their education, schools offer a variety of classes outside the required course load. Technology courses in secondary schools teach students to use and practice various tools. High school electives provide students with more opportunities to become involved in various fields.

Our Choice

Since reforms began to take place and China opened its doors to the world, hordes of Chinese elites have come to the United States to chase their dreams. Most of them are ambitious and are searching for success in this new land. Some of them have been successful, others are still making their way, but most of them have placed their hopes in their children and struggle to lay a smooth path for the next generation. Due to cultural, linguistic, habitual, and other differences in background, most of the elite became a generation of white-collar workers whom, although they earn enough to live comfortably, are plagued by a sensation of disorientation. Should they return to China? There are plenty of opportunities there, but what about their children's education? Instead, most choose to stay and put their faith in their children's future, loading them with the expectations of two generations. We often read newspaper reports about their children's success stories, such as winning the Intel Science Award, Siemens Prize, or some other prestigious competition. However, beneath these bright, inspirational stories, there are other ones of the hard work and suffering tears of the

Chinese parents that have sacrificed so much to raise their children on to their shoulders. Of course, nobody reports those stories.

Among our friends, there was a very intelligent and bright boy with good social skills. He received numerous awards at school, as well as at the regional and state levels, and had also advanced to the American Invitational Mathematics Exam (AIME). For such a gifted child, his parents spared no effort or expense to support his development, hiring tutors to teach him Chinese, the fine arts, piano, violin, and foreign languages, taking up all his free time, even on the weekends. He worked like a robot, constantly doing one activity after another without pause, without time to rest. Although he was eventually accepted to Harvard, the long-term mental pressure crushed him. Now, he is taking a temporary leave of absence to recover. We sincerely hope that he will be able to get through these difficult times and once again reach his fullest potential. We also met another talented child that had been accepted to Yale, but he also succumbed to too much pressure and is currently staying at home.

Unbalanced development makes some Chinese-American children become giants in academics, but they are easily dwarfed in other fields. Over time, mainstream American society developed an impression of rigid, ethnically Chinese children, and elite colleges raised their admission standards for this group of students.

Combining the best of the two cultures to foster children, in theory, may be the best choice. How to apply theory to practice, though, was an unfamiliar area. To this end, we were anxious and hesitant. In this period of enlightenment, we wondered what we should develop first. We constantly compared and debated about the arguments for and against each of the two educational methods.

According to a typical Chinese-style approach, we should immediately begin with the child's academic achievement, giving them exercises as soon as possible to teach them the basics through rote memorization and constant drilling.

Conversely, forcing a child's academic development too early could block us from fully understanding the child's strengths, potential, interests, and vulnerabilities. Imposing the parents' will on the children may also stifle the children's creativity and independence. We believed that this approach could temporarily produce rosy and tangible results, but could destroy the future development potential of the children.

What is enlightenment? We believe that enlightenment is when children first touch the real world and begin to gain an understanding of themselves. It is our duty to provide them with a full range of knowledge, including mathematics, language, astronomy, geography, history, literature, and social skills and to provide them with the opportunity to understand the reality they face. In this way, they will have a broad vision, creative ideas, and independent thinking in their futures. So we decided to allow them to do as they wished until fifth grade, for the most part.

However, we also understood that as Chinese-American children, if they wished to succeed in the United States, they needed some extra effort. In reality, we could not treat them in the same way as many white families treat their children. We acknowledged the disadvantages that they would experience in real life. We decided not to stop them from exploring the world in their own way, but we also did not let them run amok. Though they had unstructured playtime, we also played with them often with the goal of understanding, guiding, and inspiring them, as well as building mutual trust. During structured playtime, we tried to embed the concept of teamwork into them and lay a solid foundation for their future development.

After several years of practice, we strongly understood that during the initial stages of childhood development, parents need to put in more effort than simply asking their children to do homework.

We worked hard to find ways to provide opportunities for them, carefully observing their reactions to and interactions with their peers to understand them and guide them. We did everything possible to design projects where they could develop their creativity and imagination. When they were eager to do well in one of their activities, we taught them how to do so distinctively and uniquely. We showed them how to face reality, but if they were being treated unfairly, we encouraged them to fight for their rights. We carefully guided them to make sure they didn't go out of control; if they were on the wrong path, we corrected them without hesitation. In this manner, our children have inherited qualities from both cultures. This results in white people believing that we raised our children in the Chinese style, while our Chinese friends think that we raised our children in the American style. We like to think that we have truly made them Chinese-American.

CHAPTER 4

Childhood

Our Horse

In March 1990, our first child, Fanny, was born at Elmhurst Hospital in New York City. I named her Fanny because we wished her a life full of happiness, and the spelling of "Fanny" is very close to the word "fun." According to the Chinese zodiac, she is a horse. The horse occupies the seventh place in the Chinese zodiac. It is a symbol of strength and energy. The character traits of a horse include intelligence, honesty, and friendliness. A horse uses its strength and energy to always chase after its next target. We hoped she would always be a strong and fast horse that could gallop with determination and without fear toward the future.

The temperature in the hospital was kept at about 70 degrees Fahrenheit, but the nurse only wrapped the baby in a very thin sheet. I kept worrying, *Will she catch a cold?* This was the first time that I realized that the American child-rearing culture is different from China's.

Two days after Fanny's birth, we were released from the hospital and returned home.

Our home was actually just a small room in an apartment shared with others, but it was filled with our passion and love. We had especially prepared a baby bed for the newborn baby. For safety, the bed was surrounded by crib protectors. Looking at her doll-like face and her pinkish skin, my heart filled with infinite love. Fanny's birth was a new starting point in our lives, and we wanted to record this precious moment.

"Look! She is waking up." That little doll face erupted into sweet smiles. That smile was so beautiful and so charming; no flower in this world could even match it. John kept snapping the camera to capture her every smile.

"It's strange. Why doesn't she cry?" John wondered aloud, puzzled. We had hoped to take pictures of all her expressions for the first time, and we kept waiting and waiting. Finally, after several hours, John was able to snap a photo at the instant when she was crying. This made us believe that Fanny would be a happy girl.

We followed the American tradition of letting the baby sleep alone in her crib instead of in the mother's bed. Fanny always slept alone in her own bed. We believed that this was a good tradition, because when adults and children sleep separately, it ensures quality sleep for all. It is also helpful for developing the child's independence starting from infancy.

The Chinese custom is to let the baby sleep sideways or tilted. However, during the hospital training course, we learned to make the baby sleep on her stomach. In the hospital, the nurses taught me how to get the baby to sleep on her stomach, and I was very careful to learn what they taught me. During the practices, I was so nervous I was sweating. Each time I put her down to sleep, I was so afraid that I would accidentally twist her arm or neck. In order to prevent Fanny from hurting herself, I tried to let her sleep sideways or tilted. However, this made it very easy for Fanny to be woken up. In order to feel the difference, I tried sleeping on my stomach and found that it made me feel particularly at ease. So based on my personal experience, I believed that sleeping on the stomach makes the baby sleep better. Some recent medical reports have found that babies sleeping on their stomachs are more prone to sudden infant death syndrome. I guess that whether it sleeps sideways, tilted, or on its stomach, as long as the baby can sleep soundly, it should be a good sleeping position. For this reason, I let all of our children sleep on their stomachs. Later, we found that there are other advantages to letting them sleep on their stomachs. One day, we were surprised to discover that Fanny had turned her face from the left to the right by herself. When she woke up, she could push herself up with her little arms and lift her head to examine her surroundings. Wow, what a nice exercise! With this sleeping position, the baby can exercise the muscles of his neck, arms, and back. They are also free to practice crawling without parental assistance. Furthermore, this exercise is performed by the baby with its own strength. Because it is natural, it will not cause injuries normally associated with external forces imposed by others.

Because Fanny was our first child, we had to learn everything about parenting and nursing from books.

The book says that if a baby keeps crying, it means that he is hungry, has a wet diaper, or is sick. Therefore, whenever Fanny was making even a little noise, I always hurried to her to check what was wrong. Every night, I checked on her so much I disturbed everyone.

"Check on her only when she is really crying, or she will not sleep well," John advised me. However, I could not stop myself. Eventually, John suggested, "Let me take care of her for a few nights and let's see what happens."

He got up only when Fanny was actually crying. When Fanny hummed softly, he did not do anything and stopped me from doing anything. Aha! It worked! Fanny soon slept until dawn.

I do not know if other mothers have experienced this or not, but I always worried about whether the baby had enough to drink.

In the hospital, the nurse told me to feed the baby every three hours and then gradually extend the feedings to once every three and a half hours. The nurse said that approach was the best for the baby's digestive system. At the beginning, it was very hard to follow this routine. I tried to let the baby drink water before the proposed feeding time to solve the problem of her not drinking enough. After struggling for a few days, she finally became used to this feeding schedule.

On another occasion, about two months after her birth, the volume of the milk Fanny was drinking dropped substantially. It made me very worried, so I kept feeding her milk. When she fell asleep, I would nudge her awake and try to feed her a little more. Unfortunately, forcing her to drink more caused her indigestion and diarrhea that lasted for more than a month. For the same reason, when we educate children, we have to consider each child's ability to handle new materials and ensure that they absorb the materials they have already taken in before we give them more than they can handle.

"Is the baby hungry?" Mother Nature always hounded me. I remember once, when Fanny was about a year old, she had no appetite due to illness. I struggled to make different foods to help her regain her appetite, but each time I offered her the spoon, she always turned her head to the side. It was exhausting, both physically and mentally. I was angry and anxious and could not stop myself from impatiently shouting, "Why don't you eat it?"

John was shocked, because I had never used that tone of voice before.

"She is sick and has no appetite. Have you forgotten her diarrhea when she was two months old?" His words startled me into reality.

Fanny learning how to walk

Now I can look back on those days with amusement and the realization that, very often, parents press their own thoughts and aspirations onto their children, without considering whether or not their efforts are necessary or beneficial. Sometimes, this proves to be a hardship, even a disservice, to the child, for which it will not thank its parents, making them angry and anxious. Maternal love is so selfless and noble, but it can also be blind and paranoid. Handling it correctly is a huge challenge for first-time mothers. Love is beautiful, but knowledge and rationality can make it perfect.

Here Comes a Monkey

In March 1992, Kathy was born at the University of Utah Hospital. This time we received a monkey. We named her Kathy. The monkey occupies the ninth position in the Chinese zodiac, and its personality traits include curiosity, playfulness, and a natural intelligence and creativity. Kathy's personality consistently matches these descriptions. Real monkeys are also active, healthy, and energetic. Indeed, Kathy is robustly healthy and rarely gets sick. During the flu season, she is always the last one to fall sick and the first one to recover. We all jokingly call her "King Kong."

According to Chinese zodiac theory, the horse and the monkey do not get along well. But in our family, the "horse" and the "monkey" often speak in unison. It is amazing to hear two voices saying the exact same words at the same time. We wonder, "How can that happen? How can they speak in unison so often?"

When Kathy was born, Fanny was two years old. Fanny became a good little helper for me. When I would take a break, she would play with Kathy, showing her toys and rocking the baby basket. The newborn baby was Fanny's new interest. Fanny enjoyed gently touching Kathy's hands and playing with her younger sister.

Kathy's infancy was marked by her extra loud voice. When she was crying, we had no place to hide. John always joked, "Kathy's loud voice can help her become a great leader in the future."

As long as Kathy was awake, I had to pet, rock, or tease her. Although I had a good helper with Fanny, I was exhausted at the end of every day. At night, in order for me to get some rest, John had to get up and take care of Kathy.

Compared to Fanny, coaxing Kathy to sleep was the easiest job in the world. After finishing her milk, Kathy would fall asleep instantly. Even now, Kathy still sleeps well. This helps her maintain her high energy level.

Linda with her two little girls

Innocence

Fanny has been chasing perfection since she was a baby. I remember when she first started chewing food. Every time I gave her a cookie, she took it happily. However, after she took a bite, she would stare at the cookie blankly and ask for a new cookie. This phenomenon happened again and again and confused me greatly. Unsure of what to do, I just kept giving her a new cookie. If I offered her a broken cookie, she refused to take it; but if I gave her a whole cookie, she would give me a heavenly smile. After repeating this process, I finally understood that she wanted the cookie to be perfect.

Now, I faced a dilemma. I couldn't just let her take one bite of a cookie and throw away the rest. How could I explain this to someone that young? Concerned, I struggled with this problem, trying to figure out a solution. In a sudden burst of inspiration, I hid the box from her sight and only gave her one cookie. If she refused it, I would eat it instead, refuse to give her another one, and watch her reaction. Ha, ha! Now that she realized she would only get one cookie, if she really wanted it, she would have to eat it, regardless of whether it was broken or whole. From her childhood to the present, regardless of whether she was doing homework or taking notes, she always paid attention to being neat, clean, and perfect. When she did her homework, she could have crossed out her errors; but instead, she preferred to rewrite the homework when she made mistakes. Even taking the SAT exam was no exception. When I saw her SAT essay answer sheet, I was stunned. It did not look like rushed handwriting but, rather, like a piece of art.

During the teething stage, children like to bite hard objects. Our children also went through this phase. At that phase, Fanny liked to bite hardcover books, so we bought plastic books for her instead. In most bookstores, you can easily find this kind of book specifically prepared for children at this stage. I discovered, though, that this confused her because she could not understand why she could bite the plastic book but not the other books. Very often her innocent eyes stared at me, puzzled. They were all books, so it didn't make sense that she could bite this book but not the other books. When I realized this, I made some changes accordingly. Whenever Fanny began to bite a book, I would no longer give her the plastic book. Instead, I would scold her, "Do not bite books." And I would immediately give her a cookie and tell her, "Bite the cookie." This clarified a vague concept in the mind of a young child.

Children also love to play with water. One day when Fanny was three years old and Kathy was one, I was busy in the kitchen. I had not seen the girls for a while or heard any sound of them playing. It was unusually quiet, and that put me on high alert. *What were they doing?*

"Fanny, Kathy, where are you?" There was no response, so I began to search for them. Finally, I found them in the bathroom. They were playing with their plastic boat in the toilet bowl and having so much fun!

"Don't you know that the toilet water is very dirty?" I sounded angry, but I also wanted to laugh. They both looked at me innocently. After my initial reaction, I calmed down as I began to think about the situation more rationally. They only knew that playing with water was fun and didn't understand the concepts of clean and dirty. If I did not make my point clear, they would misunderstand and believe that playing with water was not allowed. So I took them to the bathtub and told them, "Let's play with the boat in the bathtub."

For young children, when we tell them what they are not allowed to do, we also need to show them what they can do instead. Otherwise, children will be afraid of doing the wrong thing and making their parents angry, and then they will not dare to do anything. Over time, children will lose their initiative and self-motivation, blocking their further development.

Learning and Playing

I was excited about any progress that Fanny made.

I rarely let Fanny watch television. I was worried that spending too much time watching television would hurt her eyesight. Also, I did not like to see her relying on the television. Watching too much television could make her lose interest in the environment around her and hinder her interactions with other people.

Whenever the weather allowed, I took her outside to exercise and explore our environment with activities like looking at flowers, watching the ants, and just playing childish games. On sunny days, I usually played with Fanny on the lawn. Once, when I lifted my arms and legs, Fanny imitated my actions one by one. She looked so cute.

"Quick, quick, take a picture of this!" With a smile, John recorded this scene with his camera.

During bad weather, we stayed inside, enjoying music, reading books, listening to stories, or playing with other children. Fanny's favorite place to go was the nearby library, where there were unlimited treasures—books, storytelling, activities, and games, as well as many other little friends. The library introduced Fanny to a new world of endless wonders. Therefore, I often took her in her stroller to the library to explore the new world. Each time, we came home, buoyed by our rewarding experiences.

I still remember the time when we saw another child playing with a puzzle in the library. Since that was the first time that Fanny had ever seen a puzzle, she was fascinated and patiently watched as the other child snapped the pieces together. We waited until the child had finished, then Fanny excitedly began her attempt. As this was her first time putting a puzzle together, she had to be especially patient and perseverant. Piece by piece, the puzzle began to form a picture, and whenever she encountered difficulties, I encouraged her to go on. In order to pursue a goal, being interested is not enough; even though it was just a game, she still needed to work hard in order to succeed. As the minutes ticked by, Fanny continued her efforts. Although it took a long time, she eventually completed that puzzle. She looked up at me and exclaimed, "Mom, I did it!" Her little face was filled with pride and joy at her accomplishment.

"Good girl! Great job!" I praised her, giving her a warm hug and a kiss. We were learning to use the American method of rewarding children with positive reinforcement, such as hugging. However, we also made sure that our children understood that no matter how smart they were, if they did not work hard, they could not succeed.

Not All Day Cares Are Created Equal

At that time, our software company was also in the early stages of development, and much work still needed to be done. A few months after I delivered Kathy, I needed to go back to work and took Kathy with me. At the same time, we decided to send Fanny to a day care.

For children under the age of three, they are in the initial stages of learning. Since they start with a blank slate, toddlers mostly learn by mimicking the actions of other people around them, so parents should pay close attention to their environment. If they decide to send their children to a nursery or a kindergarten, they must carefully select a quality day care. They need to have a comprehensive understanding of the workers there, the quality of the care they provide, their regulations, their code of conduct, and so on. When we chose Fanny's day care, we visited a number of day care centers to compare their environments. We ultimately chose a place called Love Land. The staff and teachers there were very polite and also offered an interesting curriculum while enforcing good standards of conduct. At Love Land, Fanny started learning English.

When Fanny first started to attend Love Land, she was very susceptible to sickness. We visited her doctor frequently, and I became very anxious. However, I learned that it is normal for children to frequently contract minor illnesses when they start attending a day care. Interacting with other children and adults helps children build up their immune systems by exposing them to a variety of bacteria and viruses. Therefore, each time Fanny recovered, we would send her back to her day care.

Soon Kathy was one year old, so we also sent her to a day care. Hers was a different day care, because Love Land was full at that moment. Not knowing much about this nursery, I decided to look around during their usual working hours. To my surprise, I saw an incredible scene.

In order to make their jobs easier, the nursery staff tied a baby to the back of a chair when it was time to feed the baby. We wanted Kathy to receive better care, so we decided to hire a babysitter for her instead of sending her to the day care. The babysitter took very good care of her.

Unexpectedly, hiring a babysitter created another problem for Kathy. One day, I took Kathy to the library. When a younger boy tried to approach her to say hello, she panicked and burst into tears. *Why did that happen?* It made me feel very strange. Subsequently, after several similar experiences, I finally understood that Kathy was afraid of meeting strangers!

I discussed this phenomenon with John. After a careful analysis, we believed that Kathy did not have the ability to handle an unfamiliar environment or a stranger. Other than us and her babysitter, she had almost no contact with other people. Her environment was too simple. We needed to expose her to more people and expand her comfort zone, so we sent Kathy to the same day care as Fanny.

In kindergarten and day care, children learn how to interact with others and build their social skills. These skills not only help develop a balanced child, but also keep them healthy in the long run. In the nursery, there were all kinds of children, and we learned to pay serious attention to our children's mood changes. For a while, Kathy kept complaining of a stomach ache and did not want to go to the day care. She had passed the initial barrier of becoming familiar with the children and teachers there, so we couldn't figure out why she did not want to go. During that time, the nursery called us frequently to report that Kathy had a stomach ache. I would have to leave work to check on her. Interestingly enough, each time I arrived at the day care, her stomach did not hurt anymore. *There must be something else going on!* The next day, after I delivered her to the nursery, I decided to stay there for a while to see what was going on. Shortly afterward, I saw a boy approach her and push her again and again. Kathy fell to the ground and started to cry. I ran to the boy and angrily shouted at him, "Stop! You cannot push her!"

I also told Kathy to shout "No!" at the boy. After that incident, Kathy's life at the day care became much easier.

This event taught her a very important lesson. In certain situations, she has to say "no" in order to protect herself. In this world, many things are not fair, but children must learn to face them and deal with them from a young age. Sending children to nurseries or kindergartens is a good way to introduce children to the real world. They will meet challenges and solve their own problems in order to learn some fundamental skills.

Fight for Your Right

In 1997, both Kathy and Fanny were attending Edgemont Elementary, a local public school. Kathy was in kindergarten, and Fanny was in second grade.

Edgemont Elementary had a reading contest. Students were encouraged to read books off a provided list, and after they finished each book, they could answer questions to gain points. Every month, the school would honor the students with the highest scores from each grade by publishing their names along with a photo in the school newspaper. Attracted by the prize, Kathy began to read. Soon, she became the front runner in her grade. She was very happy, and we were very happy for her.

One day, she came back from school and started crying.

"What happened?" I asked.

"Ms. V is not allowing me to continue to read," Kathy cried. When I heard that, I could not believe my ears.

Why? With this question, I visited Ms. V. She told me, "Kathy reads the books too fast. If she continues at this rate, soon she will have no books to read."

I had never heard such a ridiculous theory, so I decided to take this situation to the principal. He was also incredibly confused and wondered aloud, "How could that be? How could Ms. V do that?"

Later, Kathy told me that a white girl in her class also loved reading. The two girls were competing against each other, and we believed that Ms. V wanted that girl to be the next winner. If that was true, it would be utterly unfair for Kathy. We have no objection to fair competition, but in the face of unfair treatment, we have to seek justice.

Finally, Ms. V apologized and let Kathy continue reading, and Kathy continued to appear in the school newspaper. Being a winner is a good thing, but more importantly, Kathy learned to fight to get what she deserved. We told Kathy, "If it's your right, then you should fight for it."

Compassion

In 1993, on a snowy day, Fanny was sick at home. When my mother was throwing out the trash, she slipped and fell on the icy road. Fanny began to cry and rushed out of the house to try to help her grandmother stand up.

"Grandma, I can throw out the garbage. Next time, let me do it," she pleaded.

After I had returned home from work that day, my mother told me the story in an emotional voice. "Look, Fanny cares so much for others even though she is less than four years old!"

In 1997, my mother died suddenly. At the time, Fanny was seven years old, and Kathy was five. I decided to make the trip back to China to attend her funeral. I was afraid that this news would frighten the children, so I explained to them, "Grandma is sick. I need to go to China to visit her."

Fanny immediately ran upstairs without a word and made a card. "Please take it to Grandma. I hope she gets better soon!"

I could no longer hold back my tears, and I hugged her tightly. "Thank you, Fanny. I hope Grandma will get better too!"

After Kathy was born, I often took the two girls outside to explore our environment. Since the stroller we had was only for one baby, each time we left home, Fanny had to walk beside me. No matter how long the walk took, she never complained. Sometimes, when I noticed her faltering, I would ask, "Are you tired?"

She always just responded with a smile. It aroused my deep sympathy and affection, and when we passed the ice cream shop nearby, I would buy a small ice cream cone for her as a reward.

When she was small, Fanny was very cute and considerate. Now, she is still very careful to think about others' feelings. Even when she has been treated unfairly, she tries to find an excuse for the other person. We have never heard her seriously complain about anyone. Because of her easygoing personality, she never encountered any problems when she tried to get along with other people. We did not teach her how to protect herself, as we did with Kathy. Forgiveness is a good character trait, but if you have been treated unfairly, you must learn to fight to protect yourself and your rights. By the time we realized this, Fanny was already in high school and set in her ways. Now we know that no matter how smoothly their children develop, no matter what their personalities are like, parents need to teach them basic skills to protect themselves.

Emotional Intelligence

Many parents pay too much attention to their children's academic performance but ignore their development of emotional intelligence. Children are often overloaded with homework, extra practices, and other activities. These busy schedules leave them with no time to think for themselves or to develop their basic social skills. Some people think that a child's emotional intelligence is innate, but we believe that everyone has room to improve. We can teach children some social skills and improve their social behavior. Children can also learn many social skills by observing and interacting with other people, such as cooperation, empathy, conflict resolution, emotional control, and listening skills. Parents can provide opportunities for children to start this training process at a young age.

Kathy is a good example. Before two years old, she was afraid of meeting strangers. Whenever a stranger approached her, she would panic. When we became aware of this issue, we sent her to a day care where she could meet more people. We constantly introduced her to new people and taught her how to communicate with others. Working with her has changed her life dramatically. Now, she likes social activities, enjoys working with people, and possesses strong social skills.

We have always wished for our children to live happy and successful lives. When they were growing up, we tried to balance the development of their academic and emotional intelligence. We have helped our children find opportunities to access the real world and get a taste of real life. Instead of locking them indoors to do exercises all day, we let them go outside to interact with others. We also encouraged them to observe the world independently so they could decide what the real meaning of life was for them.

Due to Fanny's somewhat introverted character, compounded by the fact that we were living in a predominantly Caucasian area at the time, it was difficult for her to make friends. To remedy this problem, we invited her friends to participate in many fun activities such as seeing movies, visiting parks, or having parties. These types of invitations are more likely to be accepted than rejected. To help our children develop friendships and maintain contact with their friends, every year we organized a number of parties: for birthdays, Christmas, Thanksgiving, summer break, and more.

In preparation for their parties, we let them know that it was their party; and as such, they were responsible for planning and running it. We taught them how to take care of their guests by greeting every guest at the front door, helping their guests hang up their coats, introducing the guests to each other, and performing other small courtesies. When they cut the birthday cake, they should serve the guests first; and when they received a gift, they should say thank you. By doing all of this, they had more interaction with their guests and also made the party an enjoyable experience for everyone.

After every party, we reminded them to send thank-you notes to their guests in order to let each of their friends know that their attendance was greatly appreciated. This simple expression of gratitude allowed them to build closer relationships with their friends.

For small children, it is impossible for them to handle all of these details by themselves at once. However, we started simply and trained them to do each task one by one, repeatedly. Eventually, as with their multiplication tables, they developed and learned how to apply their new skills.

In 1996, Fanny was in first grade, and her teacher suggested that she skip a grade in school. Because the teacher felt that Fanny was smart and studious, she thought that the first grade material would be too easy for her. We seriously considered the option of moving her up to second grade. However, unlike many parents who only emphasized their children's academic performance, we believed that for Fanny, making friends was more important than skipping a grade. When we discussed this issue with Fanny, she agreed with us. She hoped to have more friends and showed no desire to skip a grade. If she had skipped a grade, most of her classmates would have been older than her, and it would have been more difficult for her to make new friends.

We encouraged Fanny to make new friends not just to have fun. Through playing with friends, she learned many things and achieved a balanced development. Given Fanny's introverted nature, learning how to make new friends and be social was particularly necessary. Fanny handled her homework easily, which gave her more time for the activities she enjoyed, such as painting, reading, arts and crafts, outdoor activities, and playing with other children.

A Crisis of the Bookworm

Fanny also joined the Edgemont reading contest, and she would read whenever she had an opportunity. She read in class, during recess, at home, and in bed. Without a doubt, she was the winner of her grade, but we were not happy to see that. On more than one occasion, her teacher noticed Fanny hiding a book under the table to read in class instead of listening to the lesson. This also reduced her interaction with other children in class or during recess and made us very worried.

The same thing may occur to different people with different results and may need to be handled differently. Loving to read was a good thing for Kathy, because she usually did not read. We were happy to see that the reading contest inspired Kathy's enthusiasm. However, Fanny was a different story. She loved reading too much. We wanted her to play more with other kids and not be so addicted to books. We were seriously concerned about Fanny's obsession because it could harm her social development, so we had to find a way to solve the problem before it caused irrevocable damage.

Generally speaking, reading is not a bad thing at all, but anything taken to an extreme can be harmful. To force her not to read was not the right approach. We wondered how we could guide her out of her current situation without hurting her enthusiasm for reading.

We started looking for different activities that could be of interest to the girls. One day, an advertisement for dance classes caught my eye. There are a number of benefits to dancing, such as learning to enjoy music and dance and developing a different hobby. When I told the girls about my idea, they were delighted and anxious to begin, so we sent Fanny and Kathy to ballet class.

Ballet class consisted of hour-long sessions after school, three days a week, every week. I enjoyed taking them to their class and watching them, dressed in pink ballet tutus, dancing along with the music. The class seemed to come to a close too soon, after just three months. When I noticed their great interest in continuing to learn how to dance, I proposed, "Do you want to try tap dancing?"

"Yes! Yes! Let's do it!" they exclaimed excitedly. Tap dancing is a completely different style of dance than ballet. It involves fast, energetic movement and coordination to make the metal pieces on the heels and toes of the shoes strike the floor to make a pleasant sound. The girls would giggle as they jumped, listening to the tapping of their shoes as they hit the ground. They enjoyed the music and were happy to dance.

Because of her natural elegance, Fanny learned ballet quickly and did very well. However, Kathy's high energy level added an extra dimension to her tap dance.

The First Note of a Piano

We tried not to influence our children with our preconceptions. As parents, we spent as much time with them as possible in order to understand them. In everyday life, we interacted with our children by playing with them and helping them explore their world. During those moments, we paid attention to their interests, strengths, and uniqueness.

In 1992, Fanny was almost two years old, and our family was invited to a friend's house to celebrate Chinese New Year. When our friend proposed that all the children take a picture with his piano, most of the children became very shy and hid behind their parents. However, Fanny showed no fear and walked over to the piano, sat on the bench, and began to touch the piano keys. Furthermore, she posed herself like an expert piano player. This made everyone laugh, but her actions told us that she liked the piano and being the center of attention. If we had not paid attention to this moment, we might have missed this insight into her thoughts. In order to further understand and develop this side of her, we bought her an electronic keyboard. She really enjoyed playing the keyboard. Anytime she had the chance, she would pound on the keys. In third grade, she started piano lessons.

Fanny's first piano teacher was Ms. R, an amiable old lady. Fanny liked her very much. Once a week, I would take Fanny to Ms. R's house for a forty-five-minute piano lesson. At home, Fanny practiced for thirty to forty-five minutes a day without any prompting. I could see that she really enjoyed playing the piano.

Every time Fanny passed a lesson, Ms. R would add a colorful small sticker to her music book to encourage her to continue practicing. These stickers represent the recognition of the teacher and give children a sense of accomplishment.

Every year, Ms. R would hold a piano recital. One day in October, she told Fanny that the next recital would be in December and that she hoped Fanny would be able to participate. With only a little more than two months to learn and perfect a recital piece, and Fanny having learned to play the piano just three months ago, I wondered, *What could she play?*

John and I were hesitant about whether she should participate or not. We decided to discuss it with Fanny to get her opinion. Surprisingly, Fanny firmly told me, "Mom, I want to be in the piano recital."

When we reported her decision to Ms. R, she suggested that Fanny choose a simple and short etude. But Fanny protested, "I don't want to play an easy song. I want to be an overnight success!"

We were very pleased by Fanny's self-confidence and courage to challenge herself. These traits would be essential to her future success. Fanny, John, and I worked together to find a suitable piece for her and finally found one called "The Great Smoky Mountains."

When Fanny told Ms. R about her decision, Ms. R was very surprised and cautioned her, "Are you sure you can play that? There are many notes you have not learned yet. Typically, this level of music is for children who have been practicing the piano for two or more years."

Fanny's answer was simply, "Yes, I can!"

The piece seemed very complicated, but most of the music did not require both of her hands to play notes simultaneously. From this perspective, if Fanny was willing to put in more effort when she practiced, I also believed that she could do it.

Because she set this goal for herself, Fanny's enthusiasm was particularly high. Whenever she had free time, she would sit down to practice. Sometimes she would play a couple measures repeatedly until she mastered them. I was impressed by her dedication.

"Hard work pays off," I told her as she practiced.

During the recital, I was so nervous and excited for her. When Fanny played, all I heard was the smooth flow and crashing power of the music. For a moment, I forgot about everything else; my mind was filled with her music. After she finished her performance, I was brought back to reality by the audience's enthusiastic applause.

At the end of the recital, a parent asked me, "How long has your daughter been playing the piano?"

I answered, "About a half year."

The parent responded, "Wow! What a blockbuster."

This experience is a testament to the Chinese adage: "Nothing is impossible, as long as the man will try."

Dancing and playing the piano were both enjoyable activities for Fanny, and they were also opportunities for her to broaden her horizons and explore her artistic potential. If our children demonstrated interest in a field, we tried our best to give them an opportunity to try the activity in order to increase their self-confidence and develop new skills. We had no intention of forcing them into a never-ending pursuit of perfection in just one activity, unless they possessed an extraordinary potential and interest in that area. If we did that, their enjoyment would have become resentment at a chore and a loss of motivation to practice and excel.

A Little Speaker

When Fanny was in second grade, she was selected to deliver a speech at her school entitled "I love America." Since we had so often taught Fanny to never settle for less than the best and to act in a way that would make her stand out in the crowd, we realized that this was an excellent opportunity to put our lessons into practice. Every member of our family worked hard to help her speech become a complete success.

When she had memorized the speech, I worked on her speaking speed, posture, and eye contact. After my basic training, we asked her stand on the staircase while we all sat on the floor below to watch her performance. In order to let her see her performance from the perspective of the audience, John purchased a video camera to record her speech and played it back to her. Since her enunciation was always flat and without cadence, we asked Kathy, the most eloquent of our family, to coach her in speaking loudly and clearly. We did not forget little Bill either; he served as an excellent member of the audience. Everyone had a job in this joint endeavor, and everyone did their best.

One time, I suggested that Fanny look up; but another time, John asked her to lower her eyes. When she was enthusiastic, we kept offering suggestions to help her improve. When she was in a bad mood or frustrated, sometimes even declaring that she would just give up on the speech, we desperately tried to cheer her up, encouraging her with words like "You're making a lot of progress!"

At the time, my friend Lisa was a university lecturer; so in order to produce better results, we asked her to help train Fanny for her speech. Based on our progress, Lisa added gestures and body movements to enhance Fanny's performance. It kept our entire family excited and very busy for almost two weeks.

"I love the United States. It is a free country, where there is freedom and human rights . . ." Success! Her speech was delivered at the right speed with the right tone, coupled with appropriate gestures. When Fanny's speech was completed, the sound of applause filled the auditorium, and many students and parents came to congratulate her warmly.

"Your efforts made you successful. Do you still wish you could give up?" I joked. She responded, as she always did, with a small, embarrassed smile.

Lost Scouts

When we first heard about the Girl Scouts, we thought it would be a very worthwhile group for our girls to join. We believed that it would offer the girls more opportunities to learn about American culture, make friends, learn survival skills, and develop their own leadership and teamwork abilities. Both Fanny and Kathy also thought that it sounded like an interesting organization, so they registered for a troop and anxiously waited for the first meeting of the Girl Scouts.

A week after their registration, our phone rang. When I picked up the phone, I whispered as loudly as I could, "It's the Girl Scouts!"

When Fanny and Kathy heard that, they ran over to me excitedly, waiting impatiently for me to get off the phone and tell them now what the woman on the other end of the line had said. Unfortunately, it was not the good news we expected. The Girl Scouts could not find a good troop leader, and they also could not fund a new troop.

It wasn't until we moved to New York several years later that Fanny and Kathy finally joined the Girl Scouts.

Spiders and Dogs

There is a common species of long-legged spiders in Utah colloquially known as "daddy longlegs." There is another species of jumping spiders that are smaller than raisins and often seen in the house.

Initially, both Fanny and Kathy were afraid of the spiders because they thought all spiders were poisonous. To clarify this misconception, we took them to the library to read the books about spiders. The children quickly learned that there are many types of spiders in Utah including the garden spider, gold spider, black widow, brown recluse, and jumping spider. The black widow with a glossy black body and red marks on the abdomen and the brown recluse with a violin-like body are two of America's most dangerous and poisonous spiders; but the others, including the daddy longlegs, are not poisonous. We spent time playing with the daddy longlegs, and sometimes I let the daddy longlegs crawl up my arm. Gradually, the girls became used to the spiders and also enjoyed playing with the daddy longlegs.

One time when Fanny was a baby, I was taking her to the library, and a large dog kept following us.

Does the dog have rabies? I wondered. I was very worried that the dog would suddenly jump on us. To protect Fanny, I hid the stroller behind me and walked backward, my eyes constantly switching back and forth between the dog and my baby. When a driver saw my situation, he was kind enough to park his car to stop the dog. He told me, "Do not worry. I will watch the dog for you. Please go ahead."

"That is very kind of you. Thank you very much!" I said gratefully before quickly running to the library.

Another time, I took Kathy to a nearby convenience store to buy milk. A small dog broke free from its owner and ran toward us, barking. I was so scared and tried to chase the dog away with the milk carton. Kathy could only hide behind me, not even daring to breathe. I told myself, "If you are afraid of the dog, the child will be scared to death."

When John heard this story, he told me that the best way to solve this problem was to get a dog ourselves. On that day in 1998, when we shared our decision with our children, they were excited and anxious, giving them strange expressions. Interestingly, when we were discussing what breed of puppy we should buy, the two sisters sided with me in arguing for a powerful German shepherd, while the two men wanted a small toy dog. I wonder if there is a psychological explanation behind our preferences. Since each party was firmly entrenched in their decision, the argument lasted for a few days without a resolution.

In the end, we activated our family voting system, where a child's vote counted for one vote each, and an adult's vote counted for two. Originally, it was set up to ensure that the parents' alliance would have the upper hand over the children's alliance. Now, it allowed the women's alliance to rule over the men's. Of course, Fanny, Kathy, and I were very pleased with the situation; but it was a totally different story for the men. Angrily, John and Bill jumped up and down and tried to find another way out, but we refused to give up even an inch. Finally, John obeyed the results of the vote and acquired a German shepherd puppy.

The puppy was so lovely and adorable, as well as fuzzy and naive, and we named him Lucky. Each day, after the children came home from school, they called, "Lucky, Lucky!" nonstop and had a great time playing with the dog. Occasionally, John would take the puppy to school to meet Fanny and Kathy when school was over. While the other children were also having fun playing with Lucky, he would see a proud expression on Kathy's face. We had a great time with Lucky! This proactive approach was indeed effective; since then, we have no longer been afraid of dogs.

"Do not let the children lose at the starting line."

During elementary school, children are full of curiosity, energy, and a strong desire for knowledge. This golden age of development is the best time for parents to educate and guide them. As parents, we wanted to take advantage of this, but how to make the best use of this precious time is a problem we have not yet found the solution to.

"Do not let the children lose at the starting line." This is a slogan many parents are familiar with. How can you judge whether a child is a winner or a loser at this age? Consider two people building a house: one is careful to lay down a solid foundation before beginning construction on the buildings; the other builds the house first, then tries to reinforce it. In the short term, the latter individual establishes a visible product first, but when the former finishes the foundation, he can move forward without needing to look back. A winner or a loser is determined by their ability to reach the ultimate goal in the long term.

Indeed, early education cannot be ignored and is necessary for children's future success. However, this does not mean that studying should occupy all their time, neglecting other activities. We gave our children free time to play and think independently so they could develop their imaginations and initiative.

We do not endorse a one-sided emphasis on early childhood education because early education and training gifted children do not share a correlation. Early education can contribute to the success of a child, but using early education to push children ahead of others their age generally does more harm than good. It will increase a child's psychological burden and block his or her physical and mental development. A proper early education should pay attention to and respect the child's personality, abilities at different ages, and individual differences so that the child can achieve a complete, balanced development.

The Prep Program

In 1997, Fanny was in second grade at Edgemont Elementary School when her teacher recommended that she take the entrance exam for a preparatory program organized by the school district.

The prep program was conducted at another school, Alta View Elementary. Fanny successfully passed a series of exams, but she did not want to go to the other school because she did not want to leave her good friends at Edgemont. We explained to her that this was a great opportunity for her to be around many other gifted children and to interact with them. By doing this, she would better understand herself. We also promised her that if she decided that she did not enjoy the program, she could come back to Edgemont at any time.

Finally, Fanny decided to give it a try.

A few months after Fanny joined the prep program, we went to a parents' meeting. At that meeting, we learned that the materials that were used for the gifted students were the same as for the regular classes. However, the gifted students were expected to accelerate their learning ahead of the regular classes by three to six months. In order to reach this goal, the gifted class would have less social activities and more homework.

What? We were shocked!

Later, we discovered that any student from the regular class who wanted to enter the prep program needed to take an exam that covered the material that the gifted class was learning—three to six months ahead of the regular student's class. This ensured that the gifted class would outscore the students from a regular class in the screening exam.

What a joke!

Moreover, in order to finish their extra work, students in the gifted classes would have reduced social activities, such as field trips. That was something else that we did not believe would do Fanny any good. The goals of the program were at complete odds with our philosophy. We expected the prep program would help the gifted kids learn the material in a broader and more thorough manner, develop their leadership skills and creativity, and promote their team spirit. In reality, this prep program just mechanically pushed the learning process forward by a few months to ensure that the "gifted" students could perform better than the regular class in the next screening exam.

We were very disappointed and decided to take Fanny back to Edgemont Elementary School. The teacher for the prep program did not understand and argued, "Fanny is doing well here. Why would you take her back to Edgemont? She will be bored there."

She did her best to discourage us from removing Fanny from the program. Despite her protestations, we believed that going back to Edgemont was the right decision. Although we withdrew Fanny from the prep program, we were able to see from her performance until that point that she was very intelligent and could hold her own against other students of a similar level.

However, our decision greatly confused and upset Fanny. She cried, "Why would you send me to Alta View one day, then later send me back to Edgemont? How can I keep my friends at both schools now?"

We understood her feelings, but she was our first child, and elementary school was still a new land for us too. Therefore, it was inevitable that we would make mistakes and have to take some detours along the way. We also felt sad for her, and to cheer her up, we held a party and invited her friends from both schools to have fun together. Finally, we were able to see her smile again.

From this experience, we realized that it is not enough to simply ask children to follow us when they are young. We also need to pay attention to their feelings and make sure that they understand the intentions behind what they have been asked to do. Otherwise, little by little, the misunderstandings will start to pile up; and they will try to distance themselves from us, making it more difficult to guide them and give them a proper education.

The Myth of the Child Prodigy

I still remember the time when Fanny was in second grade and she received a score of 65 out of 100 on a statewide exam. Did that score mean that Fanny had lost at the starting line? If so, how could we explain her later success?

For parents that have already raised children, looking back, we can see that our children's test scores before fourth grade have no impact on their future development at all. I remember that I took the situation very seriously, but when I spoke about it to John, he didn't even blink. Instead, he told me a story.

One day, when he was in elementary school, a farmer was invited to give a lecture to the students for a political reason. The farmer told the students that before the communists liberated him, he worked for a landlord. The landlord treated him and his colleague brutally. During the winter, there was nothing to do in the field, but the landlord would still drive him and his colleague to the field and force them to dig deep in the field. Interestingly, during this lecture, the farmer also mentioned that, for unknown reasons, the crops grown in that field were better than those grown elsewhere in the following year.

The farmer's story caught John's attention. For a while, he puzzled over the relationship between digging and growing good crops. Finally, he realized that digging deep was a symbol for gaining a complete understanding, which is the key to the success in many situations. In his later studies, he spent as much time as possible cultivating a deeper understanding without consideration for the benefits he might receive in the short run with shallower methods. This approach helped him stand out in an extremely difficult environment at a later time.

At this point, perhaps some of our readers may be confused. Since "digging deeper" is the key to success, isn't the way that many Chinese parents drive their children to do extra practice "digging deeper"?

No. Those methods are just a narrow-minded way of "digging deeper." We believe that if children practice without passion, motivation, innovation, and autonomy, their efforts will produce no more than repeatedly planting the soil without digging it up first.

Our understanding of "digging deeper" means broadening the vision, gaining a deeper understanding of both basic and complex concepts, developing creative thinking, and applying the knowledge they have gained. We must give them space to grow and breathe freely, like the plant roots in the loosened soil. Only by digging deeper in this way can we reap a comprehensive and extensive harvest.

In later chapters, you will see more stories about Fanny and Kathy. They both missed many great opportunities. Several times they fell behind, but they always caught up again. During these situations, the solid foundation of mutual trust and understanding we built when they were young paid off. Because of our close relationship, we understood their strengths and weaknesses. We knew how to set reasonable targets for them at the different stages of their development, and they were happy to accept our recommendations and follow our guidance. As a team, we worked together to help them achieve their goals.

During a child's enlightenment period, we believe that the most important thing is to build a solid parent-child relationship. Parents need to understand their children's interests and how to explore their children's potential. For young children, learning social and other skills by playing with other children and interacting with adults is more effective than just studying a textbook.

The parents' behavior also plays an important role in a child's education. Parents are children's role models, their heroes. The parents' values and view of the world will have a great impact on their child's. Parents should take full advantage of this prime opportunity to guide their children toward the right path. Once the children mature and their world view has taken shape, it is extremely difficult to change it.

We want to see children of sound mind. Raising children is like building high-rise buildings. We want to build skyscrapers that can pass the test of hurricanes, earthquakes, and time. In order to do this, we must first lay a solid foundation and never cut corners. Even waiting for the cement to dry requires time. Therefore, we must not be anxious. Everyone develops at a different rate, so we should allow children to develop naturally and not try to push them further than they can handle. Otherwise, the results may not be what we expect or desire.

This is a real story that we have witnessed. Every year, the Johns Hopkins University Center for Talented Youth (CTY) program offers summer camps for gifted children. These camps allow the children to select any one of a number of fascinating academic courses that they attend during the day, interspersed with various social activities during a break time in the afternoon and evening where they can interact with other intelligent youths. To be eligible for this program, the applicants are required to take the SCAT (sixth grade or lower) or SAT (seventh grade and upper) exam and obtain a score that meets certain criteria. One of our friends' children took the exam, but unfortunately barely failed to pass the required threshold. We believed that this indicated that the child just needed extra preparation before he tried again next time. However, his parents were so eager to raise his score that instead of offering the child extra help, they simply asked the school to let him skip a grade in math. Since the SAT was designed for high school students, by skipping a grade in math, the student could take a shortcut to raise his math score by learning more complex concepts that other students his age had not learned yet. Well, things worked out as planned. The boy passed the test the next time and happily enjoyed the CTY summer camp. What he and his parents didn't realize at the time was that the knowledge gap left behind by skipping a year would cost the boy a great deal. Soon after, his math performance at school also jumped, but it jumped downward, not upward. Both of the parents had excellent educations and had received postgraduate degrees, but made such a simple mistake. Why?

When educating children, parents should be patient and let nature take its course. While they can help their children reach their full potential by offering them extra practice, they should not push them to meet unrealistic expectations, and they should ensure that their child has a solid foundation. Even if a child is actually a genius child prodigy, he or she can still be destroyed by neglectful care.

CHAPTER 5

Practical and Innovative Ability

Developing motor coordination begins in childhood. Playing with toys can promote a child's sensory development and hand-eye coordination. Coloring, cutting paper, folding origami, and building block structures are all very good activities. When children start to learn new skills, imperfection is inevitable. However, imperfection is only an indication that more practice is necessary, so we should encourage children to use their newfound skills until they have mastered them. We can patiently guide them, but we cannot do the task for them.

We taught our children how to fold paper airplanes and send them soaring under the blue sky, as well as paper boats that floated on the surface of the water. We also taught our children to make paper monkeys to decorate their rooms and cut snowflake patterns to hang in their windows. In the spring, we made kites to fly in the park and taught the children to collect flower petals and leaves to make bookmarks and greeting cards with later. Young children often feel that these types of activities are fun and interesting, and through them, they can learn and play at same time. Even though they only make very simplistic creations, they can see and touch them, the tangible symbols of their efforts. This creates a feeling of accomplishment that will further fuel their interest.

Different children have different interests, and the same child may develop new interests at different stages of development. Therefore, we should take these factors into account when we are teaching them new skills in order to provide suitable hands-on experiences.

Little Scientists

Playing with Dough

When Fanny was about two years old, she saw me kneading dough and enthusiastically began to watch me, occasionally poking the dough herself with a finger. When she saw her small fingerprint left on the dough slowly changing, she gurgled with laughter.

"Is this fun?" I asked her. She nodded and laughed louder when I encouraged her, "Press it harder!"

This small incident sparked an inspiration: to allow preschool children to play with dough.

When my children played with dough, I first showed them how to use a cup to measure the proper amounts of flour and water, and then we all had fun working with it. I still remember once, when we were preparing the dough, I looked up at their faces and could not stop laughing at them. They were all baffled. When their initial confused reaction faded and they looked around, they all started laughing too. All of their faces were painted white from where they had touched them with their floury hands. When they realized this, they began to use the flour and newly-made dough as weapons to smear more flour over each other. For a time, the kitchen was filled with hazy white smoke, and when the dust had settled, each of them had become a clown.

"Silly play is boring. Let's make something with the dough, okay?" I urged them. I could not stand the mess, so I had to find a quick way out of the situation by diverting their attention.

"Yes, Mom!" the two sisters replied in unison. I really do not understand how they could do that so often without rehearsing at all.

Kathy made a long twisting snake by rolling her dough back and forth between her hands and the table. Fanny created a face by first making a flat disk and then using peas for eyes and carrots for the nose and mouth. Little Bill rolled a small ball, circling his hands over and over to try to make it perfectly round. After they finished, each of them exhibited their creations on the table proudly.

"Mine is the best."

"Hey, mine is better than yours."

"Mine is a true masterpiece."

Despite having just resolved the flour war, it seemed a verbal war was imminent.

"You all did a great job. How about adding some color?" I hastened to smooth things over.

Eagerly, they mixed their dough with food coloring; and the snake became a green snake, the human face become yellow, and the plain white ball changed into a colorful ball. This made their works of art look richer. Each of them took their creations to their rooms happily.

Soon, I found that playing with dough can be beneficial for children. Kneading the dough can increase children's finger strength, which is useful when they start learning how to write. Dough can also be used to teach children how to count. I used food coloring to dye the dough different colors, rolled the dough into strips, and then broke it into pellets for them to count. The more they counted correctly, the more pellets they received. They were all happy to participate.

I also used the brightly colored dough to hold their attention and teach them colors. We played another game where I mixed all the differently colored pellets together and then asked them to pick up only the pellets of a specific color and to count them. We also used the dough to teach them shapes such as rectangles, squares, circles, cubes, spheres, and cones.

Later, we found a product on the market called Play-Doh that could serve a similar purpose. We bought some Play-Doh to continue the exploration process with our children. In order to develop their ability to observe and compare different objects, we also bought a set of plastic animal models. After shaping the Play-Doh into a giraffe and elephant, I asked them, "What are the characteristics of a giraffe? What are the special features of an elephant?"

Seriously, the children studied the giraffe and elephant models and responded, "The giraffe has a long neck. Elephants have long noses."

"And? What else?" I asked.

"Oh, the giraffe's legs are long and thin, and the elephant's legs are short and thick," the children rushed to answer.

Magic Carnations

I remember that one day, the children and John suddenly disappeared. When I was starting to wonder what they were up to, they reappeared in front of me with mysterious smiles, John's hands hidden behind his back. Anxiously, Fanny ordered, "Mom, close your eyes!"

"Why?" When I saw their strange expressions, I was afraid that they were trying to do something to make fun of me, so I opened my eyes even wider to stare at them. Undaunted, Kathy and Bill rushed forward to cover my eyes with their little hands.

"Happy Mother's Day!" the children shouted in unison. Kathy and Bill let their hands fall as a bouquet of carnations, as white as snow, were pushed into my face!

"This is very nice, thank you!" I exclaimed, surprised.

"Mom, we know your favorite color is red, but the red carnations were sold out," Kathy added regretfully.

The next morning, in front of the doors of the children's bedrooms, there was a box labeled "Magic" and wrapped with a colorful ribbon.

"Magic? Let's see what's inside!" Bill excitedly began to open it, revealing a bunch of red carnations inside.

"Wow, how did they all turn red?" the children wondered aloud curiously.

"Do you want to learn the magic trick?" I asked them.

"Yes, Yes!" They all nodded and looked at me expectantly.

To learn the magic trick, we moved to the kitchen. Everyone received a transparent plastic cup and a white carnation, and then each of them picked a food coloring: red, blue, or green. Fanny moved fast and grabbed her favorite color, red, while Kathy picked blue, and Bill took the green. When they were ready, I issued my instructions.

"Fill your cup with water until it is about three quarters full. Then add thirty drops of food coloring."

"Why thirty? Can I add less?" Kathy asked. While she was asking her question, she forgot to continue counting and exclaimed, "Uh-oh, I forgot how much I added."

"Oops, I added too much. What can I do?" Bill asked nervously.

"It's okay. Don't worry about it." I reassured them.

"Now, the last step is to cut two inches off the stem and put the flower inside your cup." They all followed my instructions carefully.

"Mom, why isn't the flower changing colors?" Bill asked impatiently, resting his chin on his hands.

"Why will the flower change colors?" Kathy added, looking at me expectantly.

At that moment, my best answer was, "The flower will become the same color as the water because when the flower absorbs the water, it will absorb the color too."

Fanny has always enjoyed playing with colors. When she heard my explanation, her mind worked quickly. Since we have always encouraged our children to be creative and to explore the different properties of objects, she took the opportunity to practice in this situation. She mixed the red food coloring with the blue food coloring to produce a cup of purple water and repeated the same procedure as before. Surprisingly, she did not get a purple carnation; instead, the cup held a red carnation.

"Why?" everyone asked. I was also puzzled and had no answer for them.

More surprises followed as, magically, that flower gradually changed color, remaining mostly red, but also tinged with purple. By the second day, it had turned entirely purple, although not the same purple as the water. It was fantastic, and we were all astonished.

"Fanny, you are soooo great! You're more powerful than a magician!" Kathy praised Fanny with an admiring expression and a shaking voice. I thought hard, but still couldn't find an explanation for this phenomenon.

"I am going to ask Daddy," Fanny announced, hoping that her omnipotent father would have an idea. However, when she demonstrated the experiment for John, he was astonished too. It was rare for him to not have an answer to the children's questions, but that day, he was speechless.

John and I decided to go to the library to search for an answer. We studied biology textbooks to educate ourselves, and each time we learned something new, we would discuss it together and exchange ideas. After several discussions, we finally realized that since the different colors are made from different materials, they have different molecular sizes, resulting in a different rate of absorption in the flower stem. Since purple is composed of two colors—red and blue—the red molecules were absorbed first, causing the flower to be red. When the blue material was absorbed afterward, the flower gradually become purple. What a lesson! Fanny's accidental exploration opened another door for us to understand some of the many mysteries of nature.

When I tried to explain this to the children, none of them could understand—I could tell from their puzzled faces. After all, the girls were only in elementary school, and Bill had not even started school yet, so concepts like molecular size were too complicated for them to grasp.

How could I explain it otherwise? It became a challenge for me too, but I suddenly had an idea. I explained it to them like this: "Let's look at it this way. Our house is like the end of the stem and the flower petals are the ice cream shop near us. There are ten people who want to go to the ice cream shop from our house. Five of them are in red, and another five are in blue. They're like the water—with equal parts red and blue. It will be purple, right?"

"Yes!" they agreed, recalling the way they had mixed paints before to obtain different colors.

"Everyone tell me, before they leave our house, how many are in red?" I asked.

"Five!" they answered quickly.

"How many are in blue?"

"Five too."

"When they go to the ice cream shop, the people in red ride bicycles and the people in blue walk there. Which color will arrive first?"

"Red!"

"So if you take a look at the ice cream shop, what color it will be inside?"

"Red." It was obvious to them.

"Slowly, when the people in blue arrive, the color inside the ice cream shop will turn purple. Is that right?"

"Yes!"

They were all happy with the answer.

I then explained to them the importance of paying attention to unexpected phenomena because they often offer the opportunity to explore the world around them. For instance, Fanny's discovery had helped us learn something we did not know before. Kathy and Bill listened drowsily, but Fanny was fascinated and hung on to my every word.

"What if we can't explain them?" she asked, concerned.

"Never mind that. You can publish them and work together with other people to find the explanations. Professor T. D. Lee, who brought your father to this country, won a Nobel Prize because he discovered a new scientific principle while he was trying to explain an unknown phenomenon in physics."

"Oh, science is so much fun! I will be a scientist when I grow up," she decided. In this way, science set its roots in the brain of this little girl.

Fanny's little experiment, which produced such thought-provoking results, opened a door to our deeper understanding of science. What was originally intended to be a small project turned out to be a wonderful lesson for all of us, far beyond my expectations.

This incident touched us greatly. If we hadn't encouraged our children to indulge their curiosity and let them have the space to explore their world independently, it would have been impossible to have this experience. Many Chinese parents on the one hand want to see their children do better than themselves, but on the other hand want their children to follow them step-by-step in everything. Isn't this a contradiction?

Volcano Experiment

The volcano experiment is one of the most popular projects for children, regardless of their age. It essentially involves a chemical reaction of baking soda and vinegar to produce large amounts of carbon dioxide gas, resulting in an eruption similar to that of a volcano.

I remember a party we held when Fanny was in seventh grade. We had invited all our children's friends over to play. Due to the age difference, we divided the children into two groups, and the younger children were making volcanoes. They made model volcanoes out of Play-Doh, and when they saw the red "lava" erupting from them, they shouted excitedly. They constantly kept running between me and the experiment table, asking, "Mrs. Wang, can I get more vinegar?" or "Mrs. Wang, may I have more baking soda?" Of course, I happily obliged them.

When I was busy, Fanny came over to me and said, "Mom, my friends also want to make volcanoes."

I looked at her, surprised. "They are in seventh grade, and they still want to play this game?"

Eventually, more children joined the younger ones in making and playing with volcanoes, and we quickly began to run low on supplies. Just when I thought I would have to end the fun, John appeared with a large bottle of vinegar and a few packages of baking soda. Everyone cheered loudly when they saw him before returning to their volcanoes.

The volcano experiment requires the following materials: Play-Doh, a plastic bottle, red food coloring, baking soda, white vinegar, dish detergent, and a plastic or foil tray.

The procedure for creating the volcano is as follows:

1. Make a model volcano in the tray: knead the Play-Doh until it is soft and use it to cover the plastic bottle in the shape of a mountain, making sure that the bottle is upright and its opening is not covered by the Play-Doh.
2. Fill approximately three-fourths of the bottle with warm water.
3. Add ten drops of red food coloring, two tablespoons of baking soda, and a few drops of dish detergent.
4. Add some white vinegar. Instantly, the red "lava" should erupt from the bottle similar to a real volcano.

Why is this experiment so popular with children? I think it appeals to children because of its two main features: a "magic" explosion and color.

This experiment introduces children to chemical reactions and leaves a very strong impression on younger children. For the older children with some knowledge of science, I asked them to think about the science behind the magic. Why do vinegar and baking soda react with each other, and can other materials be used to produce the same effect?

Alkaline Test Kits

Boiling red cabbage produces a purple juice that can serve as a harmless pH indicator. When mixed with an acidic or alkaline solution, the juice will change color according to the properties of the solution. We gathered a variety of colorless liquids, including clear soda, vinegar, liquid soap, distilled water, tap water, and a baking soda solution to test the juice on. In order to easily observe the color change, we used clear plastic cups to hold each solution. To train our children in basic scientific methods, we gave them a dropper to add the cabbage juice into the solutions. Initially, the children eagerly added the juice into the solutions dropper by dropper without controlling the amount. In this way, we could not compare the colors, so the tests kept failing. We then taught them to be patient and to add the juice one drop at a time to make sure that the same amount of juice was added into each cup. When they started doing this, then the children saw the color differences.

Why was there a color change? Why did some drinks have a similar color change? Why did dropping the cabbage juice into the colorless solutions produce different colors? What role does the purple cabbage juice play? We guided our children to think about these questions and discover the answers by themselves.

Identifying Oxygen and Carbon Dioxide

Carbon dioxide and oxygen are colorless and odorless gases, but they play very different roles in our lives. Carbon dioxide is heavier than air and can be used to isolate a fire from the oxygen in the air; some fire extinguishers use this principle to produce foam to smother a fire. On the other hand, oxygen is necessary in order to keep a fire burning. Burning is just a chemical reaction of flammable materials with oxygen. The following experiment can be used to illustrate these facts in an intuitive way for young children:

Place a candle in the center of a wide-mouthed jar, then add some baking soda to the jar. Make sure the baking soda does not cover the candle. After this, light the candle and pour some vinegar into the jar, being careful not to pour it on to the flame. The mixture of vinegar and baking soda will create a bubbling solution, and the candle will soon go out.

After this, we posed more questions to our children. Why did the mixture of vinegar and baking soda create bubbles? Why did the candle go out? Why can the candle be lit up outside the jar, but not inside the jar now? Sometimes I answered the question for them, sometimes I encouraged them to find the answers on the Internet, and sometimes I took them to the library to show them how to search for books and how to find the answers in a book. These are all very important skills for students to learn. Whenever our children found an answer to a question, they would excitedly rush over to me with a feeling of accomplishment. We were always happy to see those proud faces.

Different parents may be experts in different fields, but all of them can use their knowledge in their field of expertise to make learning fun for their children. Local libraries often have many books that teach parents how to help their children design easy experiments to develop their children's curiosity and intelligence.

Little Performers

Fanny has enjoyed performing since she was young. Her school, Edgemont Elementary, held talent shows every year.

One day, when she was in second grade, Fanny told us that she had registered to participate in the school talent show. She was planning to show one or two science-related projects.

We were fully supportive of her enthusiasm and passion. The next day, we took her the local library and bookstore and shuttled between these two locations to find ideas for her projects. In the evening, the whole family sat together to discuss how to make her project interesting, creative, and appealing to the other students. Everyone offered her ideas and suggestions. Finally, she decided to make a model rocket and a model UFO. The materials she used were very simple: paper plates, toilet paper rolls, drinking straws, decorative stickers, and other small items. After several days of preparation and testing, the projects were successfully finished.

Fanny's Model Rocket

At the talent show, Fanny stood up on the stage to present her rocket and UFO models and introduce their working principles. The children in the audience kept shouting, "Let it fly, let it fly!"

When Fanny threw the UFO into the air, the children shouted and jumped out of their seats, trying to seize the UFO. The show was pushed to its climax.

Another time, Kathy also had an opportunity to perform in the Edgemont Elementary Talent Show when she was just in kindergarten. Although she was still little, this was a good opportunity for her to learn how to perform on stage, so we encouraged her to give it a try. Since Kathy liked to tell stories, we suggested that she do just that. Storytelling was a good choice for her because, even back then, her voice was strong, and she spoke very clearly. At the time, *The Gingerbread Man* was her favorite short story, so we took her to the library to collect different versions of the story and let her use her own language to organize the story. Then, we had her practice her stage presence and her storytelling cadence with our family as her audience. At the talent show, she was a very calm and vivid storyteller.

Halloween is most children's favorite holiday because they can go door-to-door asking for candy, visit haunted houses, and carve pumpkins. When Fanny and Kathy were at Edgemont Elementary, we took them to a pumpkin farm to pick pumpkins and play in a corn field maze. By chance, we discovered that there was a Halloween costume contest at the farm. Fanny became very excited and asked, "Mama, can we go to the costume contest?"

I used my makeup to make Fanny's and Kathy's faces look like Queen Amidala from *Star Wars* and dressed them in black, white, and red clothes for the contest. The contest was divided into several different age and character groups. In order to let the children learn how to make their own decisions, we let Fanny and Kathy choose their own competition. Fanny won first place in her group. Kathy was exceedingly jealous and regretted selecting the wrong group. She asked Fanny, "How did you choose your category?"

These activities provided learning opportunities for our children, exercised their courage, and also enhanced their self-confidence. Parents must not constantly fear failure on behalf of their children and prevent them from exploring new opportunities, or else their children's efforts and enthusiasm will weaken and eventually disappear.

Fanny is very quiet, but she enjoys performing in front of people. Every time she notices a camera pointing at her, she smiles. When she was little, she was very cute. One day, she dressed up herself, held a colorful umbrella, and posed like a model at a photo shoot. We could not stop taking pictures of her. Since then, she will suddenly appear in front of us with a creative appearance, such as wearing a swimsuit in the winter or sunglasses on a rainy day. Of course, we never missed these chances to use our camera. She enjoyed it greatly, but we had a lot of fun too. In many situations now, she seems to be shy, but definitely not in front of the camera lens.

Our First Memorial

In 1998, Fanny was in third grade, and Kathy was in first grade. To celebrate their birthdays, we bought them a computer, making them incredibly happy. To make the computer a learning tool, John suggested that they work together on a project.

"What about writing a game?" Kathy suggested.

"Oh, that is too difficult for you guys. You are not ready for it yet."

"Is drawing in Microsoft Paint okay?"

"If you do it for fun, it is too easy, and you can do it anytime. If you try to paint seriously, it will be too hard." That idea did not appeal to John either.

"Well, what can we do?" the sisters asked.

"You guys like birds and flowers. How about collecting pictures of birds or flowers and adding descriptions of each species to make a booklet?"

"Wow, what a great idea! I can imagine how beautiful it will be!" Fanny had already fallen in love with the idea. She closed her eyes and tried to imagine their future masterpiece.

"Hey, silly, stop dreaming. We haven't even started working on it yet." Kathy tried to tease Fanny.

"What's wrong with dreaming? Without dreams, you won't have hope. I like to dream, so there!"

"Well, it will not only be yours. Don't forget my share."

The two sisters began to exchange words heatedly. Noticing that they were about to start a verbal battle, I reminded them, "Do you want to continue fighting, or do you want to start your project?"

"The project!" they responded in unison, like they did so often. As always, it made me smile.

The next step was choosing their subject: birds or flowers.

"I like flowers," Fanny said. She has always liked colorful things, so her choice didn't surprise anyone.

Kathy immediately grabbed the chance to continue teasing Fanny. "Do you really like flowers? I think birds are more interesting."

"Let's do flowers," their dad decided.

"Papa, that's not fair. Why you always support Fanny?" Kathy pretended to pout.

"Okay, let's do what you said, then."

The ball had been kicked back to Kathy, and she admitted, "No, no! I was teasing Fanny. Actually, I like flowers too."

Finally, with the decision made, they started their work.

It was easy to talk about such a project, but when they actually started working on it, many questions arose. Where could they find the pictures? How should they edit them? At the time, we did not have high speed Internet at home, so they had to explore different ways to gather the images and information. Despite all the questions and problems, they remained in high spirits. After one week of work, they had collected about twenty pictures and descriptions of different flowers and compiled them into a preliminary draft. The picture sizes, font sizes, and font types were inconsistent; and the pictures and descriptions were scattered randomly across the pages. In order to give them a rough idea of how to edit their booklet, I showed them a pamphlet with photos as an example of how others formatted their work. After they understood this new idea, they rushed to their father, asking him how to resize pictures and change the font size and type. With the new techniques they learned, they unified the picture sizes, font sizes, and font types; and their project started to take the shape of an edited booklet.

As more and more samples were collected, their booklet began to look a little boring. Every item was listed in the same format down every single page. We then suggested that they separate each page into two columns so they could place each picture at a different location relative to its description to bring more life to the booklet. They agreed to make the changes, and after a few months of hard work, they finally had a beautiful booklet with a few hundred flower samples. They titled it "What a Wonderful World," and we printed and assembled it into our first family memorial. Many times, we were surprised to discover that our children knew much more about flowers than we did. For example, there is a species of flower known as the "bleeding heart." Its name derives from its shape, because its outer petals create a heart shape, while its inner petals droop out like a drop of blood.

At the request of the two sisters, we printed a few extra copies of their work as a gift to their teachers. Their teachers were very impressed by their work. For a long time afterward, whenever we met their teachers, they would talk about the booklet. I still remember when one of the teachers told us, "I always keep it handy so that when I have spare time, I can open and read it. It's not only beautiful, but also very knowledgeable."

This booklet was not just our first family memorial; it soon became a driving force for our children's exploration of the world. Since then, each time we go hiking or camping or visit the botanical garden, the children bring their flowers book and use it to identify a variety of flowers and plants, sometimes picking specimens for closer examination. After returning home after each excursion, they carefully preserve the samples they have collected. This process not only enriched their knowledge of nature, but also trained their hands-on skills. Most importantly, this was done on their own initiative, and they enjoyed it every step of the way.

Encouraging children to do projects is very useful. During the process, they learn how to set goals and use the resources around them to achieve their goals. In addition, these experiences often improve their communication skills, broaden their creativity, and develop their team spirit. When they finish the project, they will have a sense of accomplishment that encourages them to explore more opportunities in the future and chase after even greater success. Of course, projects also offer parents the chance to interact with their children and learn more about their individual interests and characteristics. This will lay a solid foundation for parents to provide proper guidance to their children.

Embracing Nature

Childhood is carefree and innocent, and if the sky should fall, children can always count on their parents to hold it up. However, as children grow older, they will inevitably begin to feel the effects of more and more of life's stressors. The burden on their shoulders will become heavier as they face increased competition and pressure to successfully ride out the storm. Children need to be optimistic and self-confident, but they also need to learn various methods of releasing their stress and burdens. Loving nature and life as well as pursuing hobbies can help them relax when life gets too difficult; it gives them a break before they have to dive back into the problems they need to solve. Precisely because of this, we expressed to our children that although academic achievement is very important, they also need to learn how to enjoy life to make it even more worthwhile.

Our backyard always has flowers, fruit trees, and a vegetable garden. In order to develop the children's hands-on ability with plants, John always kept a part of the vegetable garden for the children's experimental garden. While we took care of the main garden, with their assistance, the experimental garden was theirs alone to plant and maintain. Once, Fanny read in a book that it was possible to graft a tomato plant with a potato plant, so she decided to try it herself. Based on the book, it seemed to be a very easy project, but in the end, it took her three years to succeed.

The first year, she planted a potato in their experimental garden. When a potato plant started to grow, we bought a tomato plant for her. Once she received the tomato plant, she immediately moved it to the field. It grew well too. A few weeks later, when she thought it was time to perform her experiment, she discovered that they were planted too far away from each other. Therefore, she decided to move the tomato plant closer to the potato plant. However, when she had first planted the tomato plant, it was spring. Now, it was hot summer, so the relocation was not successful. Two or three days later, when she revisited the garden, the tomato plant was dead!

The second year, Fanny took the lessons she learned the year before and planted the tomato and potato plants close to each other. When it was time to graft them together, she did everything the book said. First, she found a good stem in the potato plant and cut a small piece of the stem off. Then, she found a stem in the tomato plant that matched the height and also cut off a small piece of the stem. Finally, she pressed the two cuts together and stuck the plants together with chewing gum. It seemed like it was well done. Unfortunately, it failed again.

The third year, Fanny decided to plant the tomato plant in a large pot so that she would have more flexibility in grafting the stems together. This time, during the grafting, she paid great attention to making sure that the part of the stem that transported water and nutrients matched in both plants before sticking them together. When she sealed the cut, she made sure that it was well sealed and that no fluid would seep through. In addition, she moved a large wood board to shadow the newly grafted plant. With all of this extra effort, she succeeded! She was so proud of her work that she frequently brought her friends over to show them her "pomato" plant. This success did not come easily, but because of that, she learned a great deal from it, especially the importance of not giving up.

When we were still living in Salt Lake City, we planted watermelons. When the watermelons were ripe, we ate the big watermelons and let our dog, Lucky, play with the small watermelons. The children kicked the small watermelons far away, and Lucky chased them and brought them back to the children; it was as if the children and Lucky were playing a soccer game in our backyard. One day, Fanny came back with an interesting question for her dad. "Papa, have you seen a square-shaped watermelon?"

"No, never" was the answer.

"But I saw a square-shaped watermelon in the newspaper. Is it a new species?" she continued.

"I do not think so. Maybe we can try it out next year."

Next year, Fanny and her father discussed how to make the watermelons grow into different shapes. They made a square-shaped wooden box and bought a large transparent plastic box. When the watermelon grew to be slightly larger than a softball, they put them into the boxes, one for each box, and left the box open. Interestingly, when the watermelons grew larger, they fit themselves to the shape of the boxes. Now they had square-shaped watermelons, one in light green and one in yellow.

"Oh, the square watermelons were grown this way!" Fanny was satisfied.

I also remember another time when we were in Utah, in order to let the children see how peanuts grew, John planted some peanuts in the children's experimental garden. One day, Fanny rushed in to happily tell us, "Mama, Papa, I have pulled up all of the weeds in our experimental garden."

"Good girl! Great job," I praised her as I always did.

"Wait! Do you mean everything?" John asked, looking worried.

"Yes, yes!" Fanny nodded.

John rushed to the garden to take a look. She had pulled up all of the peanut plants too! This story provided Kathy with an excuse to tease Fanny for a long time.

One spring, we noticed that a local farm had placed an advertisement in the newspaper, offering to teach people how to collect and make maple syrup. The children were all very interested, so we decided to give it a try. Unfortunately, each time I called the farm, nobody picked up the phone.

"Hey, are we being silly? We have maple trees in the backyard. Why can't we try to do it by ourselves?" John suggested. We picked a maple tree and on the side facing the sun about three feet off the ground, we cut the bark to leave an opening about an inch long. Before long, the sap began to seep out, and the children eagerly extended their fingers to catch some and taste it.

"Wow, it really is sweet!"

"Yes, if we boil it, it will concentrate into maple syrup."

Another year, we planted gourds, and when the gourds were large enough, the children each carved their name into a gourd. As the gourds grew day by day, their names also became larger and larger, and we enjoyed seeing their excitement as they watched them grow. When the gourds were ripe, they used the gourds in their rooms as decorations. They asked, "Why is the gourd's shape so strange—like a small head and big belly?"
We answered, "We are waiting for you to find out!"

In the summer, the children built a butterfly house to keep the butterflies they caught. In order to make a butterfly box, they cut out the sides of a large box and covered the frame with transparent plastic. They poked holes in the plastic to let air in and put branches inside so the butterflies could rest on them. Then, they covered the bottom of the box with wet grass to keep the inside humid and placed sugar water in a shallow dish with a sponge.
To prevent mold or bacteria from growing, our children changed the sugar water every other day and observed the butterflies sucking the sugar water with great interest. Unfortunately, the butterfly house was too small to keep them indefinitely because the butterflies could not freely fly inside. Eventually, the children released the butterflies. When they saw the butterflies soaring in the blue sky, the children smiled and called to the butterflies, "Fly, you are free!"

On breezy and cloudless summer nights, our family set up a tent and telescope in our backyard. We shared the sky, the stars, and the beauty of nature. We talked about subjects such as black holes, planets, and wild animals. The children often fell into a deep sleep while John and I stayed awake all night. We enjoyed the relaxing and enjoyable family time.
At night in our backyard, the crickets were chirping, and something was always twinkling in the night. The children's firefly conversations went like this:
"What is that?"
"A firefly. Its tail is flashing."
"Wow, it's so bright!"

"Maybe a lot of fireflies could make a flashlight!"

"Do you want to try to make a firefly flashlight?"

Sometimes they used butterfly nets to catch the fireflies. They discovered that the firefly's head is red, while the lower part of the abdomen has a lot of white patches. We caught dozens of fireflies and put them into a transparent bottle, watching as their tails burst with fluorescence. The children even brought a book outside and held the bottle above the book—with all the light the fireflies made, they could actually read with it! Fireflies really captured their curiosity, and their biggest question was, "How do fireflies light up their tails?"

In an encyclopedia, they found the answer. The fireflies' light is a type of bioluminescence. The fireflies' cells contain a chemical called luciferin and an enzyme called luciferase. To make light, luciferase combines luciferin with oxygen. During this process, only a very small part of the energy is released as heat, and the rest as light, so fireflies will not overheat and burn. So far, humans have not created any light source that is as efficient as a firefly's light. Jokingly, we ask our children, "Do you have any interest in developing such an efficient light source to benefit humanity?"

One autumn, we decided to do another project: building a birdhouse, in order to teach the children how to use different tools. John bought some wood and helped our children cut out the pieces and put it together into the shape of a house. After that was done, the children wanted to decorate it; so we bought paint, stickers, and other small things they could glue on. From our daily observations around our yard, we had seen a bird nest in a tree made of natural grass, small twigs, and mud. The children copied the real bird nest and inserted hay, soil, and twigs into the homemade bird house, to try to make it more comfortable for any birds that might come.

Autumn is also the harvest season, so we often invite family and friends to go apple-picking, see the autumn colors, or have a picnic. As we revel in nature's beauty and the picturesque scenery, we get so wrapped up in the view that we lose track of time. The magic of nature never fails to renew our body and mind.

Enjoying the cherry blossoms

In the winter, the trees are dormant, so it is the best time for us to take family vacations. We went to the warm climate of the Californian coast to play in the water and sand, watch sea lions, feed the seagulls, go to Disneyland, and see performances. We also traveled to Las Vegas, where we saw several shows and visited an indoor circus and amusement park. Later, we visited Disney World to experience the childish and magical fun of a fantasy world.

One winter vacation, we went to Miami Beach. When we were at the beach, with the breezes coming off the water and the ebb and flow of the tides, we walked with our bare feet in the soft sand and felt a cool, comfortable pleasure. Soon, we saw a transparent blue bubble on the sand. I looked at it and wanted to step on it with my bare feet like a child. My children quickly held me back and said, "Mama, no! This is a Portuguese man o' war, and stepping on it will be very painful."

I was skeptical and thought they were playing a joke on me. To help me believe them, they pulled me back to the hotel and found a picture with a description on the Internet:

> *The Portuguese man o' war is a jellylike marine invertebrate. Stings usually cause severe pain to humans, leaving whip-like, red welts on the skin that normally last 2 or 3 days after the initial sting, though the pain should subside after about an hour. A sting may lead to an allergic reaction. There can also*

*be serious effects, including fever, shock, and interference with
heart and lung function. Stings may also cause death.*

I laughed and said, "Thank you for saving your mom's life!"

This experience was surprising because I did not really expect
children to know more than we did. At the beach, our children kept
telling the other children to keep away from the Portuguese man o'
war.

In 1997, we took a family trip to Yellowstone National Park. That
trip is one I will never forget, and I am sure that the children also
feel the same. Yellowstone National Park is America's largest and most
famous national park. It covers an area of 8,983 square kilometers,
and its wildlife and many geothermal features are well-known. Popular
attractions at Yellowstone National Park include: lakes, canyons, rivers,
mountains, grizzly bears, wolves, bison and elk, buffalo, waterfalls, and
geysers.

To be honest, our experiences during our Yellowstone National
Park trip can be summed up in one word: disappointing!

To watch the eruption of the well-known Old Faithful geyser, we
craned our necks, stretched our legs, and eagerly awaited the show. We
waited ten minutes, twenty minutes, thirty minutes . . . By the time
Old Faithful finally erupted, not only our children, but also John and
I had nearly lost all our patience. When it erupted, the jet of water
soaring to the sky only lasted for one disappointing minute. Kathy
complained, "The fountain show in Las Vegas is better than this."

Next, we drove to a spring basin, where the hot springs touched
each other. They are a particularly bright, strange color, and they are
amazing. However, since the children were little, they were not really
interested in the beautiful landscape. Eventually, John decided to
drive around in the park to find wild animals in order to stimulate the
children's interest. Who knew that it would actually make the children
very disappointed? After driving for several hours, we had yet to see
one animal. Finally, a buffalo showed up, and everyone wanted to take
a closer look; but after that, we didn't encounter another creature.
No wonder the children said, "Yellowstone National Park is really
boring."

On the way back to our hotel, we passed a lake. Our children played in the water and on the beach with great enthusiasm. This trip helped us understand that little children and adults have very different perspectives on what is fun. They love hands-on activities more than beautiful scenery, and they reminded me that we should let them help us plan our next trip.

Our children's footprints remain not only in school, but also in zoos, museums, and everywhere in nature: mountains, caves, canyons, forests, and more. Our experiences outdoors, inspired by the stunning majesty of nature, have allowed us to forge more intimate ties with our children. As parents, we work with our children, play with them, and learn with them. We should offer them different activities, a variety of books, and a wealth of knowledge that comes from every possible source. Through these activities, they will discover their interests, abilities, and potential; and we will all increase our understanding of each other. Only parents can ever know their children so intimately, and by having a solid foundation of mutual trust and respect, we can guide and assist them in seizing the opportunities that will help them succeed in life.

Science Fair

Fanny is creative and dedicated. To release her potential, we constantly sought opportunities to promote her creativity. In 2002, Fanny found out from her best friend, "M," that Rockland County held a Science Fair every year. They decided to participate but struggled with the dilemma: "What project should we do?"

"Build a robot," one of them proposed.

"What about conducting a study?" the other asked.

They continued to bounce ideas off each other, but were not quite satisfied with any of them. One day, Fanny and her friend were working together to solve a maze, and that sparked John's inspiration. He suggested, "What about building a three-dimensional maze?"

"That's a good idea. Let's do it!" they agreed enthusiastically.

To make their 3-D maze, they discussed several options and finally picked a laser-mirror model. In their design, they planned to use wood to make a 3-D maze similar to a corn maze, but with multiple levels.

When people played the game, they would place a laser at the maze's entrance and use mirrors to guide the laser beam out of the maze. Players could also use a periscope-like set of mirrors to move the laser beam between the levels. If two people wanted to play at the same time, they could each place a laser at the entrance and exit and see whose beam reached the center first. Furthermore, their maze would have many doors so that each time people played with it, they could design their own game by closing some of the doors. After they finished their design, the two girls were amazed by their imaginations.

Over the next couple weekends, John was busy working with them on their project. He took them shopping for supplies and supervised their work. Pretty soon, though, we realized that the initial plan wasn't going to work; even though they struggled very hard to cut the pieces of the maze out of the wood, the cuts were jagged and uneven. As they puzzled over this dilemma, John suggested, "If you cannot cut the wood well, how about using cardboard?"

This change made their job much easier, and the final result looked much more refined. Each weekend, Fanny invited her best friend over to our house to work on the project. Several times, little Bill tried to offer his help. Unfortunately, each time, by either crashing into the maze or breaking the mirrors, he did more harm than good. At a certain point, the two inventors had to declare him unwelcome.

Fixing a base to each mirror required that the base be fixed firmly and at a strict perpendicular angle; it was a very difficult job. They tried many methods and strategies without any success. Concerned, they turned to me for advice. Since I had used hot glue to make other projects before, I suggested that they try hot glue. To their delight, it worked! When I saw them happy, I was happy too.

With our help and supervision, they finally built a beautiful laser-mirror maze. We all played with it and enjoyed it very much.

On March 2, 2002, Fanny and her best friend, "M," took their invention to participate in the Rockland County Science Fair and received the "Most Marketable Invention" award.

Fanny's Science Fair Project: Laser Mirror Maze

In March 2003, Fanny and "M" combined their joint efforts again to work on a new project: the Optical Fiber Skylight. For this project, they took advantage of the flexible, light-transmitting properties of optical fibers to guide natural sunlight to any location indoors. The materials they used were very simple: a bundle of optical fibers from a novelty toy and foam boards. They used the foam boards to create a model house and tied the optical fibers together to form a path to guide sunlight into the rooms of the house. In order to improve its efficiency, they placed a thin lens in front of the entrance of the optical fibers to focus the light. This project was aimed at saving energy and being more environmentally friendly. Again, their new creation was honored as the "Most Marketable Invention."

Participating in science fairs can be the first step in guiding children to seriously work on a project because they have to finish in time to present it to the public. Throughout the process, they may encounter problems that require flexible thinking and creativity to solve. They will also learn how to choose a topic, design and create the project, and showcase their work. This knowledge typically cannot be learned in the classroom. Of course, winning awards will encourage them to pursue future endeavors, and the reward money can fund their future projects.

Basement Laboratory

After Fanny decided to focus on excelling in the sciences, she continued exploring new opportunities to expand her knowledge. In the summer after tenth grade, while still busy with independent study and volunteer work, she and Kathy built a laboratory in our basement to perform their own experiments. On the weekends and during any breaks, they spent much of their time in the basement laboratory, conducting a variety of experiments across different scientific disciplines: growing bacterial cultures, preparing slides of biological samples and examining them under the microscope, performing chemical experiments such as titrations, working with circuit boards, and refining their soldering technique; there was nothing they didn't do.

Although the lab was rather small and simple, it helped them develop their laboratory skills and the confidence to solve real problems in our everyday lives.

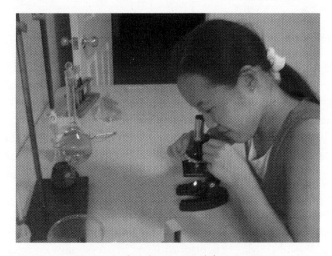

Fanny in her basement laboratory

We know that learning is not confined to textbooks and that children can also expand their knowledge by examining the world around them through research. When people discuss students doing research, many parents naturally think about working with professors or entering the Intel Science Talent Search or Siemens Competition. If students have the resources to do so, participating in these programs provides them with a great opportunity to delve deeper into scientific research and stand out among their competition. However, most high schools cannot provide students with the resources for such activities. Even so, we believe that encouraging students to make the best use of what they have will benefit them in the long run, even if they cannot enter such competitions.

A few years ago, we heard a story about a middle school boy who, through independent research, proved that the water in his school's water fountains was dirtier than the water in their toilets. His discovery attracted much public attention, and many schools took measures to keep their water fountains cleaner afterward. Although he did not receive any high profile awards, he still made a significant contribution to our society. When Fanny and Kathy were in high school, we told them this story to encourage them to pay attention to their surroundings during their daily lives and seek out ways to make their own contributions. With our encouragement, both of them did well. Eventually, Kathy even developed a new cleaning formula to help me clean kitchen grease. In one of her essays, she described this experience:

> I have always been enthralled by the endless possibilities of science, which have pushed me to delve deeper into this fascinating field. A few years ago, I built a lab in my basement with my sister where I spend many hours dabbling in different experiments, like examining bacterial cultures, carrying out titrations, and preparing slides of diverse substances. I also created a small garden where I grafted "pomatoes" and tested the effects of different conditions on plant growth. Each year, I actively participate in various science competitions, where I have won numerous awards. These successes motivated me to solve problems in real life. When I noticed my mother spending hours cleaning tenacious oil stains in the kitchen, I decided to find her a better solution.
>
> I was confident that I could resolve the problem by determining which dish detergent was the most effective. To my surprise, there were no noticeable differences among the detergents. Struggling for results, I changed the concentrations, furiously stirred the solutions, and combined detergents, but all my efforts were in vain.

An experiment from my Columbia University Science Honors Program Organic Chemistry class came to mind. We were given a procedure to produce a luminescent solution, but when it turned out poorly, I altered the experiment, exposing the solution to different conditions and modifying the amounts of certain materials, to determine the most effective procedure. Inspired, I started in a new direction, selecting several materials to add to the solution and carefully recorded my observations. After repeated testing, I discovered that baking soda had the best effect, which made sense. Baking soda was alkaline, a property that helped break the bonds in oils. To optimize my mixture's efficiency, I continued my efforts to test several other variables, such as temperature and concentration, until I was satisfied.

The next day, I showed off my magic solution. Tossing oil-coated knobs and racks into a pot of my mixture, I brought the concoction to a boil. After a few minutes, with a simple wipe of a sponge, the stove parts were shining clean. My parents were extremely happy with my magic formula. Each time they talked about cooking experiences with their friends, they would introduce my formula to them [. . .]

However, not all of Fanny's experiments turned out this well. When she was in ninth grade, she participated in a regional Science Olympiad competition. For some reason, the student who had signed up for the circuit lab event did not appear, so the team advisor sent Fanny to fill the spot, disregarding the fact that Fanny had not even learned physics yet. Fanny had always been a very calm and nice person, so she simply followed the advisor's orders. Since Fanny was so calm, the teacher was confident too. Well, once Fanny walked into the laboratory, she was understandably astonished. Faced with all the unfamiliar electronic units, she had no idea where to even start.

She thought, *Well, since I am here, I should at least try to do something. Maybe good luck will be on my side.*

However, for someone who didn't even know the basics of circuitry, not even resistances or capacities, the chance of doing something right was practically zero. The persistence that she had developed in the past simply drove her forward. We do not know what she actually did. All we know is that once she turned on the power, smoke started to rise from the circuit board in front of her. Despite the smoke, she stayed calm and tried her best to fix the problem, to no avail.

When she came home with this story, even though she described it as briefly as possible, we all laughed hysterically. When we asked her why she hadn't just told the team advisor that she couldn't do it, we received a completely unexpected answer.

"If I hadn't participated in the competition, we wouldn't have received a score. Even if I had burned everything there, since I turned up, I could at least get one point for my school."

What team spirit! As it turned out, she had actually won seven points, essentially just for showing up. She was a true math champion; even facing the rising smoke, she kept a level head and made clear calculations. Wordlessly, we just smiled and shook our heads.

Two years later, with the experience accumulated from the basement lab, it was a totally different story. On one cold winter day, the heat in the upstairs portion of our house suddenly would not turn on. Fanny immediately jumped up, volunteering to try and fix it. Although we did not expect anything to come of her efforts, since she had volunteered so readily and with such enthusiasm, we couldn't turn her down. Surprisingly, she did manage to identify, isolate, and fix the problem! In one of her college application essays, she describes her experiences with the basement lab and the process she used to fix the heater:

> *I have always been intrigued by the practical applications of science in the modern world. Two years ago, I built a working lab in my basement. Since then, I have spent countless hours poring over independent research while constructing circuits, performing chemical experiments, and studying bacterial growths. My lab is my stage—a space of endless possibilities where I astound my siblings with the wonders of science. It is also the workshop where I construct bridges and towers to represent my school in the regional Science Olympiad competitions. For the Rockland County Science Fair, I created a 3-D Laser-Mirror Maze and a model of an Optical Fiber Skylight; both won the award for the "Most Marketable Invention."*
>
> *In addition to enriching my academic performance, working in my lab has provided me with the skills and confidence to*

fix everyday appliances around my house. A few days before Christmas last year, our upstairs heater stopped working, and I persuaded my parents to let me try to fix it. Confronted with the complex heating system, I divided it into two fundamental parts: the hot water flow and the controls that directed it. Using my knowledge of circuitry, I mapped out the control system, which involved valves, thermostats, and circuits. Then, I compared the furnace and pipes to different elements of circuits. Through this process, I identified how the two parts worked together. Since the heater did not work upstairs, I deduced that the control system was malfunctioning; and after carefully studying the diagram I had sketched, I narrowed down the problem to a few places. After repeatedly examining and testing each component, I finally located the faulty relay and replaced the broken motor in that valve. The sense of accomplishment I felt in completing this job further fueled my passionate interest in science and engineering and my deep desire to learn more [. . .]

In her essay, Fanny expressed her enthusiasm for and dedication to science and technology and demonstrated her creativity and extraordinary hands-on ability, both of which are very impressive in a high school student. When she received her admissions letter from Columbia University, Ms. Rachel Fried of the admissions office included a handwritten note at the bottom of the letter:

Fanny,
Congratulations!
   Your passion for and talent in the sciences is impressive.
   I love that you built a lab in your basement!
   I think you'll really enjoy the research opportunities at Columbia. I hope to see you on campus this spring!

CHAPTER 6

Frustration and Rebuilding Confidence

The Story of Mencius's Mother

In China, there is a well-known story about the mother of Mencius. Mencius's father died when he was young, so Mencius's mother raised him as a single parent. In order to find a better environment to raise and educate her son, she relocated three times. With her persistent efforts, Mencius finally became the most famous philosopher after Confucius and played a very important role in Chinese history.

John and I also believe that the environment has a strong influence on children's growth. This idea is reflected in the Chinese saying: "Know nothing, doubt nothing." A child's mind is immature and very susceptible to the surrounding environment, which may help or hinder their development. This theory does not seem limited to only Chinese parents; studies have found correlations between higher house prices and better school districts in both America and elsewhere. Although the environment is not the only variable which determines the quality of a child's education, it definitely has a significant effect. Eventually, John and I decided to follow the example of Mencius's mother and move to a better educational environment for our children.

Kathy and Bill were born in Utah, and we brought Fanny to Salt Lake City—where they all grew up—when she was only a few months old. Their friends, with whom they had shared so many memorable moments, were all from Edgemont Elementary. The fruit trees in our garden gave them something to look forward to every autumn; and our family dog, Lucky, filled their lives with so much joy. To leave all of these blessings behind was emotionally difficult for them. When we told the children that we were planning to relocate, Kathy jumped up and was the first to object. "Mom, Dad, I don't want to move! Why should we move? Can't we stay here?"

Fanny, always the docile child, said, "I'm worried that I will lose friends, but I will obey your decision."

Our youngest, Bill, did not know what it meant to move. He thought we were taking another vacation and excitedly asked, "Will we stay in a hotel again?"

We compared the educational profiles of many states and believed that California and New York were the two best candidates. We now had to make a choice: to move to California or to move back to New York.

The Temptation of California

While living in Utah, we had visited California several times for family vacations. Discussing California evoked memories of warm weather and sunny beaches. We could still recall the roar of the sea lions, the smell of the ocean, and the adorable giant pandas in the San Diego Zoo. Of course, the children also could not forget their exciting experiences in Disneyland.

The first time we visited Disneyland, Fanny was barely tall enough to meet the height requirement for the ride Splash Mountain if she had a parent accompanying her. She insisted on going, so John had no choice but to ride with her. Kathy and I waited for them at the exit, and when she came out, Fanny's face was as white as a sheet. I asked worriedly, "Are you okay?"

John answered for her, "After the free fall, Fanny couldn't respond to me for a few minutes. She was frightened."

We all thought that the experience would stop Fanny from riding Splash Mountain again. To our surprise, the next time we visited Disneyland, she continued to ride Splash Mountain again and again with great enthusiasm. She looks gentle and soft, but she has the determination to challenge herself to the utmost. This aspect of her personality can also be seen in another story.

As I mentioned previously, the children's school held a reading competition for the students. Since she quickly devoured most of the books on her reading level, Fanny gradually began to read books at higher and higher reading levels. In second grade, she picked the book *Black Beauty*, a book typically suitable for students in junior high school. She failed to finish; but the following year, when the reading program began again, she picked *Black Beauty* as her first book to read. This time, she finished it and passed the test.

Kathy has a very different personality; she does not enjoy roller coasters, Splash Mountain, or rides with a free fall. However, she has always enjoyed socializing with other people. Whenever there is a crowd of people, she can usually be found there.

California was full of temptations for the children, and they initially decided that they would rather move to California.

The Charm of New York

New York was an unknown place for our children. However, New York City was where we had taken our first step into this country. It was also the place Fanny was born, so we had special feelings for New York. The most important factor during our considerations was the fact that many prestigious universities—such as Harvard, MIT, Princeton, Yale, and Columbia—are located on the East Coast. Because of this, we believed that moving to New York would be more conducive to children's development. To tempt them, we asked the children, "Do you want to see the Statue of Liberty?"

As expected, they cheered, "Yes!"

To try to change their minds further, we told them, "If we go to New York, we can visit the Statue of Liberty! We can climb to the crown and see all of New York City!"

Our children also enjoyed hiking and fishing. We told them that we knew about secret places on mountaintops with beautiful lakes that were the perfect places to fish. We promised that if we moved to New York, we would go to those places every summer. Eventually, we persuaded them that moving to New York would be an exciting adventure, and they began to look forward to the change of location.

Our next dilemma was finding a good school district. Although, on average, New York schools were better than Utah schools, we wanted to find the best school possible for our children. Thanks to the convenience of the Internet, we easily found information about school size, student-teacher ratio, school reputation, and other relevant data. If Mencius's mother was still alive, she would be delighted by modern information technologies. With the information we had collected from the Internet, we narrowed down our options to three areas: New York City, Long Island, and Rockland County.

New York City has a large Asian population, with most of them living in Queens or Brooklyn. If we chose New York City, our children could integrate into communities with similar cultural backgrounds. Furthermore, the public transportation system in New York City is well-developed and would make it convenient for our children to get around without our assistance. Most importantly, though, New York City has excellent educational resources. It harbored three well-known American high schools: Stuyvesant High School, the Bronx High School of Science, and Brooklyn Technical High School, as well as the rising Hunter College High School.

As we were considering the options available to us, our children pelted us with questions.

"What does New York City look like?"

"How big is it?"

"Is it easy to get lost?"

"Are New Yorkers friendly?"

In the end, we took them to visit New York City so they could discover the answers by themselves.

First, we visited the hospital where Fanny was born and the area where we used to live: Elmhurst, Queens. When they saw the windows and doors armed with iron bars, they stared at them. Kathy asked, "Why do the houses look like prisons?"

Fanny looked around doubtfully. "I was born here?"

We explained to them that when we lived there, we had heard many stories about robberies. To protect the tenants, the landlords had to equip their houses with these extra measures. We also told the children that when we first came to New York City, we were told that we should carry twenty dollars all the time. That way, in case we were robbed, we could give the robber enough money to buy our safety. When the children heard this, they were alarmed.

When we took the subway, their curiosity was soon replaced by a sense of anxiety. They could not help trying to hold their breath against the sulfurous smell, and the graffiti inside and outside the subway stations was shocking. To relax their tension, John joked that the people who drew the graffiti would call it abstract art. The children held our hands tightly with sweaty hands, afraid of wandering off.

It was a culture shock to come to a place like the "Big Apple," New York City, from a quiet place like Salt Lake City. They were shocked. They did not like it. From our previous experience and others' opinions, we felt that as an international metropolis, New York City did not represent mainstream American culture. Therefore, we decided that New York City was not a good choice for us.

Pearl River

After we eliminated New York City, we focused on Rockland County and Long Island. Long Island is a wealthy residential area with a good educational system, but it is known for traffic congestion on I-495 and its high cost of living. Since Rockland County proves a high quality education, is safe, and has a reasonable cost of living, it became our first choice. The natural environment of Rockland County is absolutely gorgeous. It has scenic mountains with many beautiful lakes, accessible by highway from all directions. On weekends, it attracts a large number of people from New York City who want to enjoy its beauty and have a picnic or barbecue. More importantly, it is a good place for children to familiarize themselves with mainstream American culture.

In the summer of 2000, we settled in Pearl River, a small town in Rockland County. Kathy enrolled in third grade at Franklin Avenue Elementary School, and Fanny entered fifth grade at Pearl River Middle School. Due to a shortage of classrooms in their elementary schools, the school district had moved the fifth graders to the middle school and the eighth graders to Pearl River High School, marking a distinct difference between typical American schools. This gave students extra time to adjust to a new environment so that they could reach their fullest potential during their critical years.

New Challenges

Soon after we settled into Pearl River, we were met with a flood of problems and difficulties. Since we had just moved, our children didn't have any friends. Due to the differences between New York and Utah education, they performed terribly on the statewide exams and academic competitions, and both Fanny and Kathy were unable to enter their schools' prep programs. Furthermore, as they were among the very few Asian-American children in the predominantly white community, they were sometimes treated unfairly. Their confidence was shaken, and their anxiety was written on their faces. They seemed to be lost in a dark and empty sea, wondering, *Where is the other side?*

John and I wondered how we could work together with our children to overcome these challenges. We understood that we could not solve all the problems overnight. Instead, we had to prioritize the problems and conquer them one by one. After a close analysis, we believed that we had to solve our children's social issues first in order to stabilize their feelings and emotions. Later, we will discuss how we worked toward this goal, but for this chapter, we will focus on our combined efforts to overcome their academic deficiencies once we cleared that first hurdle.

Academically, we decided to start by building on their strengths, helping them excel in mathematics to increase their self-confidence before attacking reading and writing. Our tactic was to not launch an incomplete attack; instead of shallowly spreading out our efforts across all the subjects, we dug deeper to ensure they had a firm foundation in all the subjects, one at a time. Once we started, we employed all of the available resources to get the job done.

A Rallying Cry

Kathy played a lot in elementary school and did not always pay attention to the school rules. During a parent-teacher conference, we were told that Kathy spoke a lot in class. She not only talked to the classmates next to her, but also walked over to others to chat while the teacher was teaching. This kind of behavior greatly displeased her teacher.

In fourth grade, Kathy learned that outstanding students could receive the Presidential Award for Academic Excellence when they graduated elementary school. She was interested and approached her teacher to learn more about the opportunity. However, her teacher coldly told her, "It is impossible for you to win."

It was like a bucket of ice water had been poured over her. When Kathy timidly told us this story, John realized that Kathy was starting to demonstrate a desire to explore her own potential. Around fourth grade, a child's self-consciousness and sense of identity gradually begin to develop as he or she starts to explore the environment independently. If children lack social experiences, they can easily lose themselves or fall into the wrong crowd. For parents, this may be the most important time to provide guidance because children are learning to explore by themselves, but they still respect their parents and expect their parents to help them. Before third grade, most children are innocent and moldable. However, after fourth or fifth grade, they form different social groups and begin to develop their future personalities.

John had a long talk with Kathy. As always, he started by talking about trivial matters, then he cut to the chase. He firmly told Kathy that she would be able to receive this award. To convince her, he listed all the reasons for his confidence and then helped Kathy plan out the steps to achieve this goal. He motivated her by joking about how, by working hard, she would prove her teacher wrong. Children are always glad when their parents fight for them because, especially at an early age, they need support and encouragement to gain the confidence to stand up for themselves. Inspired, Kathy declared, "Okay! I will get the Presidential Award to surprise my teacher."

Suddenly, Kathy began to change. Without the need for reminders from us, she began to study hard and gave up a lot of playtime in exchange. We were very happy to see these changes and very supportive of her efforts. Following Fanny's footsteps, she was diligent about doing her homework and looked for extra practice in order to excel.

Her hard work paid off. In the New York statewide exams, she received almost a perfect score in both English and mathematics, and she became an outstanding student in her class.

In June 2002, Kathy graduated from Franklin Avenue Elementary School with the Presidential Award for Educational Excellence, signed by U.S. President George W. Bush. Her name was listed in the local newspaper, *Our Town*, for the first time on October 16, 2002. What we remember the most about this accomplishment, though, was the unrestrained smile on her face as she ran to us with that certificate in her hand.

Kathy has always been a very independent child, often needing a reason to do something instead of following instructions without question. If she was properly motivated and had access to the right resources, she could achieve any of her goals, regardless of the difficulties she faced. This experience significantly contributed to the solid relationship of trust between us and Kathy, which laid an important foundation for her future conduct and our continued guidance.

The Prep Program

As soon as Kathy discovered the prep program at Franklin Avenue Elementary School, she asked us for permission to join. I immediately recalled Fanny's negative experiences with the prep program in Salt Lake City and became worried. I asked her, "Is this like the prep program in Salt Lake City?"

"No. It is different," Kathy informed me. She had learned that the children who were enrolled in the prep program attended regular classes and learned the same curriculum, but did more group projects and other activities that applied their knowledge. The program's mission was to cultivate the children's ability to think independently, gather information, and foster their team spirit. This was exactly what we wanted, a perfect match with our philosophy.

We quickly filed an application, but after we didn't hear back from the school, I tried to ask Kathy's teacher if she had been accepted. "No comment" was always the answer. *What was going on?*

I recalled reading a book that said written materials were considered more formal in the U.S. For serious matters, it is better to submit a written inquiry rather than just calling with questions. Therefore, I decided to write a letter to the school's principal to learn about the progress of Kathy's application.

Finally, we heard from the principal that Kathy needed a recommendation from her teacher, so we went to her teacher to ask for help. Her teacher responded that whether or not a student was enrolled into the prep program was determined solely by the school's principal, and there was nothing she could do about the situation. Kathy was just kicked between the principal and her teacher, and despite our best efforts, she was unable to enroll in the prep program.

Fanny had a similar experience at Pearl River Middle School. Like the elementary school, the middle school also had a prep program with similar goals. Fanny was determined to obtain the recognition of both her teachers and her classmates in this new environment, and she believed that the prep program would be the best opportunity for her to demonstrate her abilities. Thus, her first goal was to enroll in the prep program. However, she was flat-out rejected. When she submitted her application, the teacher in charge of the prep program bluntly told her, "I do not think you belong in the prep program."

Challenging the Prep Program

When Fanny and Kathy were both rejected from the prep programs, it hurt their enthusiasm and self-esteem. In Utah, they'd been considered highly intelligent and talented; but in New York, they were just average, or maybe even below average. Children especially need their parents' guidance and support when setbacks occur. While these experiences can turn into stumbling blocks that close the door to further exploration and make them satisfied with the status quo, when handled correctly, they can also become new sources of motivation to push the child forward. Knowing this, John and I tried our best to turn their frustration and disappointment into an outlet for their creativity.

I told Fanny and Kathy that people's lives cannot always be smooth. They needed to learn how to handle the obstacles that appeared and to not let themselves be dragged down by sadness and regret. We combined adages from both of their cultures—"Every cloud has a silver lining" and "Without a tiger in the mountains, the monkey is the king"—to try to help them understand. We were now living in New York, a place with better education and more competitive schools. The town's average household income was higher than the national average, and families paid more attention to children's education. It was natural to see many students with excellent academic performances, but they had to maintain their efforts and strive to improve themselves in order to bridge the gap. That was the purpose for which we had moved to New York from Utah; we wanted to challenge them to prove themselves in a more difficult environment, which we knew they could. If they did not want to be looked down upon and given the cold shoulder, they needed to work even harder.

John was not like me; he was hesitant to comfort them because he believed that it would not solve the problem. Instead, he thought they needed strength, faith, and determination. He asked Fanny and Kathy to treat the experience as a challenge and prove they were better than the prep programs. He confused all of us, so we asked, "You want us to defeat the prep program?"

He responded, "Yes, use your actions to prove that you are the best. Maybe you cannot do that now, but one or two years later, you certainly can."

John's confidence infected all of us and aroused the ambition in Fanny and Kathy. After the children had gone to bed, I whispered to him, "Do you really think that Fanny and Kathy can do it?"

John laughed. "Everything has a dual nature, and they have both been rejected from the prep programs. If we can't join them, then let's beat them!"

Breaking through the Math Barriers

In fifth grade, Fanny participated in the Math Olympiad competition. It was the first time she had a taste of real competition, and she performed poorly. There were a total of twenty-five questions in the contest, each worth one point. She only scored fifteen points and barely reached the average level of all the participants. Her eyes were filled with tears of humiliation. We were surprised because we didn't think she would perform so badly, even given the difference between New York and Utah.

Failure and frustration are not the most terrible things, though; the most terrible thing is not learning a lesson from failure. After our initial frustration, we calmed down and tried to discover the reasons for such defeat. We quickly understood that our mistakes were twofold. First, we did not know anything about this competition. If we had known it was a five-round competition, we would have been able to better prepare Fanny for it. Secondly, there was so much work to do after we moved to Pearl River that we did not pay enough attention to the children's schoolwork, since we believed they could handle it by themselves.

Fanny's failure in the math competition sent us a clear message: we needed to work hard with our children. We reviewed Fanny's problems together and encouraged her with proverbs such as "Failure is the mother of success."

Mathematics is Fanny's strength. It is also the subject in which we could help her the most. Therefore, it was the most likely area for us to make a breakthrough. We decided to go all out to overcome this barrier and rebuild her self-confidence.

We suggested that Fanny begin to prepare for the following year, since she would have the opportunity to participate in the Math Olympiad again. Now that we knew the basic rules of the game, we could plan out the best way to achieve her goal of being the top scorer in the competition.

John suggested that Fanny search the Internet in order to find more details about the competition and understand it in-depth. Online, Fanny found a book of practice problems: *Math Olympiad Contest Problems for Elementary and Middle Schools*, by Dr. George Lenchner. Without any hesitation, we bought the book as a training resource.

Experience had taught John that the most effective way to practice is through intensive training. Intensive training can concentrate children's attention span and achieve progress in a short amount of time.

In the summer of 2001, after a brief family vacation, we started to help Fanny train for the Math Olympiad. During the training period, she worked in the morning and took a break in the afternoon. In the course of her practice, we focused on the problems she had difficulties solving. Each morning, she first worked on a set of previous contest problems and made a note of the questions she couldn't solve or had solved incorrectly. After all of these had been located, we would ask her to try to solve them by herself one more time. Then, in the evening, John would teach her how to attack the problems that she was still struggling with. When they encountered a topic she had not learned yet, John would patiently teach it to her, then create more practice problems. She digested each problem completely, making sure that she not only knew how to do it, but also fully understood the concepts behind it. Each week, they would summarize the problems into categories and compare the different skills they used for each of the problems within the same category. After two weeks of training, Fanny's problem-solving skills had made visible progress. Each time she went to her father, she had fewer questions, and the interval between her questions gradually began to grow longer, until she almost never had to ask for his help.

On May 15, 2002, one of our neighbors came to us with good news: Fanny was in the newspaper! The newspaper, *the Journal News*, reported:

> *Math Olympiad: Several Pearl River Middle School students were award winners in this year's Math Olympiad . . . Fanny Wang won first place and placed in the 98th percentile of all participants . . .*

In the 2001-2002 Math Olympiad, Fanny had become the champion in her school, even though she was also competing with students one year older than her. This breakthrough rebuilt her self-confidence and encouraged her to compete in other contests.

Fanny discovered that Pearl River Middle School also participated in a Math League competition. The annual competition results were published on its official Web site: www.mathleague.com. Those results included school rankings, top students in the region, and the state's top twenty-five students.

In order to collect more information, John suggested that Fanny take the sixth grade competition without targeted preparation. Thanks to her stronger general foundation in mathematics and improved problem-solving skills, she performed well and took second place in her school. So far, we had collected information on Fanny's performance under three different situations: without any preparation, with targeted training, and without targeted training. Since our goal was to help Fanny excel on a statewide or national level, we needed to understand her in great detail. This information helped us work with her to make a long-term plan for her future.

In the eyes of others, it was a significant achievement that Fanny went from being an unknown to the Math Olympiad champion. She received much attention from her fellow classmates and teachers. Out of curiosity, her math teacher let her try the seventh grade Math League contest problems. Despite the fact she was only in sixth grade and still had not learned some of the topics covered by the questions, she solved twenty-seven questions correctly out of forty.

In order to push Fanny to the state level, John carefully studied the Math League Web site. From the published information, he concluded that Fanny needed to score thirty-six or higher to have a chance of being listed as the top twenty-five students in New York State. The goal was within Fanny's striking distance.

When he told Fanny his findings, she confidently declared her intention of being on the list and asked him to work with her again, like they had for the Math Olympiad. In order to do targeted practice, we purchased a collection of previous competitions from the Math League Web site. Since Pearl River Middle School would hold the contest in February of the coming year, we decided to do the training over winter break so it would not disrupt Fanny's regular schoolwork.

After taking a brief two-day break, the training process started. Fanny was in high spirits as I used a stopwatch to keep track of her time. Initially, she had a problem finishing the test within the time limit and also made mistakes on easy questions. Confused, we asked her, "Why are you making mistakes on the easy questions?"

"I was afraid that there wouldn't be enough time to do the rest of the questions, so I rushed through them," Fanny answered.

"Well, that is not the right strategy. Each question, easy or hard, is worth one point. You shouldn't miss the easy points." John pointed out. When she heard this, Fanny changed her tactic and secured the points from the easier problems before tackling the tougher questions. As with before, John would make Fanny attempt the problems she answered incorrectly or skipped a second time before explaining how to solve the ones she really could not answer. He coached Fanny to solve the same question with several different methods. Sometimes Fanny would feel annoyed and argue. "I already know how to do it, so why should I find other ways?"

However, John would not give her an inch. "This is a competition. You need a cutting edge to win. It's not enough to know how to do the problems. You have to be able to do them well."

She understood what he was saying. After a few days of training, she no longer ran out of time and could typically score thirty-seven or thirty-eight out of forty questions. Occasionally, she received a perfect score.

We were excited and told her, "Fanny, you are ready for the contest!"

Over the next few days, we went to the movies, went shopping, and played mahjong. We believe in the tenet of "work hard, play hard," so we thought the children needed a good break before the new semester. In February 2003, Fanny participated in the New York State seventh grade Math League competition and became the top scorer at her school and in the region, which includes five counties: Duchess, Orange, Putnam, Rockland, and Ulster. She was also ranked twenty-second in New York State.

Stumbling into Carelessness

In 2002, Kathy entered fifth grade and also decided to participate in the Math Olympiad competition.

Kathy's intelligence, coupled with Fanny's experience, made her the front runner in the five-round competition. After the first four rounds, Kathy was ahead of the other students. However, before the race was over, she became arrogant and called herself the champion of Math Olympiad. She proudly declared, "It is too easy!"

"She is going to fail," John told me calmly.

"Why don't you advise her?"

"Kathy is different than Fanny. She cannot take it seriously because of her current position. In her mind, she has already won. Letting her take a lesson now is better than her stumbling later."

John believed that sometimes, children could learn more from a failure than a success. Remedying Kathy's shortcomings while she was still young would be easier than doing it later. If she could not master the required attitude to do a job well, she would never be promoted from a pawn to a queen. We remained silent, and as expected, poor Kathy performed terribly in the final round and didn't even place in the school ranking. As the saying goes, "Don't count your chickens before they hatch."

"Life is too boring!" Kathy was mad at herself and hated her negligence.

"Math Olympiad champion, what happened?" Bill teased. Anticipating the outbreak of a fight, we quickly put out the fire and sent Bill outside to play. We tried our best to calm Kathy down before explaining to her why she had failed and how she could avoid making the same mistakes in the future. This experience made her more mature.

Kathy wrote an essay to record this unforgettable experience in her life:

My life has been filled with good days, bad days, and days I no longer can remember, but one day I will never forget is _____

It was the fifth and final contest of the Math Olympiad, a day that would prove unforgettable. The sounds of crumpling papers and furiously scribbled out work came from corners of the room. My best friend sighed in obvious frustration. Absentmindedly jotting down answers without bothering to double-check them, all I thought about was how the winner had to be me. When time was finally called, I turned in my paper, grabbed an answer sheet, and compared it to my answers scrawled on scrap paper. Looking back and forth, my jaw dropped, and my throat tightened. Only one of the five questions was correct. Trying to hide my disappointment, I turned away from the other kids for a moment. Even before comparing answers with my friends, I knew the first place title was not mine.

"What happened? How could I just get one right?"

Soon enough, the answers were revealed. For the first couple of contests, I just concentrated on the questions and looked at them over and over again. My scores for them were high, usually perfect or near perfect. I thought the contests wouldn't need too much thinking, and my concentration on doing my best was broken. After that, my focus was spent on daydreaming after answering a problem, not diligently checking it. But not concentrating was only half the reason behind my failing.

Once in the lead, a bubble of conceited thoughts had enveloped me. I became too confident that the coveted first place title would be mine. Constantly, I bragged to my friends that I was bound to be the winner. I should have known the risks of gloating so profusely: losing would make me have to eat my own words. My lack of humility and overconfidence had blinded me.

It placed me under the false impression that for every contest, winning was my destiny, so my efforts were minimal. After realizing this, I understood I was far from being the best, and losing taught me many more things that winning would have.

Benjamin Franklin once said, "After crosses and losses, men grow humbler and wiser." I agree, because after losing, I learned so many lessons that can and will help me through life, like humility, concentration, and that you "can't count your chickens before they hatch." With these lessons in mind, I won the Math Olympiad in sixth grade and became more adroit in the things I did. Most importantly, what I learned will be carried with me throughout my life. The lessons will help me when I am alone in the outside world, when I have to really work to survive and become successful. They will guide me when I need to jump a particular hurdle or go past an obstacle.

Although my life has been filled with good days, bad days, and days I no longer remember, one day I will definitely never forget is the day I lost the Math Olympiad and learned lessons that will stay with me forever.

In the 2003-2004 school year, Kathy was in sixth grade. Having learned the harsh lessons from the previous year, she didn't relax, and her persistent efforts brought home the Math Olympiad trophy.

In February 2004, she scored thirty-seven out of forty in the New York State Math League and was first place in the region and eleventh place in New York State. In 2005, Kathy continued to work hard and once again scored thirty-seven out of forty, tying her for first place in the region and fifteenth place in New York State. Through this experience, we firmly believed that, for minor issues, children should be given the freedom and the space to fail. While constant failure will diminish children's self-esteem and motivation, in moderation, it can be an even better teacher than success. Now, when Kathy succeeded, she was proud but not arrogant.

A Huge Gap

After our family moved to Pearl River, the problems seemed to keep coming one after another. Fanny performed terribly on the New

York State Educational Record Bureau (ERB) writing exam. Her score was below the fifteenth percentile of all fifth graders.

We saw the gap and couldn't believe it! The educational difference between New York and Utah was huge. When we moved, we had expected to see some gaps, but none on a scale such as this. It shocked us.

If we let this situation continue, our children would soon lose their self-confidence. Facing this dilemma, we hoped to do something to help Fanny achieve a breakthrough like she did in math. *But how could we help her achieve it?*

We knew that many Asian-American students attended tutorial schools to improve their academic performance, and wondered if that was the solution. We decided to have both Fanny and Kathy to try a writing class, so we started looking for tutorial schools nearby.

I found such a school in Fort Lee, about twenty-five minutes away from Pearl River, that offered summer writing classes and was run by a Korean-American. At the time, Fanny was in fifth grade, and Kathy was in third grade. Although there was still time for Kathy, we were worried that her writing would not be any better than Fanny's; and Fanny wanted to have someone she knew with her, so they both signed up.

The writing class lasted for about three weeks. The school had no air conditioning, so each time I picked them up, their faces were as red as apples. Occasionally, I stopped by a nearby McDonald's to buy them some ice cream to help them cool down. They always protested, "Mom, we are not hot." And they tried to save my money. I appreciated their consideration, but their big hearts pleased me even more.

One day, after their class, I asked the girls, "What do you think of this tutorial class?"

"Oh, they keep changing the teacher with all kinds of excuses," Kathy complained. "Students don't listen to the teacher, and the classroom is noisy."

Fanny did not like the tutorial class either, and I thought, *This appears to be futile.*

At the end of the class, we received performance reports from the tutorial school. Interestingly, both of the girls received an A. Even more amusing—but also worrisome—was that the teacher's comments about the girls were exactly the same, word for word. I guessed that the teacher did not know they were sisters; otherwise, he would not have so obviously written the exact same evaluation for both. We wondered how much progress the girls had really made.

Skeptically, I waited to see some improvement in Fanny's performance during the next school year. Not surprisingly, Fanny's sixth grade writing exam score wasn't much better than the previous year's. Kathy's writing scores were below average. We lost confidence in tutorial classes. Of course, this may just be an individual case; we have also heard of children having excellent, fruitful experiences in tutorial schools.

Improving Writing Skills

Writing is very important in real life. No matter what the children may do in the future, proficient writing skills will help them express themselves and demonstrate their talents clearly. Writing is a golden key to their success.

Raising children is not an easy job, but it is still a pleasure for many parents. We decided to help solve the girls' writing problem ourselves, even though it would be a huge challenge for us, as new immigrants with only an acceptable grasp of English. Aware of this deficiency, we bought several writing books from Barnes and Noble and started to develop our own plan.

As the first step, I guided them in changing a simple sentence into a complex sentence, since their writing often did not contain many adjectives, adverbs, or interesting details. For example, we started with a sentence: "A boy is fishing." We expanded it to: "A boy is fishing on a lake." Then we changed it further to: "A boy is fishing on a beautiful lake." Finally, we modified the sentence to: "As the sun rises, a boy is fishing on a beautiful lake." To make this process interesting, we developed a game. I gave Fanny and Kathy a simple sentence and told them that whoever could create the most interesting complex sentences would receive a small gift as a reward. They really enjoyed the friendly competition and would race each other to see who could make the most creative sentences. When one of them received the reward, she would smile brightly while the other congratulated her. In the end, they could expand a plain sentence into a paragraph or a short story. After they mastered this skill, I asked them to do the opposite by simplifying a complicated sentence or a paragraph of writing, since this would improve their reading comprehension skills.

The second step was teaching them how to change their sentence structures. We picked a sentence from a book and had them change it into a declarative, interrogative, exclamatory, or imperative sentence. This taught them the different types of ways that they could say the same thing in order to make their writing more interesting instead of a flat recitation of words.

After they had finished practicing with sentences, we started them on writing paragraphs. They began with descriptive writing, focusing on objects and phenomena that they observed in their daily lives. Since they loved our cat, Blacky, he became a natural subject. Sometimes, they wrote about how lovely the cat was, with his black fur and white paws; and other times, they chose to comment on how silly he was, like when he chased his tail in circles. Once, Kathy even wrote about how he was too lazy to even use his litter box properly; this made us all laugh. Soon enough, they became adept at descriptive writing and using different narrative techniques, including straight narrative and flashbacks.

It became even more interesting when they practiced argumentative essays. To start them off, we would pick an issue in current affairs for them to discuss. Once we gave them the topic, they began arguing both on paper and in person, writing essays supporting their side while furiously debating with each other. We looked on with amusement and did not intervene because it demonstrated their interest in the topic and also helped them organize their thinking and develop clear verbal skills. One time, the topic related to environmental conservation and industrial development. Fanny and Kathy just kept arguing and arguing; neither could persuade the other to abandon their position. Finally, Fanny took a very bold approach, writing two clear, strong paragraphs supporting a moderate approach, a balance between industry and the environment. After reading Fanny's writing, Kathy just stared at her in shock—usually, she was the one who won such confrontations—and had to retreat.

Finally, it was time to put all these skills together to write their essays. For each essay, we practiced different narrative techniques and writing skills to make the essay interesting to read and to familiarize our daughters with all the options available to them when they wrote.

Before they started writing, we asked them to remember and follow a procedure. First, they had to read the topic carefully to make sure they understood what they were being asked to write about and didn't go off topic. Then, they had to brainstorm ideas, such as their argument and their examples, and organize them into an outline. Only when they had done these could they start writing their draft. After their draft was complete, they had to proofread it for any mistakes and edit it to make their argument stronger. Then, when they were satisfied with their work, they could give it to someone else—us, each other, or their friends—to read as well and to offer suggestions for improvement. In their final draft, they incorporated the suggestions and read it over again to make sure there weren't any problems before they turned it in.

The editing process was the most boring part, and they hated it. Writing is fun for some people, but for others, it is a chore. Fanny disliked writing while Kathy enjoyed it, but whether they liked it or not, it was a skill they had to learn. Since she wasn't as good a writer as Kathy, Fanny frequently had to edit her work multiple times. To her, this was very painful, and sometimes she struggled to hold back her tears. We were very sympathetic, but we never lowered the bar. That was the first time we had ever been so tough on her since she was born. Still, "No pain, no gain."

When we were training Fanny and Kathy, we asked them to write on the same topic. This made it easier for them to exchange their writings and make suggestions for improvement during the reviewing process. In this way, they could learn from and help each other.

"A Wandering Leaf" was their final essay topic. In Fanny's essay, she wrote about the growth of and changes in a leaf from spring to autumn. She described the chemical processes that occurred in the leaf and how it made its own contribution to our world. At the end of her story, the leaf fell gently on the palm of a little girl and was saved as a bookmark. Her writing style was very delicate, a reflection of her personality.

Kathy enjoys spending time outdoors and is very curious about the world, which was demonstrated in her story about the leaf. She wrote about a leaf that traveled on the wind across cities and villages, lakes, and farms. She described everything that the leaf saw and heard as it floated through the sky, a wide diversity of people and places. Her article ended with a thoughtful question that stayed on the mind of the readers after they had finished reading.

That summer was fruitful because on the seventh grade ERB writing exam, Fanny scored twenty-eight out of thirty-six. Compared to fifteen out of thirty-six in fifth grade, it was an enormous improvement. This score moved her from among the worst of her classmates to above average, and when Fanny saw her ERB report, she smiled. Despite all the difficulties she had encountered along the way and all the frustrated tears she had shed late at night as she edited her essay yet another time, all the hard work that she had put in had paid off, as we had all known it would. This helped restore her self-confidence, something that comes from improvement on an individual level and from gradual progress toward goals on a state or national level. While she still had a long way to go, she was finally on the right track—and she didn't intend to stop anytime soon.

Strengthening Reading Ability

Many parents believe in a myth: reading more will improve their children's writing skills. In most cases, this is not true. Since Fanny was a small child, she has always read a lot, sometimes without any break. Although she is well-informed and has a broad range of knowledge, it did not help her writing. In most cases, when children read, they only pay attention to the story, not to the literary skills and vocabulary. If they read too much in this way, they will drift away from reality and neglect their social development. Sometimes we noticed children reading nonstop at the dinner table, on the street, and in bed, ignoring everyone and everything else around them. Their parents were not alarmed but were proud, which only made the situation worse.

Of course, if the children learn from reading, it can be very helpful. They will not only develop better writing skills, but also build their vocabulary. The only problem is how to guide them to read properly.

First, we taught our children to understand the difference between intensive reading and extensive reading, and then we trained their intensive reading skills. We started with selecting books. In order to choose books slightly higher than their reading level, we taught them to open to a random page in the book. If they could read the whole page without seeing an unknown word, it meant that the book was too easy for them. Generally, we picked books with three or four unfamiliar words per page for them to do intensive reading. As they read, we encouraged them to first use context clues to predict the definition of an unknown word. Then they would look up the actual definition in the dictionary and write the word and definition on a flash card to memorize. This method of building their vocabulary was less boring than memorizing words off a list and also gave them an example of the word's usage. We also required that they write a summary of every chapter as they read and a book review after they had finished a book.

Of course, we could not read their books to check their work. To solve this problem, sometimes we made both Fanny and Kathy read the same book. After each chapter, we listened to their summaries to make sure they had both understood what happened. When they had both finished the book, we had them debate about its theme and their opinion of it. Since Kathy's ability to articulate her defense was particularly strong, Fanny was sometimes unable to say anything, prompting her to hide and sulk instead. When this happened, John would become their mediator to make sure each of them had time to express their statements, while the other had to listen patiently and not interrupt. Through debate, they would both understand the subject better, and each of them could also see their blind spots, building a base for their further development.

Each summer, we asked them to intensively read two to three books. This greatly enhanced their learning efficiency and reading comprehension. Later, these skills would help them stand out in the WordMasters Challenge in high school.

Children have a strong desire to seek knowledge and expand their vision. In addition to intensive reading, they also need time for pleasure reading, whether of interesting but lower reading level books or other materials they are interested in. To encourage our children to read extensively, we subscribed to several different magazines and newspapers. Each year, they would tell us which subscriptions should be added and which ones should be stopped. We also bought many books on a variety of topics: children's activities, science, history, biographies, crafts, and geography, to name a few. They were under no obligation to read any of these. We simply provided them with the materials, and they chose to read whatever they were interested in. We believed that having a broad range of knowledge would be beneficial to their future.

Presidential Award for Academic Excellence

Before graduation, Pearl River Middle School held an Academic Bowl competition between two teams: the blue team and the red team. Fanny and three other students represented the blue team, and we were invited to the school to watch their performance. Fanny's extensive knowledge and rapid response times—sometimes buzzing in even before the teacher finished asking the question—won her the trust of her teammates and the respect of the audience. Each time a difficult question was posed, we could hear her fellow students cheering, "Fanny, Fanny!"

After a slow start, the blue team pulled ahead and won the contest with ease. Fanny's elegant style, broad base of knowledge, and quick response times left a deep impression on everyone.

In June 2003, Fanny graduated from Pearl River Middle School with the Presidential Award for Academic Excellence. Despite the educational gap and initial failures as we adjusted to a new environment, in three years, she had become a top student. We were all very proud of Fanny. Our horse, which had taken its first steps on shaking legs, was now running in front of the herd.

CHAPTER 7

Leadership

We started training Fanny's and Kathy's leadership skills when they were in elementary school. Every year, we held several parties for our children, and we asked them to plan some creative activities and compile a shopping list for each party. If they brought us a plan filled with activities they had already done at previous parties, we would reject it. Once a plan had been accepted, we went shopping together for their party supplies. Throughout this processes, we developed their creative thinking, planning ability, problem solving skills, and communication. Since these were their parties, they always had great fun planning them.

Leadership and creativity are very closely related. Fanny and Kathy are two very different children. Fanny is quiet, thoughtful, and creative; while Kathy is energetic, independent, and social. Because of their distinctive personalities, we had to use different strategies to develop their leadership skills.

Opening the Door to Leadership

Kathy was a high-energy, independent, and aggressive child. If she decided to do something, she didn't hesitate to pursue it. Her character was a double-edged sword, and we had to keep guiding her toward the right path as soon as possible. Often, when she was at Franklin Avenue Elementary School, we observed her playing a supporting role and following other students around. To plant the seed of leadership in

112

her mind, we often chatted about what it meant to be a leader and why a leader could do more than others.

One day in fifth grade, Kathy complained, "Why do I always have to listen to them? They never listen to me!"

From her distress, we saw her dissatisfaction with the status quo and realized that she had begun to explore her own value. This was the moment we had been waiting for. John took advantage of the situation to analyze the difference between a leader and follower with her and encourage her to find a way to be a leader. It was easy to reach such a consensus as a family, but the difficulty would be in transforming her into a leader that her friends would listen to.

Whenever John encounters a problem, he goes to the library or browses the Internet to look for a solution. To teach this to our daughter, he took Kathy to the Pearl River Public Library to hunt for the answer to her predicament. Eventually, they found a book titled *The One Minute Manager* by Blanchard and Johnson. The book is only about one hundred pages long, but it is filled with very interesting stories and is easy to read and understand. *The One Minute Manager* teaches how to observe others' facial expressions to gather information in order to guide their thinking and decisions. The book also instructs people in how to be more self-confident and how to infect others with confidence. Furthermore, it explains the necessity of striving for lofty goals. *The One Minute Manager* very effectively opened the door to developing Kathy's leadership skills.

After both of them had finished reading the book, they discussed it together. In this book, John found several skills and principles that Kathy needed to learn, but Kathy only caught one rule: at the end of each day, take a minute to think and review how it went and think about what you could have done better. John was a little disappointed and asked, "You only found one rule?"

However, he quickly realized that this was a new beginning for Kathy and that it was impossible for her to grasp everything at once. We had to start by opening the door first, and then we could gradually help Kathy improve her skills. Keeping this in his mind, he encouraged Kathy to put what she had learned into action and was delighted by her progress.

For a while, John chatted with Kathy every evening and helped her review her day. He would ask her a series of questions—What was the best thing you did today? Why do you think it was good? What was the worst thing that happened? Why do you think it was bad? Which skills have you learned from this book that could have been used in that situation? How will you handle it tomorrow? How can you start improving your efforts at home? How can you practice these skills in school? He praised her whenever she made any progress and helped her set new goals whenever she reached smaller milestones.

One time, when Kathy returned home from school, they talked about her day; and she told him that one of her friends was sick at home. He asked her, "If you were home sick, what would you be most worried about?"

She replied, "I wouldn't want to miss my homework and fall behind!"

John suggested, "Don't you think that this may be the same for your friend? Maybe you can do something for her tomorrow."

The next day at school, Kathy collected an extra copy of the homework from all of her classes. After school, she asked me to drive her to her friend's house to drop off the homework. Her friend was deeply appreciative and happy that Kathy had thought of her, and their friendship reached a new level.

From this experience, Kathy learned how small things can really affect a relationship. Ever since then, whenever one of her friends fell sick, Kathy collected the homework they missed and delivered it them, along with her wishes for them to get well soon.

Another time, Kathy told John that it had been her teacher's birthday. The whole class had sung "Happy Birthday," but Kathy wanted to do something more. She asked John, "What kind of gift do you think teachers like the most?"

John looked at her thoughtfully and replied, "Your mother was a teacher before. Maybe you can ask her."

We all sat together to discuss this question, and I explained my point of view. "I don't want my students to buy me gifts. I'd rather that they expressed something from their hearts. That's what I would appreciate the most."

We suggested that Kathy make a special birthday card for her teacher with a personalized poem, and Kathy began working on it immediately. The next day, Kathy delivered the card to the teacher. Her teacher was moved and even read the poem out loud in class.

Kathy came home with an excited expression that day and vividly recounted what had happened and the reactions of her teacher and peers. Ever since then, she has made sure to remember her friends' birthdays; and whenever the date draws near, she always gathers a group to do something to surprise her friend. Her most recent masterpiece took place at Harvard. During lecture one day, the professor was using a slideshow to present the lecture notes, as usual. When the professor flipped to the next slide, the lecture hall burst into laughter and applause—it was a special birthday announcement for one of Kathy's friends. Kathy had created the slide and e-mailed the professor the night before, asking if it could be added to the next day's lecture, just in time for her friend's birthday.

Yet another time, Kathy admitted that she was embarrassed because she did not know what to do. She told him how, at the beginning of class, the blackboard was always dirty. Whenever the class started, the teacher had to spend a few minutes just erasing the board. Kathy felt that this detracted from valuable time that could be spent teaching and wished there was a way for the board to be cleaned before the next class. As a solution, we proposed that she get a group of students to erase the blackboards after class, in the few minutes that they had between classes. Kathy followed our advice and gathered a few friends to take responsibility for their class, making sure the boards were always clean before they left.

Through these small actions, Kathy built a good reputation among her friends and teachers, winning their respect. During this process, she was also able to develop her leadership skills and practice them at school, a difficult job in our predominantly white community.

We would like to take a moment to emphasize a very important point. When a child is about to move in a new direction, he or she needs a lot of help. Simply pointing out the right road is not enough. Parents need to work with their children to ensure that they are initially successful in order to build their self-confidence. Otherwise, if children are forced to explore a new area alone, they can easily fail, which will discourage them from pursuing their personal development in the future.

Later, when Kathy entered high school, we introduced her to another book titled *The Leadership Challenge* by Kouzes and Posner. *The Leadership Challenge* is a more advanced book about leadership.

It discusses many topics in great detail such as building personal credibility, welcoming opportunities, and supporting face-to-face interaction. Kathy anxiously applied the skills she had learned and constantly improved herself, raising her leadership skills to a new level. She learned how to do many things such as reading people's facial expressions, observing the environment, setting her own goals, and seizing opportunities. At home, she became very diligent. Whenever we needed help, she would always be the first one to notice and offer her assistance. Before a major exam, she would gather her friends together to review the subject and offer her help to others. When her friends had difficulties, she would try to help them overcome their problems. We were very pleased and surprised to see her progress, which went far beyond our expectations. Despite the fact that we were living in a predominantly white community, she had a close-knit group of friends who willingly shared both their happiness and their sadness with her and followed her.

Girl Scouts

Fanny and Kathy never forgot their dream of joining the Girl Scouts. After we had settled in Pearl River, we started looking for an opportunity for them to pursue this dream. With the assistance of the Rockland County Girl Scouts, Fanny joined a Girl Scouts troop in a nearby town, while Kathy was able to join a troop in Pearl River with many of her classmates. Kathy's Girl Scouts troop was very active, and we always encouraged the girls to participate in Girl Scouts activities.

One time, Kathy's troop was planning to bake one hundred apple pies for a fund-raiser. Of course, this required a lot of apples. Someone had to convince farmers to donate apples to help the Girl Scouts accomplish their goal, so Kathy and I volunteered for this task. It turned out that this was not an easy job at all. After we received the assignment, we called several farms and asked for their sponsorship, but we failed. *What could we do?* There was not much time left, so we decided to take an aggressive approach by visiting the farms and talking with the owners face-to-face without making an appointment. I told Kathy to be ready with her rhetoric and had her put on the Girl Scouts uniform. We also brought the letter from the Girl Scouts explaining their intentions, and then we were on our way to the farms. While

I was driving, I asked Kathy to practice her speech to persuade the owners.

To my surprise, when we arrived at the first farm, Kathy was scared. She stood off to the side and left me with no choice but speak for her. The owner generously donated two cases of apples, but Kathy's timidity had shocked me. She was talkative at home and in school and enjoyed socializing with people. How could she hide in a real situation when people were counting on her? I was angry and frustrated. I told her, "Kathy, this is your responsibility. Why did you hide like a turtle?"

When we arrived at the second farm, the owner was not there, so we moved on to the third farm. As we drove to the third farm, I started calming down and talked to Kathy. I told her, "Everything has a beginning. I understand you were scared to talk to a stranger, but what we are doing is helping others. Can you try next time?"

When we arrived at the third farm, Kathy spoke shyly to the farmer. However, she accomplished her goal, and we received another three boxes of apples. Mission accomplished! On the way home from the farm, I asked her, "Was it that terrible to speak to him?"

She replied, "It was not as difficult as I had imagined."

Finishing one hundred apple pies in one day was not a small project. We met at a church, and all the girls and their mothers worked together like an industrial assembly line: wash, peel, cut, season, and seal. Everybody smiled when they saw one hundred apple pies lined up in a neat row at the end of the day.

In 2010, the Rockland County Girl Scouts planned a Support the Troops project. They encouraged each Girl Scout to write a letter to the U.S. soldiers in Iraq on specially designed stationery and also planned to sell this stationery to raise funds for the Girl Scouts. Each Girl Scout could submit a proposed design for the stationery, but of all the designs that were turned in, Kathy's was the one that was chosen. The Girl Scouts intended to price the stationery at one dollar each, but when Kathy took her design to a local Staples store to make copies, she hit a wall. For a colored copy, it cost one dollar per copy, which meant the Girl Scouts wouldn't make any profit by selling the stationery. I encouraged her to bargain for a better price. She carefully explained the purpose of the stationery to the store manager and asked him to offer his store's support. Thanks to the American tradition of supporting the Girl Scouts, the manager offered her half price, and the problem was solved. From this experience, Kathy learned how to bargain and the importance of communication.

A Dark Cloud

Kathy's Girl Scouts experiences were not always filled with happiness and fun. We lived in a town in which Caucasians made up a very large majority, and our involvement seemed to make some people uncomfortable. After Kathy joined the Girl Scouts, she began to receive outrageously unfair treatment.

Whenever the Girl Scouts had a meeting, every child received a notice from the troop leaders—every child except Kathy. Instead, she had to constantly ask her friends when and where the next meeting would be. I wondered whether the troop leaders had lost our phone number and e-mail address. Initially, we guessed that was what happened, so I called her troop leaders to confirm their records, and all our contact information was correct. However, Kathy still never received a notice whenever they had a meeting, and we began to understand that forgetting to inform Kathy was not accidental. We told Kathy, "As a member of the Girl Scouts, it is your right to participate in the meetings and activities. You should fight for your right!"

Whenever Kathy found out about a meeting or an activity from one of the other girls, she would attend and actively participate without displaying any emotional distraction or distress. She did what she had to do regardless of others' misconduct. She learned to become tough.

In 2008, after years of hard work, Kathy received the Girl Scout Silver Award, the second highest Girl Scouts award. We were sincerely happy for Kathy because for years, she had been given the cold shoulder. It was very difficult for Kathy to struggle through it all, but she never gave up, determined not to let those who wanted to push her out succeed. The silver award was an accomplishment we didn't expect, and we believed that it showed that we had finally prevailed over narrower minds. But as they say, "Who laughs last laughs best." Cold water was poured on us again, and it was cold, icy cold!

On June 18, 2008, the local newspaper, *Our Town,* published an article about the Girl Scout Silver Award ceremony along with a photo of all the award recipients. We saw the smiling face of Kathy in the photo, but when we continued to read the report, we were all shocked. I shouted, "What? Where is Kathy's name?"

John said, "Read carefully. I do not think the troublemakers would be so obvious about it."

John was incredulous. We read the article carefully and counted the number of girls in the photo. There were forty-three children and only forty-two names. Kathy's was the only name missing. She was also the only Asian-American child in the photo. With tears in her eyes, Kathy said, "I want to ask our troop leader, why?"

I told her, "Let it go. It's no big deal."

This is reality! We do not know if other Asian-American children have had similar experiences, but Kathy's Girl Scouts experiences touched a deep nerve. One of her essays describes the journey she went through:

> Girl Scouts is a national organization with hundreds of branches across the country, designed to promote "courage, confidence, and character to make the world a better place" in its members. This opportunity to make friends and do something for the community attracted me to Girl Scouts, so I joined in elementary school. However, my Girl Scouting experiences were far from perfect.
>
> At the beginning of fourth grade, I was officially assigned to a troop, but months passed with no word from the troop leaders. Curious, I talked to a couple of my classmates in the same troop, wondering if they knew when meetings would start. To my surprise, they had no idea I was in their troop and revealed that I had missed several meetings already. Confused, I called both of the troop leaders, verifying my contact information to ensure they knew I was still interested. I also asked my friends in the troop to pass along any notices they received about new meetings. Finally, I attended my first Girl Scouts meeting, thanks to information I received from my friends. To ensure I would be notified in the future, I gave my contact information to the troop leaders once more.
>
> Time and time again, the troop leaders continued to neglect informing me of meetings, and I only learned about them through my friends. To improve this situation, I resubmitted my

contact information again and again and even appealed to the local Girl Scouts council in an attempt to remedy this problem. As the years passed by, although there were some improvements and I did occasionally receive meeting and activity times from the troop leaders, I usually had to rely on my friends for information.

On one particular occasion, all the troops in the area had a group photo to celebrate receiving their Silver Award. This picture, along with an article, was submitted to the local newspaper. When I rifled through the pages, I found the article and the photograph. Reading the caption, I found I was the only person not labeled and the only Asian girl amidst the white ones. Thinking it was a mistake, I turned next to the article, which listed all the recipients of the Silver Award, except me.

I had been treated unfairly. So many times, I was frustrated. To move past this inequity, I decided to do something by myself, so I created the Volunteer Service Group (VSG). After its inception, the VSG grew quickly as I recruited members from my school who were all similarly interested in giving back to society. We extended our reach and helped multiple causes and organizations throughout the community, carrying out several short- and long-term projects successfully. At the same time, this helped me to become aware of problems in the community that the VSG could remedy. Through our volunteering, my efforts and the accomplishments of the VSG were fully recognized and appreciated.

Now, I am still a member of Girl Scouts, but I also have another way of contributing to society and meeting new people. The circumstances with my troop are a lesson about real life. Obstacles will always appear in our lives, but we determine whether they block us or help us move forward. By seeing these barriers as an opportunity to improve, we can always find a path to success.

Tai Chi Club

In order to help Fanny make new friends, strengthen her leadership skills, and further enhance her creativity, we suggested that she create a club. By creating a club, she could interact with people who had similar interests while staying true to her personality.

We asked her, "What activity will others also like? Which club would you like to create?"

For a while, this became a hot topic in our family. Eventually, I suggested, "Sports clubs are popular. How about creating a sports club?"

Pearl River High School had numerous sports clubs already, and neither Fanny nor Kathy was very athletic, so typical sports clubs were out of the question. During school, they had noticed that there were a considerable number of students like them who struggled with regular sports but who liked gentle and relaxing activities. To fulfill this criterion, we found a special sport called Tai Chi. We all agreed it was a good idea to create a Tai Chi Club because it required less equipment, was a less demanding exercise, and uniquely promoted Chinese culture.

Creating a new club is not an easy job. It requires courage, an overall plan, administrative approval, strong organizational capabilities, and many other aspects. To this end, Fanny and Kathy decided to combine forces to establish the Pearl River High School Tai Chi Club. Since Kathy was only in eighth grade, she was energetic and had plenty of time to assist Fanny.

First, they decided to draft a club charter to attract the attention of the school officials. In determining how to write the proposal and what to include, they referred to examples that they found on the Internet. After repeated discussion and editing, they came up with the Tai Chi Club Charter:

Pearl River High School Tai Chi Club Charter

I. Goal

The goal of the Tai Chi Club is to provide a means for students of all grades and fitness levels to stay healthy, focused, and relaxed through an exercise that has been practiced for centuries: Tai Chi. The concentration gained through Tai Chi will help students study with more vigor. Tai Chi helps one's body and brain regain energy to start working once more.

II. Membership Criteria

The Tai Chi Club is open to all interested Pearl River High School students.

III. Tai Chi Club Structure

The Tai Chi Club is nonprofit. There is no membership fee. Any donations will be used to further the Tai Chi Club.

Leadership and guidance of the Tai Chi Club will be the responsibility of Fanny Wang and Kathy Wang.

Tai Chi Club meetings will be held after school on the day most convenient to its members. We will meet once a week, except for midterm and finals weeks.

The Tai Chi Club provides the following benefits:

- A way for students to gain the energy and concentration needed for studying
- Improved academic and social performance
- Good health and self-discipline through the graceful movements of Tai Chi
- Good balance, posture, and breathing patterns
- The opportunity to learn about the age-old practice of Tai Chi

IV. Tai Chi Club Expenses

There are no expenses for joining the club. If any donations are received, they will be used to help the club. Any possible trips or traveling expenses will be paid by the members going on the trips. The school only needs to provide a TV, DVD player, and an adequate area with enough space to move around in, such as the gym or cafeteria.

V. Code of Ethics

All members shall conform to the Pearl River High School Code of Conduct.

With the club charter in hand, Fanny and Kathy visited Mr. F, the principal of Pearl River High School, and submitted their proposal for the Tai Chi Club.

June 5, 2006

W F, Principal
Pearl River High School
275 E. Central Avenue
Pearl River, NY 10965

Dear Mr. F,

We would like to form a Tai Chi Club at Pearl River High School. Tai Chi is a series of slow and focused exercises that originated centuries ago in China. Studies have proven that the movements of Tai Chi help a person concentrate, maintain physical health, and relax. Our first encounters with Tai Chi left us sweating from the physical aspects, but we also felt free, relaxed, and ready to tackle our schoolwork. Tai Chi not only helps the body, but it also refines the mind. Our research has shown that similar clubs exist in many high schools across the nation. For these reasons, we feel that a Tai Chi Club would be beneficial to many students at Pearl River High School.

There are several reasons why the establishment of a Tai Chi Club is so important:

1. *To keep students healthy through the graceful, slow, focused, and fluid Tai Chi movements.*
2. *To keep high school students less stressed in their difficult high school years through a weekly activity that students enjoy. This would instill the strength and self-discipline needed in their everyday lives.*
3. *To develop good posture, balance, breathing skills, and concentration formed through Tai Chi.*
4. *To boost self-esteem and promote self-awareness through this meditation in motion.*

5. *To achieve fitness in the body.*
6. *To help improve academic performance and social skills.*

It is well-known that the lessons of self-esteem, concentration, and relaxation are invaluable principles in a student's academic and daily life. The concentration skills developed by Tai Chi help students achieve higher grades and encourage students to participate in class.

Enclosed are a proposed Tai Chi Club Charter and a list of interested students for your review. This proposal has been unofficially approved by Mr. E and Ms. M to ensure it meets Pearl River High School's requirements for an extracurricular club activity. We hope this proposal will be approved by next September so we will have time to prepare. Please feel free to contact us with any questions you may have. Thank you for your prompt attention in this important matter.

Regards,
Fanny Wang, Pearl River High School Student
Kathy Wang, Pearl River High School Student
Enclosures: Club Charter

After he had read the proposal, Mr. F responded, "Very interesting! Take it to Mr. E, the assistant principal, because he is in charge of these specific issues."

Therefore, Fanny and Kathy went to see Mr. E to discuss their plan. Mr. E expressed his interest in the club and encouraged them to start it. His enthusiasm delighted both Fanny and Kathy. Fanny exclaimed, "I did not expect it to go so smoothly!"

Then, Mr. E changed his tone and said, "But it all depends on you."

He talked about the problems in the U.S. economy and how the school activity funds were tight, so the school could not provide financial backing for a new club activity. He finally added, "You would have to convince a teacher to supervise your club for free."

For security purposes, each school activity needed at least one teacher as a supervisor and advisor. Normally, the school paid club advisors; but given the current situation, that wasn't possible. Finding a teacher to supervise their activities for free was a major obstacle. They talked to many teachers without any success, but one day, they came home with big smiles on their faces because Ms. M had agreed to supervise the Tai Chi Club!

After solving that problem, they cheerfully moved on to the next step. They needed to find a practice space, obtain the equipment for their practices, and recruit members. Eventually, they used the cafeteria as their practice space and borrowed a TV and DVD player from the school library to play the instructional DVD. To ensure the success of the Tai Chi Club, they used all the resources available to recruit members. In about one month, more than twenty students had joined the Tai Chi Club. Unlike most other sports, Tai Chi includes slow, elegant movements that demand a lot of energy and focus. After practice, these new members experienced the power embedded in this sport. The cafeteria was filled with comments like "Tai Chi is powerful. My legs hurt so much. Ow!" or "I just want to fall down." Finally, they succeeded in creating a new club for their school.

Next year, they met a new difficulty: Ms. M was unable to continue as the Tai Chi Club's club advisor. This meant they had to start over again.

"Don't be discouraged and continue to look for support. New problems mean new challenges," we encouraged them. Luckily, they found a new supervisor, Ms. D. She has supported the Tai Chi Club ever since.

I remember one day, over the dinner table, Fanny and Kathy emotionally told us a story. During a major storm, the basement of Ms. D's house was at risk of flooding. All the club members were worried for her and suggested that she go home to check it out. They all promised they would behave, but Ms. D insisted on staying to the end of the club activities. Her selflessness and sense of responsibility to the students taught them an important lesson.

Chemistry Olympiad Team

Fanny loves math and science and has won numerous awards in various math competitions. We had hoped that Pearl River High School would provide opportunities for its students to compete in biology, chemistry, physics, or scientific research at the state or national level to showcase its talented students. However, this was not the case. When we learned that there were annual national competitions in biology, chemistry, and physics, Fanny was very interested and tried to promote the idea of participating in the U.S. Biology Olympiad. She approached Ms. H, a biology teacher and the supervisor of the Science Olympiad Club at the time, to ask her to register the school for the competition; but nothing came out of it.

In tenth grade, Fanny took an honors chemistry course. This time, she wanted to participate in the U.S. National Chemistry Olympiad. From our previous experience with Ms. H, we understood that if she simply offered a suggestion or a request, it would not work at all. John suggested, "If you lead the project and develop a practical plan, like you did for the Tai Chi Club, what do you think will happen?"

John's suggestion showed Fanny there was still hope, so she started her research. From the official Web site of the American Chemical Society (ACS), she found detailed information regarding the Chemistry Olympiad competition, including problems used in previous competitions. She learned that the preliminary local competition of the U.S. National Chemistry Olympiad is open to all high school students, both citizens and non-citizens. However, only U.S. citizens are allowed to participate in the national exam. Each year, at that time, about ten thousand students participate in the local exam to compete for five hundred spots in the national exam.

First, we contacted the ACS regional coordinator, Dr. G, to find out the detailed requirements for a high school team. After that, Fanny lobbied her chemistry teacher, Mrs. M, for her support. With her experience from creating the Tai Chi Club, Fanny had a better idea of how to organize a team and gain support for her idea. She prepared a detailed description of the Chemistry Olympiad and its requirements and included Dr. G's contact information. She also compiled a list of benefits this club would provide for students and the school:

- Promote students' interest in learning chemistry
- Encourage more students to study science
- Inspire students to strive for excellence
- Challenge students to set higher goals
- Offer more opportunities for students to show their potential
- Enhance our learning environment

- Honor our teachers for their excellent work
- Increase the awareness of our teachers
- Increase the awareness of Pearl River High School

Finally, Fanny brought her proposal to her teacher and told her, "Mrs. M, I have prepared everything. Would you please contact Dr. G and recommend that our school participate in the competition?"

With the support of Mrs. M, Fanny was able to successfully build a team for her school and participate in the U.S. National Chemistry Olympiad.

A Community without Borders

On May 12, 2008, China's Sichuan province was racked by a deadly earthquake that measured at 8.0. For a long time, newspapers and television news programs didn't report about anything except for this overwhelming tragedy. Many charities launched a variety of efforts to help the victims of the earthquake, and our children also wanted to help.

I suggested, "Your personal power is very limited. Can you launch a donation in your school to support the victims in Sichuan?"

Following this conversation, Fanny, Kathy, and Bill collected pictures and reports about the earthquake and made a poster. During their lunch break at school, they exhibited their poster to raise donations.

In the process, they encountered a variety of problems: student apathy, issues of trust, organization, and implementation, and others. However, they overcame all the obstacles that appeared in their way and successfully raised money to donate to the Sichuan earthquake victims. The following is an essay that Kathy wrote, which tells the story of their experience:

> We are all members of a global community and as such, we all have an intrinsic duty to this community. Many times, though, we conveniently forget our obligations to our community, focusing instead on competition and getting ahead in life. However, individuals should never overlook their responsibilities to each other and their community. With the

support of Columbia University President Lee C. Bollinger, Columbia's many global service organizations have encouraged students to engage in volunteer work all over the globe, offering more opportunities for students to "bring help to every region of the world."

I also enjoy helping others; in my spare time, I offer free tutoring and actively participate in community service. To better contribute to our community, I cofounded the Volunteer Service Group (VSG), which links student volunteers to local nonprofit organizations, such as the Association for the Visually Impaired, People to People, and many others. With a larger group of volunteers, we are able to tackle bigger projects and provide more efficient services to these organizations. For a long time, I thought community service only extended to our immediate community, but on May 12, 2008, the massive Sichuan earthquake expanded my perception of community service.

As news of the earthquake flooded the television, I felt that we needed to do something for the quake victims and called together a meeting of the VSG. I proposed taking action. While some of the members were in total accord, others were hesitant and confused. The biggest doubt manifested itself in our interpretation of the VSG's domain: could such a project really be considered community service? After all, the quake victims were thousands of miles away in another country and had seemingly nothing to do with us. Although we had a genuine debate, we could not reach a consensus and left the meeting still vacillating over what to do.

After the meeting, I researched online to try and find an answer to our enigma. One association, Doctors without Borders, particularly caught my attention with its approach to humanitarian efforts. According to the program's charter, the organization stresses its impartiality and independence from economic, political, and religious factors. The volunteer doctors promote universal medical ethics, while giving up high salaries and better living conditions and even risking their lives by entering regions of armed conflict. I wondered what induced them to make such sacrifice, and, as I searched deeper and read testimonials, I gradually began to understand. As the name of the association suggests, the doctors view the world without borders or restrictions, recognizing only the sick who need their services. Their community is a global one, encompassing all populations in distress. This broader line of thinking, I realized, should be applied to our lives and our VSG dilemma. Our community is not just local, but also state, national, and global, spanning every corner of our planet. We need to work together to help each other, regardless of location and background.

When I presented this information and new understanding to the VSG, we discussed and considered many aspects of this view. With a wider perspective on the meaning of "community," we were able to look at our issue in a different light and found that we all agreed with this definition of an all-inclusive community. After additional consideration, we unanimously voted to establish an Earthquake Relief Fund and began collecting money at school. Our new global community service project was on its way.

We have long been taught that history is a record of winners and losers, warfare and strife. I believe that now in the twenty-first century, it is time to write a new page of history, focused on cooperation, friendship, and service to all.

Obama's Army

Ever since fifth grade, Kathy has demonstrated her strong leadership character. Gradually, she has developed a strong social circle that plays together, studies together, and does community service together. We believed, though, that she could raise her skills to a new level.

In the second half of 2007, the race between presidential candidates Hillary Clinton and Barack Obama became very intense. Our entire family became excited as well and repeatedly debated about who was the better candidate. One day, a new idea popped into John's head. He said, "Kathy, you like to debate, so you should go to the Obama campaign! It would be a good chance for you to exercise your skills and to get in touch with mainstream America."

Without a doubt, that was something Kathy would enjoy doing. Immediately, she jumped up to search for information on how to get involved. On the Internet, she found the address and contact information of Barack Obama's campaign headquarters in New York. John suggested, "Let them know about your insights."

Kathy hesitated and was skeptical, asking, "Will they take me seriously? I'm not eighteen, and I can't even vote. Why would they care about my opinion?"

Still, she sent her e-mail:

Bill Crossing the Line + Hillary's Presidency = Constitutional Crisis?

Hi! My name is Kathy Wang. I am currently a high schooler residing in New York. Although I cannot vote yet, I am still interested in the elections, and I am a supporter of Barack Obama. This year's elections have been so exciting and eventful. Every day, something new happens, so I'm always watching the news to remain updated on the political scene.

However, recently, there has been something that especially concerns me, and that is Bill Clinton's overwhelming role in Hillary's campaign. Traditionally, former presidents have not been involved too deeply in any presidential race. It would be unfair and would negatively affect the election process. Bill Clinton, though, has been overly asserting his presence and slandering Obama to raise Hillary up. This clear disdain for the universally understood neutrality invites so many more chilling possibilities of what may happen in the future.

The Constitution has a special provision so that a president can serve no more than two terms. It was created for fear that a president might become dictator if he holds office for too long, loses control, and becomes overly accustomed to power. Currently, Bill Clinton has broken accepted traditions and crossed the line of appropriate conduct. Because of this, I have been worried about the possibility that if Hillary becomes president, Bill would gain immense amounts of political influence at the same time. I feel that Hillary's ascension to the presidency could also secure her husband virtually unlimited power. He would be able to influence not only her decisions, but also the superior power of her presidency. Without an official title, he would have no responsibility for anything he does, and there would be no restrictions or laws to stop him.

I believe this undermines the basic principles which our country was founded upon. America is a democracy, not a starting base for a presidential monarchy. I am not trying to imply that the Clintons intend to form a dictatorship, but I feel that a situation like this invites many problems about struggles for power and corruption, posing problems in the future of our country. Although breaking precedents usually has a positive connotation to it, this time if Hillary Clinton becomes president and Bill continues to lose control with the promise of power so close, our system of checks and balances will surely crumble.

I think these points should be brought to the attention of American voters; they have the right to realize the unintentional consequences of voting for Hillary and Bill Clinton, who have already shown signs of being out of control. I am really curious about what your thoughts and reactions are to these possibilities.

Thank you so much for taking the time to read this. I hope you can respond back soon.

Let's go Obama, the right change for America.

Kathy Wang

After a while, Kathy received a response from Barack Obama's campaign headquarters in New York:

Dear Kathy,

Thank you for contacting Obama for America. The volume of messages we're receiving has gone up since Barack's victory in Iowa. While we cannot respond individually to over a thousand messages per day, the level of interest and thoughtfulness of the comments reflected in these communications are very gratifying. Your thoughts on our campaign and America's future are greatly appreciated.

Individual citizens like you are the foundation of this campaign. Thank you again for writing.

Sincerely,
The Correspondence Team
Obama for America

After that first e-mail, Kathy received campaign training in Obama's headquarters in New York to make her contribution to Obama's presidential campaign. At the beginning, she worked at the headquarters in New York City and later at the Obama Rockland County Center in Nyack, New York.

On the first Friday after the presidential election, Kathy received a message from Barack Obama:

Kathy,

You did it.

Not just on Tuesday, but every day for a year, you did what the cynics said we couldn't do.

You said the time has come to get beyond the same old tactics that divide and distract us, and you gave people—young and old, rich and poor, black, white, Latino, and Asian—a reason to believe again.

Because of your work, we won the most states and delegates on February 5th and finished strongly all across the country.

And the momentum you created won't stop now. Together we're building a campaign that will compete in the general election—and a united Democratic Party that can lead this country for the next generation.

You've set an amazing standard and provided a huge boost as we gear up for the next round of contests.

Thanks to you, we have a new wind at our backs, and we're ready to carry our message across the nation.

It's the same message we took from Iowa to South Carolina and across the nation on February 5th—the same message we had when we were up and when we were down—that out of many, we are one.

And if we are met with cynicism and doubt and folks who tell us that we can't, we will respond with those three simple words that sum up the spirit of this nation:
Yes, we can. Thank you for all of your hard work.

Barack

This amazing process helped Kathy to broaden her mind and gain a deeper understanding of the true value of this great country. The following is an essay she wrote to describe her experience:

When Barack Obama first entered the presidential race, I was awed by his vision. Closer examination of his speeches and ideals convinced me to join his campaign. After a few persuasive conversations with his campaign manager, I was accepted as a campaign intern. Working in his New York headquarters, I helped organize activities, contact potential voters, and field their questions. As the only high school student working there, I brought fresh comments and suggestions from a new perspective. My enthusiasm and active participation delighted the other volunteers, injecting new energy into the atmosphere. On election night, I joined millions of Americans in witnessing the writing of a new page in history, and I am proud to have been a part of it. Through this campaign process, I have seen the nature and witnessed the power of our country. Indeed, it is truly the people that make our nation great.

CHAPTER 8

Developing Interests

Centuries ago, in traditional China, well-educated families trained their daughters in playing instruments, learning chess, writing poetry, and painting. Although we now live in modern times, having a variety of interests and hobbies can still enhance a child's lifestyle and development. We did not expect our children to do everything, nor did we force them to participate in activities we chose for them. Instead, we allowed them to decide what they wanted to pursue, whether it was the piano, flute, clarinet, chess, art, badminton, swimming, or hiking, to name a few. We made all of these options available to them, then let them freely explore where their interests lay. This also provided us with the opportunity to understand their natural inclinations and abilities.

With so many options, parents often face the dilemma of deciding which activities are worth pursuing. Some parents simply ask their children to do as much as possible, following the doctrine of "the more, the better." To the parents, it is a logical decision; after all, what is the harm in learning more skills?

However, academics should still be the primary concern of most students. With the exception of an extremely small group of especially gifted children, we believe that there needs to be a strong emphasis on academic performance. Participating in too many extracurricular activities will detract from their time and inevitably result in negative consequences. When deciding which extracurricular to pursue, an activity is acceptable only if it does not cause a major impact on a student's schoolwork. Otherwise, it should be forgone.

How could we decide if an activity would impact their schoolwork? Our major concern was time; if one extracurricular occupied an entire day every weekend, those students would have one less day to concentrate on their studies compared to their peers, a significant 15% disadvantage. Therefore, we tried to avoid extracurricular activities that would occupy sizable blocks of time.

Broadening Horizons

Our bookshelves are packed with a wide variety of books, from novels, poetry, and biographies to dictionaries, cookbooks, brain teasers, and reference books. We did not expect our children to read every book; we just provided them with a diverse pool of knowledge. When they had time, these resources were readily available for them to look through. With all of these different genres at their disposal, our children could broaden their horizons by enriching their knowledge.

We also subscribed to four or five different journals or magazines that covered a broad spectrum of topics, including science, technology, health, news, and entertainment. Each year, as their interests changed, we would replace one magazine subscription with a new one that they requested. Additionally, we would subscribe to one Chinese newspaper for us and one English newspaper for the children. The cartoon sections were always Bill's favorites, while Fanny paid more attention to science and culture, and Kathy was more interested in political affairs and current events. Furthermore, we spent much time just talking to them about current affairs, historical events, and scientific developments, sharing stories about well-known figures and discussing the cultural practices of other societies. These all served to help broaden their interests as well.

To aid their intellectual development, we also purchased educational games and materials, letting them learn by playing with puzzles, Scrabble, Brain Quest, and other activities. We persisted in our efforts to provide them with an enjoyable learning environment; instead of using force and pressuring them to study, we used their own interests and curiosity to naturally motivate them. Through this, they learned more willingly, happily, and efficiently.

Writing Chinese characters is a very difficult task for children. In order to interest our children in learning Chinese, I started by reading them popular fables, such as "The Crow and the Pitcher," "The Tortoise and the Hare," and "The Foal Crossing the River." Each story made them laugh, and as they had fun, they developed a desire to learn more. Whenever they had spare time, they would run to me, demanding, "Mom, teach us Chinese!"

Writing is not the only hard aspect of learning Chinese. Correct pronunciation was also a new challenge. Every phonetic spelling has four tones that can easily be mixed up. However, since our children started learning out of their own curiosity, this was not a big problem. They always enjoyed themselves, and once they learned how to write a new character, they would proudly show off their work to their father or brother.

To maintain their interest, we also bought Chinese cartoons and watched them together. Monkey King grew to be their favorite character. Each time we finished watching an episode, they would chase each other around the house yelling, "*Shi fu* . . . Monkey King is coming!"

John enjoys watching National Basketball Association (NBA) games. Often, he would watch these games until late at night, and the children would join him when they could. On the weekends, he would always grant our children exceptions, letting them watch NBA games past midnight. I was always confused by this and asked him why they couldn't just study longer into the night instead of watching those games. John didn't have a genuine answer, but he replied, "Well, sometimes they have to do something exciting, right?"

Of course, all the children sided with their dad; and as the absolute minority, I couldn't do anything. Because of this, our children became well-acquainted with NBA teams and the names of many players.

The Chinese have a saying: "Sometimes you can plant a flower seed and it won't bloom, but if you toss a willow tree branch on to the ground, it will grow to cast a huge shadow." It refers to a situation that produces unexpected, and even better, results. Interestingly enough, their knowledge of the NBA actually came to their rescue on a surprising occasion.

When Fanny and Kathy visited China, they organized an information exchange program with the students there. During their first meeting, they stood at the board to introduce themselves, facing a classroom of over fifty students. Many young teachers share a common experience the first time they stand in front of a class: there are usually a few boys who will try to test and embarrass the teacher, especially in the case of young female teachers. John and the teachers at the Chinese school worried that if this happened, Fanny and Kathy would not be able to handle the situation; so they stood near the classroom doors, thinking that if anything went out of control, they could rush in and rescue the sisters.

As expected, John noticed a few boys making eye contact with each other across the room, exchanging sly smiles and knowing looks. One boy raised his hand and led the charge; he didn't talk about studying or high school or college but instead raised a question about the NBA. His thoughts had probably been along the lines of, "Well, you girls may do well in school, but let's see if you know anything about the men's world of sports!"

To his surprise, immediately after he presented his question, Kathy seized the topic, talking knowledgeably about players like Kobe Bryant, Shaquille O'Neal, Yao Ming, and Wang Zhizhi. When she described something in particularly great detail, the students applauded. When she made a joke or humorously recounted a story, everyone laughed appreciatively. Finally, she shot back at the boy, "Have you seen the games where Magic Johnson and Larry Bird faced off, or when they both teamed up with Michael Jordan? Have you seen the brilliant alliance of Karl Malone and John Stockton? Those were really cool."

The whole class went quiet in an instant, stunned by how deeply she seemed to know the sport. Once John and the teachers saw that the sisters had full control over the situation and had won the respect of the students, they felt at ease and walked away to enjoy their own conversations. Repeatedly, they could hear laughter and applause from the classroom. The two sisters had started off with quite a bang.

Playing with puzzles can be beneficial to children's intellectual development and can train their patience and powers of observation. When Fanny and Kathy were each about one year old, we introduced them to puzzles. We first started with simple ones, matching differently shaped blocks with corresponding locations on a board; and as they grew up, we presented them with more complex puzzles. After successfully solving these puzzles constantly, they became very proud of themselves, boasting that they were ready for anything. We wanted to let them know that this wasn't the case.

One day, we bought a very complex puzzle with one thousand pieces. After we returned home, we started feeling slight regrets because we knew it would be too complicated for them. If they couldn't finish the puzzle, their self-confidence and interest in puzzles would suffer. However, if we helped them, we would just be training our own patience, not theirs. Then, an idea came to us: we would raise the stakes and make it difficult for them to quit once they started. We used bright wrapping paper to cover the box, tied colorful ribbons around it, and put it in the center of the kitchen table. It would be the first thing they saw when they walked through the front door.

As expected, when they returned home, they spied the gift immediately and rushed to open it. This was the opportunity to enact my plan, so I told them, "If you really want to open the gift, you can't regret it!"

"Mom, we won't! We promise!" they both answered in unison. Ever since they were little, they had never regretted any of their gifts, so they couldn't even imagine the possibility. However, once they opened the box and caught a glimpse of all the pieces, they just stared at me.

Kathy asked, in a small voice, "Mom, you overestimated our abilities, didn't you?"

"Wow! So many pieces!" Fanny was also startled, looking at the puzzle doubtfully.

I continued to follow my plan, teasing them, "Oh, so you guys are regretting it now?"

They were too embarrassed to take back their words since they had just promised not to; so in response, they just grabbed the box, sat in a corner, and started on the puzzle. After a couple of hours, though, they had made very little progress.

"This puzzle sucks! We'll never get it!" Kathy burst out, frustrated.

"Who knew a puzzle could be so difficult?" Fanny sighed, although she was not quite ready to admit defeat.

I thought it was time to offer my help, and once I joined them, they perked up again. I suggested that they start by sorting the pieces, grouping them based on their colors and guessing which pieces belonged in the same area. I also pointed out that they could start with easier, more identifiable pieces, such as the edge pieces, which always had a flat side. Together, we worked on the border of the puzzle and gradually made progress. By this time, they had regained some of their confidence and determination.

Over the next couple of weeks, when they returned home, if they had time, they worked on the puzzle. On the weekends, our whole family sat together to work on it for an hour or so as well. As we fit the pieces together, we exchanged jokes and shared stories; the children particularly liked it when John entertained them with tales of what he was like at their age. We all had a very enjoyable time.

It took nearly three weeks to complete the puzzle, but we finally finished it. It still hangs on Kathy's bedroom wall as a testament to all of our efforts. Now that both Fanny and Kathy are attending college far away, our home is much quieter. Recalling those times when we were so happy together, sometimes we feel as though we have lost something.

This activity trained our children in perseverance and persistence and helped them realize that there are no limits to learning and practice. Since then, neither of them has ever dared to say that a puzzle was a piece of cake.

With a clattering crash, the domino tower fell again.

"Oh wow, why me again?" Bill complained, face red with barely suppressed frustration.

Playing with dominos is a welcome pastime in our family. In our game, one person makes a structure—a wall, mountain, tower, or whatever shape he or she can think of—out of dominoes. In turns, each player removes one domino from the structure, leaving the topmost dominos alone. If other pieces are knocked over in the process of removing one, the player has to take all of them. This continues until the whole structure collapses. The player with the least domino pieces is declared the winner. Since the structures are different every time, the game always challenges the builder and the other players.

This game trained their hands-on skills, patience, and powers of observation as they built, analyzed, and removed pieces from the structures. With this game, they also exercised their imaginations and creativity, approaching it with the critical eye of an architect or engineer. Whenever it was their turn to create the structure, they tried to build in small loopholes and tricks that only they would notice so that others would be forced to knock down more dominos.

Every time the children finished building, John would always walk around, carefully examining their structures before we started the game. Sometimes I would be impatient to play and urge him, "Hey! Let's start the game already!"

Finally, he smiled at me and explained, "There's no rush, my dear wife! Have you noticed something interesting? Look carefully—there's a lot of information inside these towers. Whenever Fanny builds, she does so symmetrically, with a particular shape in mind. When Kathy does it, there isn't as much regularity, but you can always see that she adds an unusual, purposeful twist. It's a great match with their personalities, don't you think?"

When I looked at it this way, it made sense. I hadn't realized that even such a simple game could give us so much insight into our children's personalities.

Every time we play this game, we carefully contemplate our moves, walking around and around the tower as the others egg us on playfully. Even now, whenever our daughters return from college, they still enjoy playing this game.

"The Kitten Goes Fishing"

Fishing is another activity that everyone in our family enjoys. We love fishing because, first, it trained our children's patience and focus. Second, it is always great fun for everyone. Third, of course, we all enjoy the fish that we catch!

When we lived in Utah, there was a fishing pond not too far from our home, so we went there almost every weekend. Those mornings, when we got up, everyone jumped into action: the children dug up worms, John prepared fishing poles and gear, I made lunch, and we packed the car, eager to start casting our lines.

The first time we went fishing, a problem emerged: the children were afraid of putting the worms on the hooks. We had to repeatedly encourage them to overcome their squeamishness, and eventually, they were able to do so successfully. Of course, it often took a long time for the fish to take the bait; and since children have short attention spans, they lost their patience very easily.

"Mom, it's been a long time. Where are all the fish?" they complained. In response, I told them a story about a kitten that went fishing with its mother.

One day, the mother cat decided to take the kitten fishing. As they sat by the water and waited for the fish to bite, a dragonfly flew by. The kitten, immediately distracted, put down the pole to try to catch the dragonfly. When the kitten returned to his fishing pole, a butterfly fluttered past him. Again, the kitten left to chase the butterfly. When the kitten finally returned, of course he still had not caught anything, but his mother had caught a whole bucket of fish!

"Ha, ha, Mom, we get it now!" They all understood what I meant and settled down with their fishing poles. In the end, they all caught their own fish, and we went home in high spirits.

Kathy catching a fish

Our fishing experiences helped Fanny stand out during a fishing competition hosted by our town. In the summer of 2002, the town announced a fishing contest open to all children. According to the rules, fish caught by adults would not count for anything; only children could receive awards for their fish. These awards were separated into different levels depending on the weight of the fish they caught. Since the town did not put too many fish in the pond, catching them would not be easy.

It sounded like fun, so we invited another family to go with us and enjoy this event. The morning of the competition, we prepared our fishing poles, dug up worms, and stocked a cooler with refreshments. It was a small pond, so in order to find the best spot, we arrived early. Shortly afterward, many more people arrived, and the shores of the pond became busy as people crowded around.

Everyone had fun, enjoying the sunshine and the music in the background. We chatted, laughed, and had a small picnic; but the whole time, none of our children saw any signs of fish. However, every so often, they would hear the loudspeakers announcing that another child had hooked a fish and received a prize.

Overcome with a sense of urgency that heightened with every new announcement, Fanny asked, "Dad, can I move to a different location?"

Once she received our permission, she immediately walked to a quieter location. While we were sitting on the grass entertaining ourselves, Fanny called to us excitedly, "Mom, Dad! I caught a fish!"

She ran to us with a fish dangling off the end of her fishing pole. "Let's go get the award!"

"Congratulations!" the organizer said with a smile as she ran up, and he checked the fish's weight. It turned out to be over five ounces, which was quite large, so he handed her a trophy. However, there was still some time left before the end of the competition, so Fanny wanted to try again. She dropped the trophy at our feet, grabbed her fishing pole, and ran over to the pond once more. We joked to each other, "Wow! It seems like Fanny is attracted to trophies!"

Soon afterward, to our surprise, Fanny caught another big fish and received another trophy. The son of the other family, Kathy, and Bill still had not caught anything; but now Fanny had two prizes. To her credit, Fanny was very generous; she gave one of her trophies to the other family's boy and let Kathy and Bill hold her trophy in turns. That day, everyone returned home happily.

No Miracles in the Pool

When Fanny was seven years old and Kathy was five, we noticed that they enjoyed playing in the water very much and seemed to have a natural affinity for it. One day, we curiously asked them, "Do you two want to learn how to swim?" They jumped up, cheering, so we signed them up for swimming lessons immediately.

The first time they entered the pool, they did so without any fear or hesitation, immediately stepping into the water. Enthusiastically following their teacher's instructions, they learned how to hold their breath, kick, tread water, and float on their backs, never once needing my support. After a full session of classes, they quickly learned several major swimming styles: freestyle, backstroke, and breaststroke.

On the last day of swimming lessons, John came with us to see what Fanny and Kathy had learned. When he saw they could do all the swimming strokes, he was surprised by their progress and commented, "Well, I learned to swim, and I've practiced for almost thirty to forty years, but I still only know one style: the dog paddle! If they've been able to learn all of this in just a few weeks, maybe they have some real talent!"

After hearing John say this, I grew excited. Together, we discussed how we could potentially train them to be swimming stars. Through careful research, we discovered that very few Chinese had really stood out in swimming. However, diving was a completely different story; the Chinese almost completely dominated this field. Maybe our family held two superstars, the next Fu Mingxia (a multiple world champion and Olympic gold medalist in diving). As our thoughts developed more and more in this direction, we became eager to explore this idea. Without any hesitation, we registered them for diving classes.

On the first day of their diving class, John took the day off from work so we could drive both of them to the pool and observe them. We sat in the bleachers, watching expectantly as a long line of other children gracefully jumped off the diving board. We were impressed and hoped to see our children perform similarly, to pull off some miracle to prove their innate genius. Finally, our daughters climbed the tall ladder and stepped onto the diving board.

They slowly inched forward. Once they reached the middle of the diving board, we could see their pale faces as they trembled with fear. Over and over, we tried to catch their eye to encourage them, but they were unable to take even one more step toward the edge. Our dreams of diving stars came to a screeching halt, and we had no choice but to take our daughters back home and cancel their lessons. We realized then that if we didn't understand our children's talents and abilities and just planned something according to our own personal fancies and desires, our efforts would be doomed to fail.

Joy in Art

A bird and a flower, a tiger by a stream, a running horse . . . Kathy's bedroom was like an art gallery, with all the drawings and paintings she was particularly proud of hanging on her wall. Time and time again, we would look into her room and find ourselves drawn to a certain painting or picture, stepping closer for a better look. Was she an art genius? It's a long story.

Kathy's interest in art started with "abstract" art. When she and her sister were younger, we provided them with paper, brushes, and paints. She would draw a thick, wiggly line and then run to show me. "Mom! I drew a snake!" After painting a few squares, she brought the paper to John. "Dad! Look at my house!" Her sister would do the same.

What else could we do besides encourage them? Every time, we just told them, "Good job!"

Whenever these two sisters heard our praise, they would get excited and smile with great satisfaction, then run off to again continue their artistic creations. Each time, they would hang every piece on their bed frame with a great sense of accomplishment.

Many other people continued to praise her work, distorting Kathy's perspective of her abilities as the flattery went to her head. One day, when Kathy was in high school, she told me, "Mom, my friends say I'm talented in art. I want to take lessons."

Coincidentally, she had a friend who had real artistic talent, a girl whose pieces had been showcased in their own galleries. One of her pieces had even been selected for exhibition on Capitol Hill in Washington DC. To deflate Kathy's ego, I took her to her friend's exhibit so she could compare herself to others on a broader scale. When we arrived and saw the amazing work of her friend, I asked Kathy, "So how do your pieces compare with hers? Do you think you have this much talent?"

I explained to her, "If you take art lessons on the weekends, you will need to spend two or three hours traveling and then at least another hour for lessons. After you come back, you will still need to practice. By that point, an entire day will be gone. Right now you're heavily loaded with schoolwork, and you still have so many extracurricular and social activities. Can you really handle it all?"

Finally, Kathy understood the situation. Since she has always been good at setting priorities, she gave up her original idea of art classes and instead chose to teach herself in her free time.

A Chess Player

When children learn to play strategy games such as chess or go, they also learn to think critically and develop the ability to coordinate several things at once.

When Fanny wanted to learn to play chess, we faced a small issue: neither of us knew how to play western chess, but we wanted to encourage this interest of hers. Eventually, we decided that John would teach her—since he was the man in the family, this sort of job was his responsibility.

Faced with this task, he went to the bookstore and bought a very thick book on chess techniques. Every day, Fanny and John studied that book to learn how to play chess, sometimes laughing, and other times arguing until they were both red in the face. When I had enough of their bickering and tried to mediate between them, they turned on me and defended themselves: "It's one of the joys of the game!"

Slowly, Fanny's interest in chess developed further; she constantly wanted to play, but John was very busy and did not always have the time to play against her. However, we couldn't expect this little girl to understand the problems of adults. The moment John returned home, she would be ready and waiting. Sitting at the table with the board already set up, she would look at her father and demand, "Play!"

She was a smart girl and picked up on a key pattern: the more tired her father was, the more he would lose. Furthermore, poor John, after losing the game, would still have to pretend to be happy and congratulate her, "Hey, Fanny! You've made more progress!" Fanny only grew more enthusiastic about the game under this praise and would then ask for one more game.

"What? One *more* game?" His face would grow pale, and he would sigh to himself. "What a balanced development . . . I'd rather give her a bunch of difficult math problems to struggle with so I can finally have a break!"

Fanny playing chess with her father

It is true that playing with children and encouraging their hobbies can be much harder than simply loading them with extra practice and walking away. However, John was more experienced in the ways of the world. Soon, he formulated his own strategy to handle the situation: he bought chess software for the computer. Once he installed it, he shouted to Fanny triumphantly, "Fanny, come here and play! You can pick any level that you want!"

For the first few days, Fanny played against the computer happily, but we had failed to see a major flaw in John's plan. The computer was just a machine; it did not understand human emotion. When she won, the computer did not flatter her. When she lost, it did not try to console her. So after a while, she came back, asking her dad to play against her once more.

This lasted for a few years until Fanny entered high school, where there was a chess club and other people who would play against her, lifting quite a burden off John.

A girl playing chess is not common in the U.S. In her high school club, Fanny was the only female chess player.

Dig a Hole, Find a Gold Nugget

Undeniably, some children are given offers by prestigious colleges because they are talented in certain sports. We knew of one girl from

Pearl River High School who had been accepted by Princeton for her skill in swimming. Such instances created misunderstandings in the community; some people believed that in order to attend an elite college, students needed to do sports. Kathy was one such person affected by this idea.

In tenth grade, her best friend joined the high school track team and encouraged Kathy to do the same. Kathy enjoyed running and seriously considered this option. When she asked us for our opinion, John asked her a few questions in response.

"Has your running ever advanced you to the state level?"

"No . . . ," she replied.

"Do you think the track team will unleash your potential more than other clubs?"

"I think other clubs could be better."

"If you join the track team, will you still have time to join other clubs?"

"Maybe not."

To us, the answer was clear, but Kathy still did not completely agree. In the end, John suggested, "For now, continue with your club activities. If there are no conflicts, you can join track. Is that okay?"

Satisfied with this, Kathy followed his advice. However, when she went to join the track team, she discovered the coach had very rigid rules: anyone who joined had to attend practice every day. Kathy finally realized she had to give this up.

Kathy had also tried her luck with softball, but we all quickly realized that she had no talent for it—in the entire season, she didn't even hit the ball once. Interestingly enough, her team still came in first place, and she happily received a trophy. The incident soon became another family joke. Just as she had told us, it was possible to "dig a hole, find a gold nugget."

These experiences had proven that Kathy was not strongly athletic, so we did not think it was necessary for her to continue playing softball and develop a habit of remaining on the sidelines. She had her own specialties, and these talents could be better developed elsewhere.

Physical Exercise

Physical exercise is necessary because nothing can be accomplished without a healthy body. However, it is unnecessary to push this to an extreme. Through our experiences with our children, we understood that they did not enjoy sports with excessive physical contact. With this in mind, we chose activities such as hiking, biking, fishing, camping, badminton, ping-pong, tennis, and swimming to build their physical and mental endurance.

Hiking has long been our family's favorite activity, especially during spring and autumn. In the spring, the forests are filled with the stirrings of life: trees start to grow green once more, and flowers begin to bloom everywhere. After a long winter, spring brings the whisperings of nature's revival and renewal.

Autumn is the harvest season. We enjoy hiking in the crisp air and picking blueberries along the trail. When our children were younger, they had only eaten blueberries from the supermarket. However, once we discovered wild blueberries—juicy, sweet, and all-natural—the blueberries from the store lost their appeal. In addition, the wild blueberry pancakes we made were simply delicious.

However, in order to reach the blueberries, we needed to hike up steep trails for at least half an hour, carrying backpacks of food and drinks. The first time we went, Fanny was nine years old, Kathy was seven, and Bill was five. Along the trail, they became tired and walked unsteadily on the path, stumbling occasionally. Sometimes, we had to hold their hands and encourage them to continue. They would even use their hands and feet to climb up particularly rough areas, sweat dripping down their faces and blurring their vision. Although hiking demanded a lot of physical effort, we all really enjoyed it.

After we settled down in Pearl River, we learned about a beautiful lake in the mountains where we could go fishing. The catch was that we would have to hike past two mountain peaks to reach the lake. We asked our children, "Do you guys dare to go for it?"

"Yes, why not?" they replied excitedly. Our whole family was determined to hike the trail, so we set off down the path. The road was very steep, and occasionally there were loose rocks, so we had to watch our footing carefully. Initially, the children were very enthusiastic, running in front of us and jumping from rock to rock. We had no way to hold them back, so most of the time, I lagged behind. They would often yell back to me, "Mom, come on!"

After we passed the first peak, they started getting tired and asked, "How much longer until we get there?"

"An hour and a half," I answered, and so we continued toward the next peak. It seemed like an endless trail. Exhaustion caught up with them, and they gradually lost their patience.

"It's too much!" they complained, almost in despair. However, we urged them onward.

"Yes, but we've already finished two-thirds of the trail! If we give up now, we will have failed. Each step forward is a step closer to our destination."

After another hour of hiking, the road curved around a bend and flattened out. Once the children heard the sounds of a bubbling stream and saw the sunlight breaking through the trees and reflecting off clear water, they cheered and started running again.

"We're here! Mom, Dad! It's so beautiful!" Birds sang in the trees, and fish swam in the lake, close to the shore. Flowers grew on the edges of the lake, and we spied a family of swans playing in the water. It seemed like a dream. After spending some time admiring the scene, we started fishing and brought home a decent catch.

After years of exercise, they now have no problems with hiking fifteen miles a day and greatly enjoy doing so.

The Wangster

When Kathy and Fanny were in middle school, they had plenty of free time during the summer, so they took golf lessons and learned the basic skills and rules of the game. They also participated in many outdoor activities and sports. However, in the winter, they could not venture outside to do those things; so we asked them to do sit-ups and push-ups, run on the treadmill, or exercise with weights.

When Fanny and Bill started doing push-ups, their bodies contorted like snakes; but when Kathy tried it, her back remained as straight as a rod. From the beginning, she could do at least fifteen push-ups, causing her siblings and me to cheer her on and making Kathy feel proud of herself.

Hearing our cheering, John joined us. When he saw Kathy's performance, he was struck by a sudden inspiration, asking her, "Kathy, would you like to do something that can really make people admire you?"

His question resounded deeply in Kathy's heart. Every child wants a chance to prove himself or herself in the public eye, and Kathy was no different. She eagerly asked, "What can I do?"

"Just continue doing this—practicing push-ups. I'm sure that after a while, you will be able to do forty or fifty. In your physical education class, you can show this off, and we'll see who thinks you're a nerd then!"

Kathy grew very motivated by her dad's encouragement. Every day, she practiced hard and made unexpected progress.

About half a year later, Kathy could comfortably do fifty standard push-ups. Fanny and Bill also improved, but their forms still could not compare with hers. The silhouettes of their bodies remained decidedly serpentine. From this, we could also see the importance in training children according to their strengths.

One day, John told Kathy, "You're ready now."

During her physical education class, Kathy purposely challenged a strong, physically fit male classmate to a push-up contest. That boy did very well, doing over thirty push-ups before looking at her triumphantly as their classmates applauded him. He waited, smug and confident, to see what the bookworm could do.

Kathy approached this strategically, playing up her image as the class nerd. She pretended to be shocked and shied away, but finally, driven by the other students, got down reluctantly. Then, she did fifty standard push-ups, executing each in a clean, precise manner. Everyone was astonished, the boy most of all. From that, Kathy earned the nickname "Wangster." She could now walk around the halls proudly, head held high.

We knew Kathy was neither talented in sports nor capable of performing miracles. We just used her talent in this small area for a flashy performance. As we've said before, it is always important to teach children according to their talents and use methods that complement their natures. A lot of parents tend to forget this when guiding their children.

After Fanny and Kathy went to Harvard, many of our friends often talked about them with great reverence. They all thought that Fanny and Kathy had been admitted because they were talented geniuses, but as their parents, we knew the truth. We do not deny that they are very intelligent, but they are not geniuses or prodigies. The factor that has contributed the greatest to their successes is the methods we used to showcase their talents and unleash their potentials.

As we have seen in this chapter, Kathy could put on a dramatic show; but when she did so, she did not rely on her strengths. Instead, she surprised everyone by showing off in her weakest area: sports. This demonstrates that talent is only one factor in success; how to utilize children's talent is more critical.

CHAPTER 9

Individuality and Freedom of Choice

American parents like to emphasize their children's individuality and freedom of choice. While we agree that these are important, we do not think that children should be allowed to do what they want without any discipline. It is natural for children to love playing; if we do not impose any restrictions, most of them will choose to play aimlessly all day long. This is not just the case for young children—even high school students would do the same. On the other hand, if we take away all our children's freedom, we cannot build a solid relationship with them because all of our channels of communication will be cut off. If we lack common ground, children tend to become more rebellious. As parents, we wanted to handle this properly to create and promote a harmonious family atmosphere. By maintaining good communication with our children and providing proper guidance, we can assist our children in becoming successful.

If we look around, regardless of whether we are in China or the U.S., Chinese children always have plenty of extracurricular activities to keep them busy, such as piano and violin lessons, sports practices, extra academic programs, and art classes. However, everyone's energy has its limits, and each individual has his or her own interests and strengths. No one can do everything, so we cannot just follow a path set by others; to really move forward, we need to consider each child's individuality, interests, and specialties. They need a certain freedom to choose what they enjoy and to try what they are interested in. This way, they will pay more attention and naturally devote more effort to what they are doing, ultimately obtaining better results.

Fanny and Kathy picked classes, clubs, and activities according to what they wanted; and in most cases, they did very well. Of course, sometimes they made wrong choices, choosing an activity that didn't quite suit them. When this happened, we let them choose whether they wanted to continue on and work through the problems or just drop the activity altogether. Occasionally, though, we found it necessary to intervene and force them to stop what they were doing.

Fanny and Kathy have two completely different personalities. Fanny is quiet and introverted, very thoughtful, and always chasing perfection. She is also creative, with strong romantic tendencies, but her biggest weakness is that she has a difficult time expressing herself. Although she enjoys making friends, she does not always know how to do so. For many years, we put in tremendous effort to help her develop in a balanced manner.

When she was young, we took her to our friends' houses to visit and interact with their children. We also frequently went on trips to the library, playground, and social events so she could have more opportunities to be around other children. After she started school, we would often invite her classmates and friends to our house for small parties on weekends. We tried to push her to make friends. Occasionally, we would set targets, such as one new friend a month. Eventually, we realized that the most difficult part for her was initiating contact with others, so we altered our strategies, encouraging her to participate in clubs and other social activities. In those situations, most children already share some common interests, making it easier for her to identify with and get along with them.

Academically, Fanny enjoys science and math. As she grew up, we emphasized her strengths in science, where she would be able to stand out. Based on our understanding of her, we gradually raised her short-term academic targets. When we set these targets, we tried to establish them at a level that would require her to expend genuine effort, which encouraged her to continuously move forward. In science, we urged her to explore new opportunities that would best release her potential and creativity and allow her to excel, such as by proactively participating in academic competitions, entering science fairs, and building a basement laboratory.

On the other hand, Kathy is more humorous and extroverted, enjoying the social side of everything. She does things boldly and passionately, but sometimes this causes her to be careless and inattentive to small details.

When Fanny was about one year old, John did a very interesting experiment. He placed one hand behind her back, allowing her to balance by resting her weight on his hand. When he removed his hand from her back, she would fall since the support was gone. When Kathy was around the same age, John did the same experiment. However, when he removed his hand from her back, she stayed in place and did not move at all. From this, we could see that from an early age, Kathy had a very independent personality. Later, this would prove true: she grew up to be not only independent, but also daring enough to do anything.

Based on Kathy's traits, we adopted a more open parenting strategy, letting her have more space to develop by herself. We guided her with a more social approach, encouraging her to improve her creativity and leadership and learn sophisticated social skills to more effectively interact with her peers. We supported her becoming more involved in the community and social events. In high school, she joined more humanities-based clubs, such as Mock Trial, Model UN, the school newspaper, and the Yearbook Club. As a result, she was frequently interviewing teachers, writing reports, and—outside of school—participating in campaign activities.

Because of her bold personality, while we offered her more space for development, we also paid her closer attention. Whenever we saw any signs that she was moving in the wrong direction, we immediately intervened, making sure she would not fall off the right path. We were afraid that once she was on the wrong track, it would be extremely difficult to pull her back.

Children's unique personalities and specialties are gifts. Parents should respect this and guide their children to take advantage of their strengths, while letting their children enjoy themselves in the pursuit of success. Many children misunderstand the term "unique," believing that uniqueness lies in wearing strange clothes, behaving in a disorderly fashion, or speaking impudently. However, parents should familiarize their children with a positive definition of uniqueness: thinking or doing things in a correct manner and using their unique creativity and individual initiative to lead productive lives.

Fanny's Flute

All of our children had the opportunity to learn to play the piano. Of the three, Fanny liked playing the piano the most and has maintained this as a hobby; playing piano is something she still enjoys in college.

Fanny playing the flute

In September 2000, Fanny was in middle school. She had become attracted to the flute, but she did not mention this to anyone.

In December, our family attended the middle school winter concert showcasing the school's orchestra, chorus, and band. The band's performance was outstanding; even a quiet person like me was roused by the music they had played. On the way back home, we all talked about the concert. It was strange because Fanny was not involved in the conversation at all. Instead, she looked out the car window sadly. My intuition told me she was troubled. When we got home, I asked her, "Is there anything bothering you?"

"No," she answered, but her tone was wistful. She quietly walked to her room.

I could tell there was something making her unhappy and determined to find out, I followed her to her room. Holding her hand, I sat by her bed. "Fanny, I know something is bothering you. Please look at me and tell me the truth."

A few tears squeezed out as she told me, "I want to learn the flute. I want to join the band."

"Well, that's great! Why didn't you tell us earlier?" I said, relieved to finally know what was going on.

"I want to learn the flute, but I want to continue learning the piano. Please, can I do both?"

At last, I understood why she had been afraid to speak out. She thought we would limit her to one instrument.

"Of course, why not?" I replied. If she enjoyed both and had time for them, why couldn't she learn two instruments?

She was not expecting my answer and jumped up, exclaiming, "Thank you, Mom. I love you!"

"Remember, if you have something bothering you, please tell us. We don't always say no, right?" I added firmly.

Many things in children's lives seem trivial to their parents, but if these minor things accumulate, they may create large obstacles between parents and their children, so parents need to pay close attention to their children. Because children are immature, they view things from a different perspective; often, they think differently from us but are afraid to express their true feelings. If parents do not recognize this and do not communicate with their children, their children will see them as even more distant and remote. We not only need to observe them, but also need to encourage them to speak their minds. As long as they want to pursue a positive, healthy activity, we should encourage and assist them. Even when dealing with something that is not positive, we should not simply blame our children repeatedly. Instead, we should discuss the matter using facts and logic, helping children change their ideas by understanding our reasoning.

A Penchant for Performing

In September 2001, when Fanny was in sixth grade, she started learning how to play the flute. Most of the children in the middle school band had started learning their instruments in elementary school, so Fanny lagged behind them considerably. When the band teacher announced the winter concert schedule, Fanny expressed her desire to join the band on stage. However, the teacher told her, "Sorry, you just started learning, and your playing level is a little too low. How about next year?"

Fanny was completely shocked. Ever since she was little, she had enjoyed performing on stage and had always done well. This time, it seemed like she would be unable to play with the band.

She came home with tears in her eyes and told us about how much she wanted to perform in the concert. In this situation, we recalled one of her other musical experiences on stage: participating in her first piano recital. Her tremendous efforts in preparing and performing had surprised everyone greatly. We knew the same thing would happen again with the flute if she was given the opportunity. We had always been very supportive of her passions and encouraged her perseverance, so in order to help her reach a level where she could perform with the band, we signed her up for private flute lessons. For those two months, she worked extremely hard. Whenever she had time, she would sneak down to the basement to practice her flute. As a result, she made significant progress. With a solid music background from learning piano and an earnest desire to learn, her efforts finally paid off. In December, the teacher was surprised by her enormous progress and allowed her to perform on stage during the winter concert.

Fanny playing the piano

If children are allowed to pursue their own interests, they can better demonstrate their own initiative. Self-motivation can drive children far beyond our expectations, and as parents, we cannot ignore this powerful force and should never destroy this engine propelling them forward.

I remember that shortly after we agreed that Fanny could learn the flute, we drove to Florida for a vacation. At the time, we had not yet purchased a flute for her. The whole time that we were on the road, she blew over the top of an empty water bottle. We all laughed at her and asked, "What are you doing?"

She replied seriously, "I'm trying to practice techniques for the flute."

In May 2005, Fanny participated in the New York State School Music Association (NYSSMA) Level Four Flute Exam and received a score of "Excellent."

In middle school, she also performed in the school play. Each time we saw her onstage, we could see her confidence and poise reflected in her performance and shining in her eyes. It really moved me, and I was very proud of her. When the show was over, we applauded loudly, hoping she could feel our support.

She also participated in the school talent show, always choosing to play the piano. Every time, she would carefully prepare for weeks, and her performances were greatly enjoyed by her fellow students and their parents. For all of these activities, we were her loyal audience members, happy to be her cheerleaders and to support her endeavors.

After we moved to New York, Fanny continued her piano lessons. Her piano teacher, Mrs. P, was Russian and held a master's degree in music. Under her recommendation, Fanny participated in the Rockland County Music Teacher's Guild piano competition. She received the highest honor, the Gold Ribbon Award. In May 2002, she took the NYSSMA Level Four Piano Exam, played Beethoven's *Für Elise,* and received the highest score of "Outstanding." In April the following year, Fanny participated in the NYSSMA Level Five Piano exam and played Tchaikovsky's *June Barcarolle*. This piece of music was much more difficult and Fanny received an A, but the highest possible score was an A+. We realized that her piano skills were reaching a natural plateau, but we did not feel bad about this. Playing the piano was only a source of entertainment for her. It definitely raised her musicality and was a skill that could improve her quality of life in the future, but it was still just an amateur hobby.

Recognizing this, we suggested that Fanny stop her piano lessons. However, Fanny, as a self-motivated perfectionist, refused to face this reality and did not want to give up. By her request, her piano lessons continued for one more year. During this year, we could not see any noticeable progress, and she also realized this. After that year, she took our suggestion and stopped her lessons.

Many of our friends could not understand why we did this. They were all familiar with children trying to quit and being forced to continue by their parents, but they had never heard of parents suggesting that their children quit. Some of them asked us, "What's wrong with you guys?"

We knew our daughter well and understood that each time Fanny had received the highest scores and honors, it was not because she was a musical prodigy, but because her intelligence and hard work had been sufficient for that level of playing. However, these two factors could only take her so far without natural musical ability. Once Fanny's musical resources had been exhausted, she would inevitably meet an insurmountable barrier. If we knew that defeat was inevitable, it didn't make sense to linger, fighting a losing battle. Instead, we could cut our losses and fall back, saving our efforts and resources for a new venture.

A graceful retreat was better than suffering great losses from repeated failure.

Although Fanny stopped her piano lessons, she still enjoys the piano as a hobby. When she has free time, she plays the piano for her amusement and our entertainment. One time, after watching the Broadway musical *The Phantom of the Opera*, Fanny fell in love with the music, so we bought her the piano scores. Immediately, she sat down to enthusiastically to learn how to play the music.

There is one thing that I still do not understand about her: why she liked performing so much. After all, it seems very contradictory to her introverted character. From this, we can see how complex a child's personality is. Parents should not judge their children solely based on their own views, because these views may not be fully accurate representations of their children's characters. Instead, parents need to provide opportunities for their children to express themselves freely. In this way, they can gain more information and knowledge about their children and help them to fully utilize their potential.

Kathy's Clarinet

In 1999, when Kathy was in second grade, we suggested that she take piano lessons as well.

"I don't like it," she responded.

We still encouraged her to give it a try, reasoning, "If you don't try, how will you know?"

She agreed to take piano lessons for a couple months, learning from the same teacher that Fanny had at the time. To make practicing more interesting, Fanny would sometimes sit next to Kathy when Kathy was practicing, showing her how to play or giving her tips on how to improve. However, Kathy really showed no interest in the piano. As the saying goes, "You can lead a horse to water, but you can't make it drink." Although we gave Kathy the opportunity to learn how to play the piano, she simply didn't enjoy it. Seeing Kathy's indifference toward the piano convinced us we should let this go, but we also reminded her that if she ever changed her mind, she could resume her lessons.

Since this was just a hobby, we did not want to pressure them. The children were still in their exploratory phases and, honestly, sometimes even they did not know what they really enjoyed. This is also the case for many college students; they enter college without being sure about their major, but are able to declare their major with confidence after a year of learning. Some students though, as they learn even more, will find new interests and change their majors, sometimes several times, before their third year, when most students settle down. We should give our children the space, time, and opportunities to explore their real interests. Once they find something they are really interested in and enjoy doing, it will be much easier for them to continue pursuing that activity. Even if these activities promise a tough road ahead, they will face these challenges willingly and enjoy the process.

While she started with the piano, Kathy found her true calling in the clarinet. Fanny also started with the piano, but she picked up the flute as well. We always kept our minds open in these matters. We knew they weren't musical prodigies, and our purpose was not to train them to become musicians. What instrument they decided to play, if any, was their decision entirely. All we had to do was to keep the door of opportunity open. As long as the conditions permitted it, if they wanted to try something new, we would support them.

Kathy playing the clarinet

A Birthday Gift

In March 1997, Fanny and Kathy celebrated their birthdays, with Fanny turning seven and Kathy turning five. As they blew out the candles on their cake, they made a wish together: they wanted a pet rabbit. Our children had wanted a pet for a long time, so to satisfy their curiosity, we decided to fulfill their wish. We also saw this as a good opportunity to teach them another lesson.

"Okay, we'll get a pet, but you two must be responsible for it and give it a comfortable home," I told them. First, we asked them to first understand a rabbit's habitat and figure out how to build a proper home for it. To start them off, I took the children to the library to learn about a rabbit's natural environment, dietary needs, and other important information. A couple months later, equipped with this data, we traveled to a farm to pick out a rabbit. When the children saw

162

all of the rabbits, it seemed like they wanted to bring them all home. We understood what they were thinking: they wanted their rabbit to have company so it would not be lonely. So in the end, we bought two rabbits.

A rabbit's ideal habitat needs to be clean and dry, with plenty of access to sunshine. Looking around the backyard, we picked a suitable location and built a home for the rabbits together. Even as they worked under the hot sun, the children cheerfully carried and stacked bricks for the rabbits' new home. To prevent the rabbits from running away, we fenced off a five feet by three feet enclosure, giving them enough space to comfortably move about. The encyclopedia had mentioned that wild rabbits had a range of thirty tennis courts, but unfortunately, that wasn't possible for us.

Rabbits enjoy eating certain types of grass and fresh vegetables. Since carrots were easy to plant, we allowed our children to grow them around the rabbit's enclosure. To make sure the rabbits had enough exercise, every day after they returned from school, the children let out the rabbits and happily chased them around the backyard, labeling their antics "making the rabbits do exercise."

Loving animals is natural for children. We should indulge these affectionate feelings, but we cannot let children develop the bad habit of only playing with, but not taking responsibility of, these animals. We required our children to feed the rabbits, take them out for exercise on a daily basis, and clean their enclosure regularly. We let our children know that these rabbits were alive, and since they brought these creatures home, they had to respect them. It was their duty to ensure that these animals grew happily and healthily. Through this process, they were able to develop a responsibility for living creatures and understand the true value of life and love.

Burning the Books

Harry Potter is a fictional book series written by British author, J. K. Rowling. Since it was released in 1997, it has been an international success. This book—with aspects of adventure, magic, fantasy, romance, and thriller—has captured the imaginations and hearts of children and adults all over the world. We heard many children talk about how, once they started reading the books, they just could not stop. During a party, I talked about this *Harry Potter* craze with the mother of one of Kathy's friends, mentioning my confusion as to why children made such a big deal over these books and movies.

In response, she told me, "You should read the books! I first read it with my daughter, and the story was so deeply attractive. I've also fallen in love with it!"

In an attempt to understand this phenomenon, we watched the movies with our children, trying to find a common ground. Although the movies differed somewhat from the books, the rough idea and plotline was basically the same, and we still could not see what the mania was about. I talked to my children, advising them, "You can love a movie, a character, or what they do, but do not blindly obsess over them and lose your own logic and independent thinking."

After our children bought the *Harry Potter* books, they were wildly ecstatic. They read the books over and over again, sometimes wanting to skip meals or ignore homework assignments to continue reading. Several times, we reminded them, "You guys need to regulate yourselves and develop your capacities for self-control!"

No matter how much we emphasized the importance of self-control and despite our repeated reminders, they simply could not stop. We were not against our children reading *Harry Potter*, but the way they were doing so raised our concerns. Every time we urged them to regain their composure and think rationally, they simply discarded our advice, continuing to read the book obsessively: before and after each meal, while they were supposed to be doing homework, during their bedtimes . . . When we removed the lamps from their rooms, they used flashlights instead. Faced with this situation, we had no choice but to take an extreme approach: we burned the books.

In front of the children, we threw each book into the fireplace. As they watched their beloved books catch on fire, we could see tears welling in their eyes. We did not understand how the situation had spiraled out of control this badly.

Before this, we had always treated them with respect. We would advise them, and they would heed our guidance and follow our suggestions. However, this experience made us realize that their self-control could be very weak. We had to take such an extreme approach to stop them and jar them back to their senses.

In order to test their self-control, a few weeks later, we bought a new set of Harry Potter books for them to read, but only in their spare time. This time, they were much more reasonable in managing their reading.

Smashing the iPods

Another time, our children lost their self-control again, and we had to take desperate measures to force them to regain it once more.

During high school, children are under a lot of stress and sometimes need to find some way to relax; so we decided to buy the popular iPod, one for each of them. Of course, they were all happy about this; soon after receiving them, they quickly became adept at downloading and transferring music and pictures to these new devices. After school, upon returning home, they would plug in the earbuds and lounge on the couches, completely at ease. When they went to school, we also gave these little music players a try, discovering that the sound quality was excellent and they were convenient to use.

However, a problem soon emerged: they began to use their iPods every day. Once they put on their headphones, nothing could get through to them. When we called to them, they could not hear us. They put off their homework to the last minute and worked on it carelessly. For the first couple of weeks, we understood their behavior as children enjoying a new toy. We figured that after a few weeks, the novelty would wear off.

Yet the situation did not improve; instead, it became worse. They began to forget their basic responsibilities and duties. We could not let this continue, so we told them, again, to regain their self-control. No matter how we reminded them, our efforts were to no avail. This might explain why Apple is so rich—we had once heard a saying that if you want to make money, try to make it off children first, then women; if you fail in both, your last choice is to turn to a man's pocket. Because children are so impressionable and easily lured by fashion, it seemed like this theory had some merit!

One night, I called the children to the table for dinner, but no one responded. Their dad had to approach each of them and invite them one by one to the dinner table. This was just the start, for at the dinner table, they were still reluctant to remove their earbuds. John was pretty upset but tried to be patient and kept his anger in check at the dinner table. We had a quiet dinner that night.

After dinner, instead of clearing the table as they usually did, the children just walked away, content to sit back on the couches and enjoy their music. Their actions finally pushed John over the edge. Without saying a word, he took their iPods from them and hammered them into pieces of twisted metal.

I felt pretty bad. A few hundred dollars' worth of technology was destroyed in a few seconds.

We did not buy any more iPods for a while. However, when Fanny went to college, we bought her a new iPod!

Confronting Reality

Since their birth and up to high school, our children have been provided with a variety of opportunities, and we have encouraged them to participate in a diverse range of activities. We made them aware that they were intelligent, but not geniuses; if they wanted to be successful, they had to work hard. At the same time, they should pursue their own interests and strive to develop in a balanced manner.

When we speak of balanced development, it must be first built on a strong foundation of their own specialties, using these strengths to branch out from an essential academic core. We tried our best to guide them in building a solid academic base and then expanding from there, developing other skills or interests to complement their personalities.

Today, competition is fierce and omnipresent in every level of society. Asian-Americans in particular need to put in extra effort to excel. If they want to be admitted to an elite college or find a better job, they need to work hard to stand out in their field. In America, the most prestigious colleges demand academically outstanding students. In addition to these high standards, prospective students must have demonstrated achievements in other areas.

In return, such elite colleges offer renowned faculty, abundant resources, world-class facilities, an intellectually competitive atmosphere, and strong networks with the outside world. Such benefits are difficult to find in other colleges. These top colleges also gather the most brilliant students from all corners of the world in every field. Working and studying with these people as their peers promotes the spirit of academia and motivates students to reach higher, not only intellectually. Students who attend elite colleges can learn from the unique specialties, skills, creative minds, and diversity of classmates who are chosen from the best of the best.

This is why we encouraged Fanny and Kathy to aim for these top colleges, to be part of this stimulating and challenging atmosphere, and to live among the top minds of their generation. Some children want to avoid stress and hard work, preferring to take an easier route in life. They may argue, "Well, I don't want to go to the top colleges." And this is their own choice. However, the world is always moving forward, and those who do not move with it will be left behind.

Eventually, everyone needs to face the serious problems of finding a job, paying for health insurance, saving for retirement, and the other necessities of life. We needed to make our children realize that it is necessary to have some basic survival skills when they enter the real world. The best way to be successful is to play on their strengths; no matter what people do or what goals they have, they must always work hard.

Mayor Michael R. Bloomberg Hosts Barbecue in Honor of the
2010 New York City Summer Interns
Gracie Mansion, New York July 19, 2010

The purpose of studying is not just to attend college or to learn skills to survive in the real world. The most important point is to gain a deeper understanding of the world and be able to take control of their lives. With more knowledge comes the power to enhance people's ability to determine their futures and accomplish their goals. Learning gives them the outlet to explore themselves and live a productive life without regrets.

For many years, America's top colleges have held different, higher standards for Asian-American students. Sociology professor Thomas J. Espenshade of Princeton University and Dr. Alexandria Walton Radford of MPR Associates, Inc. coauthored the book *No Longer Separate, Not Yet Equal*, which used data from the National Survey of College Experience to illustrate the disparities in the college admissions process. Their research indicated that an Asian student with a combined SAT critical reading and math score of 1550 was equivalent to a white student scoring 1410 and an African-American student scoring 1100 when it came to admissions decisions by the top colleges. It seems that the commonly held belief, that Asian-American SAT scores are reduced by 100-150 points in the eyes of college admissions officers, is not just a rumor; there are actually legitimate grounds for this claim. This just serves to underscore an important point: Asian children must work harder.

There are some families that take many vacations throughout the year and often, these parents have no problem with taking their children out of school for days in order to do so. This sometimes confused our children, because it was at odds with our educational philosophy. When this happened, we simply and clearly told them that we did not agree with those parents' actions. Different choices and environments produce different results. They needed to ignore the distractions that pulled them in every direction and stay steady and persevere on the path that would bring them to success.

CHAPTER 10

Self-Management

Training children in self-management and independence is a long-term process, but an important one that cannot be skipped. Upon entering elite colleges, some students are forced to take a leave of absence or simply drop out because they lack this essential ability. We have heard this type of news quite often and reflected upon it deeply. In order to allow children to pursue their future successfully, we need to train them to develop proper self-management skills in both academics and their daily lives, while establishing a spirit of independence. This training can be tailored to emphasize different aspects for different ages.

Self-Management Skills

There is nothing wrong with parents loving their children, but if parents try to manage every tiny detail of their children's lives and do not give them the opportunity to explore and exercise their individuality, they will block the development of their children's initiative and self-management skills.

Often, we have seen parents chasing their two- or three-year-old children around in an attempt to feed them. When their child falls down, both parents rush to scoop the child up, as concerned as if their child was a fragile vase. When these children reach high school, they do not hesitate to call out, "Mom! I'm late!" And these mothers then help them with everyday tasks like picking out an outfit or packing their backpack. Even in college, some students still need their parents to go with them in order to continue taking care of them. If we treat children like this, they will never grow up and develop a sense of independence.

Children have natural curiosity for learning and will energetically explore their surroundings. For them, everything is new, interesting, and exciting. When we raise our children, we can take advantage of this inquisitive nature to train their self-management ability. For instance, when a baby is a few months old, he or she can already hold a bottle independently. Why should the parents always hold the bottle? When a toddler falls, shouldn't the parents encourage him or her to stand up again? I think that it is better to give our children opportunities to become independent and mentally strong, rather than just taking care of everything for them.

When a child first starts learning how to use dining utensils, they often make a huge mess, painting their clothes and faces with food and knocking over cups of milk or juice; but this is completely normal. Yes, by letting them learn rather than feeding them ourselves, we spend more time cleaning up after them; but it is important for them to develop this ability by themselves. When I look back through old photo albums and see pictures of my children plastered with food or surrounded by a big mess in the closet as they look for their clothes, I am always amused.

In training a child's sense of independence, we need to start as early as possible. When our children began learning how to walk, we bought a baby walker, which had many advantages. Psychologically, our children did not feel wholly reliant on their parents. Physically, they had more freedom to move around and investigate their surroundings, which also strengthened their muscles. When they became tired, they could just sit down, giving them a sense of security. When we first taught our children to walk, John and I would stand a short distance apart and encourage them to walk back and forth between us. When they fell, we gently urged them to stand up; and when they reached us, we would give them a big hug. In this way, they learned how to walk in a relaxed, low-pressure atmosphere while we were able to develop stronger bonds with our children.

Think about it this way: if children are used to relying on their parents for everything, how can they become independent in the future? Washing the dishes, doing laundry, cleaning their room and the bathrooms, and occasionally cooking simple dishes . . . these tasks may not seem significant, but they are basic living skills. Children should learn to do these before they leave for college. We do not want these seemingly minor chores to affect their college experience, adding unnecessary stress to their daily lives. After our children entered middle school, we gradually taught them these skills, one by one.

When our children first learned to wash dishes, it wasn't surprising to hear a cacophony in the kitchen, the occasional crash of a dropped dish or the tinkling of a broken cup. When this happened, afraid we would blame them, they would come to us nervously apologizing, "Mom, sorry, I broke the plate!"

"Don't worry, it's no problem! We're just paying for your dish-washing tuition," I always answered them jokingly.

Initially, although they would spend a long time at the sink, the dishes would not be completely clean, but this was all right. After a few more practices, they would learn to clean them thoroughly and effectively; I never worried about that.

Sometimes, when they were busy, studying or playing, they would forget to do their laundry and find, suddenly, that they had no clean clothes to change into. This caused them considerable embarrassment in front of their friends. When this happened, we did not do their laundry for them, letting their embarrassment act as a reminder not to forget again. Now, whenever they come home, they do their laundry and pack clean clothes the day before they return to Harvard, in preparation for school.

During their high school years, we understood that they were very busy, so we only asked that they clean their rooms once a week, usually on the weekend, in the afternoon. However, each time they cleaned, they had to do the job well and clean both their rooms and the bathrooms.

Later, I discovered that many other families did the same thing. During a meeting of Harvard parents, I met a mother with four children, and she told me her story. She and her husband both had full-time jobs, so they had to constantly juggle their professional lives with their family life. After a full day of work, the mother still had to deal with mounds of housework and other responsibilities at home, putting even more pressure on her. After delivering her fourth child, she felt that it was too much to handle by herself, so she and her husband decided to hire a housekeeper. With the extra help, she was relieved from considerable physical work, but her children's rooms became messier and messier. When she complained to them about the state of their rooms and asked them to clean them, her children protested, "But that's the housekeeper's job!"

She understood then that she had made a mistake. If she continued like this, she would be educating her children incorrectly. Without any hesitation, the mother dismissed the housekeeper, and their lives returned to normal again.

Teaching our children how to cook was a fun process for them. I bought a children's cookbook, which made cooking seem easy to learn, and started by appealing to their curiosity and interests. Our children, like most others, enjoyed playing with different patterns and shapes; so I bought different molds for cookies and cakes. Since they liked eating strawberries dipped in chocolate, I showed them how to make this dessert. Each time they learned a new dish, they were always filled with a sense of accomplishment. Whenever we had a party or a gathering of friends, they always liked to showcase their creations: pies, cakes, chocolate strawberries, and so on. After entering high school, they started learning more serious cooking: making their favorite dishes, instead of just sweets. This was highly practical because they would eventually need to know how to cook, and it made sense to teach them how to make dishes they would actually eat.

I remember once, when Fanny was home during a school break, John and I were returning home late; so I called Fanny and asked her to prepare dinner. When we arrived home, dinner was ready with four dishes laid out: three entrees and a soup. They all looked great and tasted delicious. We all joked with her, "Fanny, when you're finished with college, you can be a top chef!"

With more skills, life becomes more convenient. Despite their busy school schedules, when Fanny and Kathy turned seventeen, they started learning how to drive; and John was always happy to coach them. After they received their driver's licenses, they had more freedom and a wider range in which to move around. They were happy with this newfound sense of independence, and of course, we enjoyed the free time we gained when they no longer needed us to be their chauffeurs.

Good Habits for Life

Study and work habits, to a great extent, can be the determining factors of a person's speed and efficiency in many situations, which often play a crucial role in individual success. Without good living habits, complete independence is hard to achieve, which inevitably causes negative impacts on family life. Without good study habits, the competitive edge needed to perform effectively will be lost. Thus, we need to help our children develop good living and study habits when they are young because they will benefit them for their whole lives.

In real life, we often see that many students have difficulty focusing while studying. When they sit down at a desk, in a minute, they may leave to get a drink. The next minute, they may be checking their phone or looking around for a pencil or pen. Although they may sit there for an hour, the time spent studying may be less than thirty minutes in actuality, with very low efficiency. Sometimes, they will realize they have misplaced something and then spend a lot of time searching for it. When they turn on their computers, they may be distracted by the Internet for hours. All of this is related to ineffective study habits and poor time management.

Fanny and Kathy studying at the library

We used many methods to develop our children's study and living habits. Every time we used them, we worked to improve and perfect these strategies. A few of them are included below:

1. Set up a central study location. Our kitchen table was the central workplace for our children because the TV was not in sight and no other distractions were available. A fixed location for studying offers several advantages, such as an association with a strong studying atmosphere.
2. Set a common location for supplies. In our household, all the pens, pencils, scissors, glue, and other study essentials were stored inside two large transparent jars in the middle of the kitchen table. This method saved time as our children no longer had to run back and forth searching for office supplies.
3. Have a clean desk. Keep the table organized and clean of any objects not related to studying. When the children are confronted with an open, clean space, they will feel more comfortable and less stressed.
4. Buy a daily organizer for each child. At the beginning of each school year, we bought planners for our children so they could write down their daily duties, homework, schedules, and appointments. This allowed them to be better organized and learn how to best manage their time.
5. Organize their resources. Have a special storage closet/shelf devoted to storing their textbooks, notes, and other reference materials in an orderly fashion so that they can easily find what they need.
6. Partition time in an organized manner. There are times when the mind works more efficiently, as well as inefficient times for studying. Identify and use these times strategically. Typically, between 3:00 PM to dinner was considered "trash time." Normally, during this time, we did not ask them to do any work that required large mental strain. They spent much of this time on exercise, extracurricular activities, volunteer work, and leisure.

When they were in high school, especially eleventh and twelfth grade, which were full of standardized tests, it was also necessary for them to take reasonable breaks. During the holidays, we always let the children take a break first, then, if necessary, encouraged them to do some independent study to enrich their academics or prepare for the next semester. Toward the end of the holidays, we also arranged for them to have another good break, allowing them to recharge for the new semester.

7. Start projects early. Projects, whether done independently or for school, normally involve a long-term effort. First, students need to do background research to collect materials and devise a plan. When they actually start the project, they will most likely meet some unexpected problems. We always encouraged our children to start their projects early to avoid running into difficult-to-solve problems at the last minute.

8. Develop efficient study habits. We have always paid attention to the effectiveness of our children's studying. Normally, after they had been studying for an hour, we would suggest that they take a ten- to fifteen-minute break. While they were studying, we discouraged them from stopping often for refreshments and did not allow them to watch any TV or listen to music because we wanted them to focus and avoid distractions. If they had homework that required them to use the computer, we asked them to complete their other homework first. After all, once they opened an Internet browser, they would forget everything; and hours would fly by before they realized it.

9. Take effective notes. When our children began taking notes, we suggested that they leave some empty space on their paper. This space could be used to add comments or questions to help them understand the material, or to record additional details, such as from their textbook, a method that enriched their learning experience.

10. Stay focused. On school nights, other than a half hour or so after dinner, we discouraged them from watching TV. The night before a major test, we always asked them to take a break and get a good night's sleep, ensuring they would be in a productive mind-set the next day.

To establish organized habits, we prepared a large plastic box as a storage container for our children's toys. In addition, we designated the lowest level of the bookshelves as space for the children's books. After our children learned how to walk, we taught them how to put their toys away in the toy box and their books back on to the shelf after they were finished reading. This helped them develop the habit of returning things to their proper places.

Every week, I also spent time with the children to help them organize their toys and books. They were always curious and happy, enjoying this time together. When they did things correctly, I would give them hugs and kisses, and they would burst into giggles and smiles. I understood that if I cleaned up by myself, I could save time and energy, but this was a lesson that we needed to teach our children.

Once our children entered elementary school, I raised my expectations of them. When we were in Utah, both Fanny and Kathy were in elementary school and enjoyed playing with their best friend, another girl in the neighborhood. One day, their friend's mother asked me, "How long does it take your children to get ready in the morning?"

"Twenty minutes," I answered.

"That can't be possible," she replied, surprised. "My girl takes at least an hour!"

After a busy day at work, I still had to prepare dinner and take care of household chores; so at night, I was exhausted. In order to manage our time more efficiently, I taught our children how to make a to-do list in preparation for the next day.

Every evening, when Fanny and Kathy finished their homework, they would put their backpacks next to the door and move food to the dining table for breakfast. Before going to bed, they would lay out their clothes for the following day and set the alarm clock. These measures greatly reduced the time it took them to get ready in the morning.

Initially, there were some problems in carrying out these plans fully; sometimes, they would forget to set their alarms or would fail to put their shoes at the door. I also told them that if they were late for school, they would have to take responsibility for their tardiness. On one occasion, they were late, so I asked them to review their schedule and set their alarms earlier so they would have more time in the morning. Through these practices, they learned to adjust themselves to their environment. Eventually, they grew accustomed to this routine and developed the habit of being prepared in the mornings.

After moving to New York, Fanny entered fifth grade at Pearl River Middle School, and Kathy entered third grade at the elementary school. Because they had entered different environments, the two sisters had to adapt to many new things. In their daily lives, it seemed as though they were always forgetting something; Fanny left her flute on the bus home from school while Kathy often called me to deliver her clarinet since she had forgotten it at home.

In middle school, there were many more things that they needed to add to their schedule, including studying, social events, and extracurricular activities. In order to deal with this, we needed to teach our children how to organize their time more efficiently and prioritize their schedules. In addition, it was also important for them to learn how to multitask in order to complete everything that needed to be done.

Fanny has always chased perfection. I remember one time, she worked extra hard to finish a project, but could not find the assignment when she arrived at school, so the teacher gave her a "zero." Fanny felt terrible and cried because she had spent so much time and energy on the project; it had taken her almost a month of work. When she came back and told me what had happened, I checked her backpack and found a mess of loose papers swimming around. Her project must have gotten lost in the clutter, so I took her to Staples and bought her a set of binders in different colors. We asked her to label each binder with a school subject and separated each binder with dividers, making sections for notes, quizzes and tests, and homework. This allowed her to organize her schoolwork and thus be able to find her assignments and papers quickly. Since then, no similar incident has ever happened.

Time Management

After Fanny's and Kathy's successes, some parents posed us the same question: "They were so busy during high school, so how were they able to do so many extracurricular activities and volunteer work? Did they have any time to sleep?"

As students, of course, academics took priority; they were not full-time activists or humanitarians. To make sure our children could manage their studies and participate in other activities, time management was key. Since they entered middle school, we trained them on how to optimally manage their time.

Each summer, we asked them to submit a daily schedule to us, a proposal as to how they would spend their time. The following is Kathy's 2007 summer schedule:

9:00-9:30	Wake up, eat breakfast, prepare for the day
9:30-9:55	Study vocabulary (ten words/day)
10:10-11:10	Practice and Review for the SAT Subject Test in Chemistry
11:25-12:25	Practice and Review for the SAT Subject Test in Biology
12:25-1:30	Lunch and break
1:30-3:00	Critical Reading and Writing Review, Debate
3:00-6:30	Break: Exercise, volunteer service, cleaning
6:30-8:00	Dinner, washing dishes, watch/read the news, family time
8:00-9:00	Prepare for math competitions or Chemistry Olympiad
9:00-9:30	Break/practice music
9:30-10:00	Shower, prepare for bed, etc.
10:00-10:30	Free time
10:30	Bedtime

I remember that the first time we asked them to make a summer schedule, both Fanny and Kathy sat at the table for hours, not sure where to start because they had so many things to do. They found it difficult to fit everything into their schedule, so we gave them a few suggestions. We first asked them to set a target for themselves, because when setting a schedule, it is important to prioritize each item. Then, they made a list of what they needed to do every day, identifying the tasks that required the most concentration. These tasks were assigned to the times when they worked more efficiently, in order to maximize their results.

Since Fanny and Kathy both wanted to please us by showing their efforts, they initially filled in their schedule completely, without a minute's break. We explained to them, "When you do work, you need to pay attention to efficiency and be aware of when productivity peaks. Do not just work without playing or play all the time."

Even for something as basic as their summer schedules, they had to repeatedly modify them, coming to us for advice before going back to edit their schedules, over and over again. Naturally, everything has its own difficulties in the beginning. Once they learned the principles behind time management and drafted a few workable plans for the summer, they would know how to set up a reasonable schedule that would allow them to balance their studies and social activities. Even during high school's most stressful years, they were able to manage their time properly and actively participate in a variety of activities, so it seemed to others that they were doing more than anyone could in a given day.

After a good night's sleep, mornings were considered the prime time for studying. Another good time for studying was during the evenings. In the summer, between three o'clock and dinner, our children always had free time. Typically, they would play, exercise, participate in community service, or do something else they enjoyed. Year by year, their neighborhood friends became familiar with this schedule and would only ring the doorbell after three o'clock to ask our children to hang out.

When school started, they would walk to school in the morning, giving them exercise and waking them up completely by the time they arrived. After school, they always stayed late to participate in clubs and extracurricular activities, which we also encouraged. Upon returning home, they would take a short break and then start on their homework. From Monday to Friday, we never gave them extra work; after their schoolwork was finished, they could take a break. On the weekends, if necessary, we would give them supplementary materials to work on, which would usually only take one or two hours. The rest of the time was theirs, free for community service, personal projects, cleaning, relaxing, or whatever else they had in mind.

In high school, Fanny and Kathy were pretty busy and always wanted to sleep in on the weekends. As a compromise, we suggested that they try to get up at nine o'clock and start their homework after breakfast. Of course, they still needed to remember to clean their rooms and do their laundry too.

Our children's ratio of free time to work fell between the Chinese and American cultural averages. They played less than typical American children; but in their situation, in order to stand out, what else could they do?

Summer Camp

In the U.S., there are a wide variety of summer camps where children can spend their summer vacations. Many colleges host summer programs tailored specifically to high school students. These summer camps are good opportunities for students to further develop their social skills and become used to living away from home. Also, these programs often attract foreign students since the camps provide a look at the American education system, expose students to American culture, and allow them to refine their English skills.

Although it seems easy to just send children away to summer camp, the experience can negatively impact them if it is not approached in the right way. We took a gradual approach to sending our children away to summer camp. Before they entered middle school, we chose day camps close to home, with programs that ran from the morning to the afternoon, ensuring they would return home every day. After they entered middle school, they were more mature and independent, so we allowed our children to travel further, participating in programs where they would be away from home for days and eventually weeks at a time.

We knew a family that took a different approach, with negative results. Every summer, the parents spent most of their time trying to enhance their son's academic performance, making him do a lot of extra practice every day. Because of their singular focus on his academics, his parents did not pay enough attention to developing their son's social skills or independence. Although the boy performed outstandingly in the academic realm, he did not know how to act in social situations. When the boy entered high school, his parents realized this problem and attempted to correct it, but they did not take a gradual approach. Instead, they immediately sent their son off to a foreign country, to a summer camp in Europe. His parents were acting with good intentions; undoubtedly, they hoped that their son would gain international experience and learn to interact with other cultures. However, they never considered the possible implications for their son, since this would be the first time he had ever left them. While abroad, the boy lived with a host family, but due to his lack of social skills, he could not connect with them. Before the camp had finished, he was forced to return home early. In this situation, the summer program did not encourage the boy's development; instead, it damaged his self-confidence.

We believe that being creative and bold is a good thing, but the actual approach to a new experience must be strategic and well-thought-out in order for it to be successful.

The Johns Hopkins University Center for Talented Youth (CTY) program is well-known in the U.S. Every summer, it offers various programs in several locations for students of different ages. After passing a qualification exam, students can select the courses that interest them and specify the locations where they want to participate in the program. In 2002, Fanny qualified for the program and chose to enroll in a three-week CTY program at their Siena College site.

Our children at the JHU CTY Summer Camp

Siena College was a two-hour drive from our home and was located in beautiful suburbs. It was quiet, with a pretty small campus, and it offered a program that greatly interested Fanny. We had considered many factors before choosing this location because, at the time, Fanny was just twelve years old, and it was her first time leaving us. We hoped that she would have a wonderful summer camp experience.

After registration, we visited the dining hall, library, and dorms to take a look around. We were pleasantly surprised to see that the girls' dorms were so nice; only two students shared each spacious room, and every room had its own personal bathroom. I recalled my own college experience: we had eight students packed into one small room—what a comparison!

After Fanny had settled in, the resident assistants called meetings for their students. From that moment, their lives would be the same as college students'. They would eat in dining halls, study in libraries, and participate in social activities, largely without constant adult supervision. While the children attended their meetings, the summer program officials hosted a special meeting for their parents. There, they tried to reassure us with words such as "safety," "food," and "fun activities" and also suggested that parents try not to call their children. They would also encourage the children to not call their parents, though if they really wanted to call, there would be a time limit for doing so. The purpose of this was to help the students develop a sense of independence. To make sure that the parents were not too alarmed, the organizers told us, "In case of an emergency, we will contact you immediately."

After we returned home, I could not stop worrying. Every day seemed to stretch on for ages. Several times, I thought about calling Fanny, but John stopped me. During those three weeks when Fanny was separated from us, my mind was preoccupied with thinking about her, and I constantly worried. "What's she doing now? The weather is so hot . . . will she be okay? Does she like the school's food? Has she made any new friends? Does she enjoy the program?"

Finally, the camp ended, and we drove there to pick her up. On the way there, I formulated a plan to collect her dirty clothes and pack the rest of her belongings. When we arrived, I spotted Fanny immediately. She was outside her dorm, already awaiting our arrival. To my surprise, she had everything in order: the clothes had been washed, folded, and packed away. Her sheets and blankets were organized and ready to go. Everything else neatly fit into her suitcases. When she saw us, she smiled and said, "Let's go home."

The only negative aspect of this camp is that she developed a lot of acne, because there had been an abundance of fried foods during meals. Even now, whenever she comes home from college, I always try to cook as many vegetable dishes for her as I can.

When Kathy was in eighth grade in 2006, she also attended the CTY summer camp at Siena. There, she made many friends; even now, they are still in contact with each other. During her time there, she wrote an essay titled, "CTY: The Best Nerd Camp Ever," describing her experience. It gave us great insight into her true feelings for the camp:

CTY: The Best Nerd Camp Ever

While I anxiously waited for my parents to open the letter regarding my SAT scores, I wondered if I would be going to CTY this year. I knew my scores could be high enough, and so did my parents, which is why they started discussing it weeks before. All of my friends and I viewed CTY as a place to learn boring things over the summer, aka, a nerd camp, so I wasn't very enthusiastic, but I decided to brave it out; there was nothing else to do and all my friends would be away, so why not? It turns out I am glad I did come to CTY.

When I finally arrived, unpacked, and my family had left, I stood in my room, unsure of what to do. I noticed the two empty beds and wondered where my roommate, M, was. Gazing around the room, I took in the individual bathroom, wide space, and enough living space for at least three people. I also felt a little sorry for the guys at Ryan Hall; they have no air conditioner. As K put it, "I suppose the living conditions are pretty nice . . . for girls, but not for the guys in Ryan Hall. It smells like mold and mildew."

D, a resident assistant (RA) in Ryan Hall also agreed. "The [Ryan Hall dorms] are horrible. It is hot all the time, it stinks there, and there are bugs from the smell and heat. Overall, it's not a great place to live in."

After admiring the living space and pitying the guys for all of three seconds, I cautiously wandered into the hall and my RA, A, stepped out of her room. After introductions, into my room I went again. Soon afterward, we had a hall bonding, telling about ourselves with toilet paper. The more squares you had, the more you had to say. That night, we played an intense game of Sardines, a hide-and-seek game where the person who finds the hider hides with him/her. The hall was filled with excited squeals, shushing noises, and all sorts of cheerful cacophony. It was just a start to the fun and closeness A's hall would have.

Then, there was class, which everyone was surprised to say, was totally fun. To the shock of my hall friends, there were only two guys in Crafting the Essay, and we all became friends, and there were even some little crushes in between. All of us were glad to see that the teacher, A, and her teaching assistant (TA), H, were really nice, young, and possessed a sense of humor. No matter what the jokes we made, they understood them and instead of haranguing us, they laughed along. Any other adult would have turned the other way, instead of hiding laughter.

The best part about class is the inside jokes we made up, like "think outside the Hank." Hank was a cardboard box we decorated and named. Inside were the contents of our narrow-minded thinking. Also, there was the "lens" handshake, which is now captured in a class photo for our yearbook. From class, we not only learned how to write a better essay, but to free ourselves from the constraints of a monotonous society.

The extracurricular activities and free times are also great because it is all a part of "mandatory fun," which we all participate in. The best part is after meals, where everyone half lays in the grass (we can't lay down totally because CTY deems it "suggestive"), and it is the very scene of idyllic contentment. Students and adults alike group beneath shady trees, toss Frisbees, get hit by Frisbees, or play a game with a large green bouncy ball called Methuselah. This is the time where I socialize, make new friends, discover new games, and just enjoy life as it is. During dances, there is hardly a person left with nothing to do as guys and girls jump and swirl to energetic beats or awkwardly sway to slow music.

On Casino Night, my hall had the time of our lives. C cleared most people of their money by playing Russian roulette, and one hall was left nearly broke. It convinced our hall that we would be winning big by the end of the night, which we did, thanks to my roommate's "bank" and everyone else winning the fake money.

Fun in the Sun: we were totally soaked to our skins and took turns attempting to dunk the RAs who we had a grudge against, always cheering the person who succeeded in dunking the adults. My hallway ordered buckets of water dumped on various people, while L and A, both from my hall, attempted to hide from the assassins, which they ultimately failed, and therefore, were drenched.

Also, during one movie, the Labyrinth, *my hall adopted a song from there. It is impossible to go through a whole day without hearing A's hall singing, "You remind me of the babe . . . what babe? . . . the babe with the power . . ."*

Apart from all the fun-filled, and sometimes wet, activities, what everyone really enjoyed was being together in each other's company. All twelve of us from A's hall have bonded so quickly that we aren't ever separated, whether it be at meals, mandatory fun, or class.

Apart from the social and personal fun, there is also academic fun during all of the classes, which are taught by knowledgeable teachers. A, the teacher of Crafting the Essay, has a masters in both Fine Arts and Creative Writing, and she runs her own classroom at a university level. She describes CTY as a "good opportunity to get away for summer and learn new things about teaching." Even H, the TA who acts more as a friend, finds it a great experience, saying that "It gives me a passion and enthusiasm to do my own work. It is very inspiring."

During the last week, all the kids are scrambling to get their new friends' e-mail addresses, screen names, and phone numbers. A, our RA, had actually gone to CTY as a kid, and had "enjoyed it when I was younger."

The enjoyable experience obviously continued. "Yes, of course I am going to stay in touch with you guys!" says K, and her sentiment is echoed by many throughout the Siena College campus, because every single person is friendly toward the next. That said, tons of people plan on returning to the CTY program next year, including the kids, teachers, TAs, and RAs.

Maybe we are nerds, but as B. B. put it in his essay, "They are a species set apart," and that is indeed what we are. So many things have happened and brought the CTY community together quickly and tightly, and most of it is from actions, not words. Everyone here is friends with each other, all sharing the common thread of being athletic, social, friendly, and just like an average person. What sets us apart from all the others is that we have an above average intelligence, and we are smart enough to understand so much more than what was in front of us, especially if you took the Crafting the Essay course. And although I am not coming back, I definitely will remember all the experiences, funny, sad, happy, and mad for my whole entire life.

Participating in summer camp is not only a good training experience for children, but also an opportunity for parents to gauge the level of their child's independence. Through this, parents can obtain a better idea of how to plan and guide their children in the future. Both Fanny's and Kathy's successful experiences in summer camp let us know that they were well on the path toward independence; they were ready to seriously start facing the future.

Effective Study Habits

Self-management also plays a very important role in studying. Before Fanny entered middle school, we did not give her any extra homework. As a result, she was more naturally curious, free to explore her own interests. Every time we visited a bookstore, the children and I would separate to look for our own books. Interestingly enough, they would always choose materials revolving around the same theme of intellectual development: brain teasers, 2-D or 3-D puzzles, modeling kits, or coloring and activity books.

One day, when she was still in elementary school, Fanny stood in front of a bookshelf for a very long time, apparently drawn to a particular book there. Curiously, I walked over to her to find out what book had attracted her so much. To my surprise, it was a math and reading comprehension practice book! I reasoned, "Well, if she enjoys it, why not buy it?"

I didn't really expect her to do the problems in the book or to take the lessons seriously, but I bought it anyways to make her happy. To my surprise, after we returned home, she really did do all the practices! When she encountered a problem that she did not understand, she would approach us for an explanation. Since she was so young, we did not want to push her to do any extra work, but if she was driven by her own self-motivation, of course we would give her our full support.

In elementary school, Kathy seemed to spend a lot of her time playing, yet we did not press her to do the same things that Fanny did. Since she was still young, we found no reason to push her in a certain direction. Now, looking back, we can see we handled her correctly; in fourth grade, when she began to show signs of initiative, we provided her with the guidance to match her personality. She seized this and immediately drove herself forward with her high energy, erupting more powerfully than Fanny had.

Looking at this from another angle, if we had emphasized only academics and pressed our children to do practice exercises from a very early age, there would have been a higher chance that they would eventually rebel and refuse to study. If that had happened, this would be an entirely different story.

Both Fanny and Kathy actively sought to improve and challenge themselves to new heights. The only difference was that Kathy had unlocked her initiative a little later than Fanny. We basically did not involve ourselves in their schoolwork; if they had questions, they were always welcome to ask us. Otherwise, we let them handle it themselves.

Since we did not become involved, Fanny and Kathy had to develop their own way of managing their time. Every day, they kept track of their own schedule. When there was a lot of homework or more demands from extracurricular activities, they gave up their playtime and focused more on their work. We would often remind them that they needed to not only work hard, but also work smart.

To prepare for competitions, we would offer suggestions, such as how to locate materials and find references, which strategies to use, and how to manage their time; but we let them practice by themselves. If they were stuck on a problem, we encouraged them to first look for a solution by either checking reference books or searching the Internet. Only when their efforts failed and they really couldn't solve it would we offer our direct help. Although this practice was more time consuming, it ultimately helped them gain a deeper understanding of the concepts and solutions.

At school, teachers would often offer extra help sessions. Fanny and Kathy went to these selectively, choosing to attend only if they had questions. Otherwise, they would skip them. We respected their choice and agreed with their thinking: if they were capable of doing well by themselves, independent study would be more productive. By doing this, they were able to use their time more efficiently.

Although many parents sent their children to after-school programs for supplementary lessons, we did not follow suit. Most of these parents had misunderstood the situation. When they saw other students seeking extra help, they were afraid that if their children did not attend, they would be at a disadvantage and fall behind. They did not ask themselves whether their children truly needed extra help. Additionally, these types of after-school programs may be productive for some students, but not for others. We have had this kind of experience.

In 2002, because Fanny did very poorly on the Educational Record Bureau (ERB) test, we sent both Fanny and Kathy to a writing class offered by a learning enrichment company. We hoped our children could improve their writing skills through this kind of program, but the year after that, their ERB tests results still showed no signs of progress. A common problem with these programs is that the teachers teach material according to the level of the average student. Although some students may have a firm grasp of the material already, the teacher may repeat it over and over. At the same time, the teachers may completely leave out certain material that some students are unfamiliar with, but need to learn. Without student-specific lesson plans, these efforts cannot be completely effective.

Some of our friends also tried sending their children to this type of after-school program, but similarly found it to be ineffective. When they talked to us, we suggested that they help their children prepare for the SAT test by themselves, with our method. Our friends took our advice and in the end, their children performed very well. This strategy improved their children's independent studying capability, and this process of working closely with their children has also enhanced their relationship, building a stronger bond of mutual respect.

Students face a larger workload when they enter high school. Some students end up studying past midnight, but doing so adversely affects their productivity the next day. If this continues over a long period of time, it places considerable stress on students, both physically and mentally. To avoid this kind of problem, we set our children's bedtime to eleven o'clock every night, with only a few, rare exceptions. This naturally forced them to finish their homework in a timely manner, instead of dragging it out over hours. Just because students have their books open does not mean they are working; they may not be focused at all. By adding a time limit, we forced them to develop good study habits and increase their studying efficiency.

Mental Strength

Mental self-management is even more important. In life, it is inevitable that people will encounter obstacles and failures. Parents need to teach their children positive thinking, perseverance, and how to look for opportunities in negative situations, turning failures into a driving force. If children have the courage to challenge themselves, they can always stand up again. An essay that Kathy wrote in eighth grade reflects the spirit and importance of self-resilience:

I Believe . . .

Ever since entering the public school system, something or another has always restricted me, whether it is a person, a failure, or a catastrophic event. Every time I was knocked down, though, I found a blaze of determination that helped me up just as quickly. This is where I learned that every obstacle is actually an opportunity waiting to be discovered.

There was that time in kindergarten, where I had read all of the simple This is Sam *readers, which was way ahead of all the other kids. Instead of congratulating me, my teacher refused to let me go any further. She complained that I was reading too fast and wasn't giving my classmates time to catch up. My mother helped me ignore this and obtained first grade books. I persisted in my reading until I became pretty good, which carries on today. This set the stage for any future mishaps.*

Another time, I was doing the Presidential Fitness Test last year in seventh grade. Needless to say, my ventures toward physical fitness failed. All the guys and lots of the girls were teasing me about how I was so slow, unathletic, and just good at school, aka, your average nerd. Although my feelings were really hurt and I cried for a while, my resolve soon became stronger to show those people that I could be strong. The next year, in eighth grade, I did a lot better, and all my former tormenters were agape. They started calling me the "Wangster," which was fine with me.

These incidents, among others, taught me to rise above the ashes, and I have tried to do so every time I fail at anything. So many times I have heard of stories where the underdog wins, and in my quixotic world, I could be the emerging underdog. I know that whenever someone persists after getting hurt, they only become stronger. It is kind of like how whenever you tear a muscle, it hurts, but it actually means your muscles are mending and becoming tougher. Because of these things, I believe that you should always get up after you fall, no matter how hard it is, because only good will come out of it.

CHAPTER 11

Teenage Rebellion

Around a certain age, most teenagers will rebel, and parenting them during this time is a frustrating experience. I remember a few occasions when I was so exasperated by our teenager's attitudes and mind-sets that I told myself, "This is it! I'm never getting involved in their business again!"

However, as parents, we will always act out of the love in our hearts and assume proper responsibility over our children. After I calmed down, I would try to talk to them rationally. No matter how frustrated I became, I believed communication was still the key to getting along with and understanding our children.

A Harmonious Home

Ever since our children were young, we paid a lot of attention to them and stayed with them as much as possible. At home, we played games, did crafts and projects, and participated in sports together. We also took family vacations every year and went on frequent hiking and fishing trips. Often, we would stay in the library for half a day with our children, do volunteer work together, or indulge in other activities. We tried to treat our children as friends and supported them as they developed their team spirit, sense of patience, and social skills. All of this allowed us to build a very strong family bond.

A spring break vacation

Whenever our children encountered any difficulties, they felt comfortable coming to us. In that situation, would sit with them to listen to their troubles, answer their questions, and clarify their confusion. We were also very supportive of their activities and interests.

We basically devoted all of our spare time to our children; when we were together, we talked about anything and everything: the news, their concerns, interesting events in our daily lives, etc. We believed that a close relationship of mutual trust would facilitate communications between our two generations, making them enjoy sharing their experiences with us. In our attempts to understand them, we started when they were young and invested tremendous amounts of time in them. Honestly, when they entered their teenage rebellious years, they behaved relatively well, and we faced only occasional small frustrations.

Since Fanny always pursued perfection, we often encouraged her to try her best and never give up in the face of difficulties. For many years, she applied these ideas successfully, but this also created problems for her. No matter what she was participating in, she always tried to win. Whenever she lost a game among her friends, she would feel frustrated with herself. Sometimes, we would remind her, "Fanny, it's just a game. Why are you taking it so seriously?"

She would look at us, confused, and reply, "But you want me to be perfect!"

"Studying and working are different from daily life. When you play, the purpose is to have fun and make friends. Learn how to interact with people and enjoy their company. If you play games so seriously, how will anyone be happy?" we tried to explain to her, but we never knew if she truly understood what we were trying to teach her.

Mahjong is a game enjoyed by every member of our family, and it has played a very positive role in our family life. It has not only provided us with hours of entertainment and relaxation, but also been a tool for relieving tense situations. Sometimes, when our children were upset or we inevitably had some embarrassing moments, after playing mahjong for half an hour or so, everything would return to normal.

Understanding Is the Key

Raising a child is a long journey, full of sorrow and joy. As parents, we need to use our love, patience, and communication skills to build a relationship of mutual trust with our children. We should guide them in the right direction and help them establish a sense of morality in their lives, laying down a solid foundation for their futures.

In educating their children, the father and mother may have different strategies and methods, but they should always share the same goal: to guide their children toward success. Therefore, if a problem arises, parents should not blame each other. It is important that they first exchange ideas and try to reach a common ground, then work together to help their children overcome any difficulties. The more difficult a situation is, the more important it becomes for parents to support each other and maintain harmony and balance in the family.

Normally, John and I do not argue with each other; but regarding our children, we sometimes do become frustrated. However, we always come to the same conclusion quickly to reduce our children's confusion about what they should do. This allows our family to act as a unified team and continue moving forward.

Our children were raised in a family with a Chinese cultural background. However, they also grew up surrounded by American culture. These two cultures would inevitably contradict each other sometimes, so we believed it was especially important for us to communicate with our children to minimize the confusion from such inconsistencies. We learned to pay attention to the nature of our children's environment and treasured the moments when they showed signs of wanting to talk to us, quickly setting aside our work to listen to them. If we were really too busy to immediately put down our tasks, we would clearly let our children know that we were glad to listen and would talk to them as soon as possible. Communication is essential between parents and children. Without open communication, parents cannot know what their children are thinking and how to guide them properly.

John and I were both busy with full-time jobs, but we always tried to make time to sit down with our children and talk to them about their school day and listen to their stories. During these conversations, we paid close attention to any signs of emotional changes or shifts in their moods.

Dinnertime was always the most valuable time in our family. We always sat down together, relaxing and enjoying the meal while we listened to our children tell us about their day. Kathy always brought a lot of interesting stories to the table and made our dinnertime extremely enjoyable. Of course, we also raised other topics to learn about their interests and different points of view, which allowed us to see their progress as well. When we chatted with our children, we could talk about anything: current events, health, life, sports, politics, or religion—we never set any restrictions on our discussions.

Most aspects of our parenting ideology were developed in China. Sometimes, to our children, these practices seemed outdated and hearkened back to the distant past. They weren't entirely wrong, so we tried to be considerate of their ways of thinking and sought to integrate more modern methods into our teachings. Since we knew that cultural conflicts would inevitably arise, we tried to understand and absorb the basic essence of American culture. Whenever we had any differences of opinion with our children, we did not try to repress them or force them to follow our ways. Instead, we sat down to talk it over with them and determine the best course of action.

Every year, Pearl River High School, like many other American high schools, holds a senior prom. Kathy enjoyed social activities, so this type of event was important to her, and we supported her participation. Prom is a traditional part of American culture; and some parents spend hundreds or even thousands of dollars on their daughters for this event, purchasing expensive evening gowns, making appointments at hairdressers and nail salons months in advance, and buying fine jewelry, shoes, and other accessories. Kathy seemed impressed by this dazzling extravagance. Quite often, she would mention that this girl had purchased a very expensive dress, or that girl had made an appointment at a professional makeup studio.

I told her that while we respected this tradition and understood the teenage desire to leave an impression, we did not agree with the lavishness of it all. Spending more money did not guarantee a better job or a nicer appearance. To convince Kathy, I took her to the mall to try on some dresses, and we visited a makeup counter to let the professionals do her makeup. Neither of us was satisfied with this excursion. Finally, we just purchased false, manicured nails, I helped do her makeup by myself, and she wore my light purple evening gown. When she appeared at prom, everyone was surprised by how beautiful she looked.

In the second half of 2009, Kathy was in her senior year, and the high school organized a trip to Disney World for her class. It cost quite a lot, so in order to help us save money, Kathy told us that she did not want to go. However, in her eyes, we could see that she was suppressing her true feelings and actually really wanted to attend. We appreciated her consideration and were impressed by her ability to control her emotions. In the real world, not everything would always go her way, and in these cases, good self-control was necessary and would prove beneficial throughout her life. However, we suggested that Kathy go on the trip. Since she was still a child, playing was a normal part of her life. More importantly, this was a school-organized activity and offered a very good opportunity for her to bond with her peers and to further develop her independence. Although it would cost much more than an evening gown, it was also worth much more than a dress.

Through these experiences, we tried to pass a message on to our children: necessity is unrelated to cost. If there was something that would benefit them in a significant way, money should not be their greatest concern. If we could support their participation in such activities, we were always happy to do so.

Change Is Necessary

During their teenage years, children experience many changes. Their thoughts develop and expand as they start thinking and questioning their world more seriously. They also begin to make more decisions for themselves. It is important that parents do not repress them, but instead pay attention to these changes. Our strategy was to listen more and speak less, carefully observing them and remaining patient, trying to understand their thought processes. When they felt annoyed, we heard them out; we understood that it was also a difficult time for them. They were experiencing a lot of internal conflict and were also under much emotional stress. Only by listening to them and sympathizing with their situation was it possible for us to offer advice that they would accept. If parents simply repress their children at this age, it is very possible that they will sever the communication pathways with their children. This only causes more confusion, frustration, and stress; in some cases, their children will just explosively rebel.

During these years, when communicating with children, it is counterproductive to lecture them endlessly. Sometimes, when parents approach them, the teenagers may look at their parents warily and complain, "Another lecture again?" When they do stay and listen, they will do so impatiently. When this happened, we realized that we needed to reconsider our approach.

Normally, when our children returned home from school, we would greet them and chat about their day and their progress in school. We also exchanged information and ideas regarding their interests, problems, or anything else that came up. After dinner, we spent more time talking with them and establishing an atmosphere of open communication.

After they entered high school, we did the same thing as before, trying to guide them and pass along our ideas to them. However, we noticed that our children gradually tried to distance themselves from us—after dinner, they would either go to their rooms or sit in the opposite corner of the room. Once we saw this, we immediately adjusted our approach and no longer lectured them, instead briefly mentioning our opinions or offering only small suggestions. This allowed our communications with them to return to normal.

One day, when Fanny and Kathy were both in high school, we heard some surprising news: a junior at their school had become pregnant. In the U.S., it is not too unusual for teenagers to become pregnant, but at Pearl River High School, a school we had spent much time becoming familiar with, this phenomenon was rare. I took Fanny and Kathy aside to have a serious, private talk about being responsible for themselves and for others, what it meant to be pregnant during high school and how to prevent it.

"Can we be involved in relationships, then, and when?" When they asked me this question, I told them to evaluate their goals and consider the different phases of a person's life. Sometimes, it was more worthwhile to wait, instead of rushing in. We hoped that they would only become involved with another person when they were mature physically and mentally and had some experience with the real world. Only then could they really experience the feeling of love, instead of being guided by whim and then getting hurt because they were not prepared. With this line of reasoning, we believed that high school was not the best time for such things. Although some of their friends were in relationships, this did not mean that they should follow suit. They needed to keep a clear mind and do what was best for them.

During their teenage years, students seek recognition from their peers. Very often, one word from their friends holds more weight than a thousand from their parents. This can cause them to cave in to peer pressure and lean toward a gang mentality. Parents should pay close attention to their children, and if they see any signs that they are headed in this direction, they must firmly intervene. Once children have fallen on to that track, it is extremely difficult to pull them out. Sometimes, even when a child is successfully removed from that environment, they will have suffered too much damage to recover.

One day, John noticed that Kathy's arm had a "tattoo." Although it was drawn on by pen, John was immediately on full alert, and he had a serious talk with Kathy. When he noticed that I wasn't taking it as seriously, he explained to me, "Tattoos normally signal the start of gang activity, as the mark of their group. If we see something like this, we have no choice but to put an end to it. It cannot continue in that direction."

This was different than when toddlers played with removable tattoos. As a small child, it is just for fun, and there is no potential for gang activity. For a teenager, it may be different. We are not saying that every tattoo is a sign of gang membership, but we had to stop it before it began.

Kathy felt very bad and tried to argue, "Well, tattoos are also a form of art. NBA players, Hollywood stars . . . they all have tattoos and are not gang members!"

Her arguments were not illogical; of course, nothing is absolute. However, we just wanted to stop a possible trend. When she recognized this and realized that the markings could cause misunderstandings, Kathy washed off the "tattoo" with soap and water without further protest.

Another common teenage phenomenon is the pursuit of fashion and becoming "cool," evidenced by popular midriff-baring shirts designed to catch other people's attention. One day, after Kathy returned home, she discussed the "fashionable" girls in her school, who wore clothes emblazoned with logos of well-known brands in styles that showed as much skin as possible without breaking the school's dress code. When high school students went shopping, they seemed to choose the most expensive items as a way to show off. Of course, we didn't believe that every student did this, but Kathy was clearly contemplating it, so we felt that we needed to set things straight.

The main issue was how to understand fashion, because we believed that everyone had their own definition. We tried to teach our children to set their own values and think independently, instead of just blindly following others to chase fashion. Repeatedly, we told them that maintaining individuality and focusing on personal goals were much more important than conforming to others' standards. Although this meant that they couldn't be the most popular students at their school, we believed that by following their own path and creating their own concept of fashion, they could find true friends and new opportunities.

In tenth grade, Kathy wrote a short piece about the meaning of "cool":

> *Many people think that teenagers are those moody, maturing kids who follow trends and that are affected by the "cool" brands of everything in life. But what is the definition of "cool"? It seems that society takes it to mean what everyone else is eating, drinking, wearing, or doing, no matter how risqué or asinine it seems. Community thinks it is something that appeals to the majority; after all, we live in democratic America. To me, "cool"*

is something that fits the individual and accentuates the strong points in a person. It is something innovative, distinctive, and different. There is no method to my madness, but that is just my definition of the overly used word: cool, which is why I am not obsessed with Abercrombie and expensive stores of that ilk.

In high school, both Fanny and Kathy demonstrated this understanding of "cool" and fashion in their actions. They were very proactive in their community service and volunteer efforts, including tutoring their peers for free. Their actions influenced other students; soon, many others began to offer similar services as well. After school and on the weekends, the library was full of many students helping others. We believed this was also a type of fashion, which our children had introduced, and which Fanny and Kathy have still remained true to at Harvard.

Motherly Concerns

One day in March 2008, after a heavy snow the night before, it was especially cold, and the roads were covered with thick layers of ice. A car stopped in front of our yard, and a young man approached our front door. Kathy answered it.

"Happy birthday!" the boy said, handing her a gift. With quiet thanks, Kathy took the gift and snuck into her bedroom.

"Who was that?" I asked her.

"Oh, it's just this guy I know," she mumbled.

This incident reminded me of something that had happened a few months ago. I had taken Kathy to the tennis courts and had noticed a boy playing tennis with an older man. When he saw Kathy, he asked, "Are you Kathy?"

"Yes," Kathy answered his strange question without any surprise. I wondered who this boy was, and how he knew her, so I asked her as much.

"He's my friend's boyfriend. We know each other through Facebook," she told me, so I pushed my thoughts out of my mind. In the present circumstances, though, the situation seemed even stranger. These two were not in the same school or very familiar with each other. Why did he know her birthday and especially go out of his way to deliver a gift in the horrible weather? However, because I didn't know anything else, I chose to remain quiet.

The next Christmas, Kathy's friends wanted to get together for a party at her friend's house. This was pretty normal because her friends were a very close, active group. However, after overhearing some of her phone conversations, I felt that something was wrong. Since the party was being held at her friend's house, I didn't understand why Kathy was contacting everyone, including the boyfriend of her friend. Curious, I asked her about this.

"Oh, they broke up," she replied.

"Well, if that's the case, you shouldn't get involved with that boy," I advised her. I recalled the day that he sent her the gift and realized something else. "Is he pursuing you?"

"No, no . . . ," she said, avoiding my gaze.

I launched into a lecture. "First of all, at this age, you should be focusing on your studies. Second, it seems like you're not his type. If you were his type, why would he go after your friend first? Also, what would people think about you if you became involved with him now? Third, this boy has changed girlfriends so frequently. He seems like a playboy. I hope you're not his next target."

Kathy tried to deflect this, protesting, "Mom, we're just friends!"

But I was still worried, so I asked her to let me check her e-mail. When I did so, I was astonished by what I found, which raised huge danger signs in my mind. In one of the boy's e-mails, he mentioned teaching her and her friends how to pass through the firewalls of their school's computers. It reminded me of a recent news article about two University of California—Los Angeles, (UCLA) girls who had broken through the firewalls of their university's computers to change their grades. Once their actions were discovered, they were immediately expelled from UCLA. This discovery troubled me greatly, so I brought the matter to John. Kathy was different from Fanny in this regard: she dared to think and act more brashly, and once she found something she wanted to do, nothing could hold her back.

When discussing Kathy's boldness, I can't help including a small story. When Fanny and Kathy were in elementary school, Fanny often hid her storybooks under her desk so she could read them during class. Her teacher notified us of this situation, and at the dinner table, we brought this up and tried to persuade Fanny to stop. Then, Kathy jumped in, exclaiming, "Mom! I also read storybooks in class! But I'm different from Fanny—I don't hide it. I just put it on top of the desk and read it openly!" Her words made us laugh, but we were also worried about where this path would lead.

We realized that we needed to do something to stop further contact between Kathy and this boy. We asked Kathy to surrender her cell phone and the password to her e-mail. Unfortunately, this was not the end of the problems.

One day in the summer of 2008, Kathy received a phone call from one of her classmates, informing her that there would be band rehearsal that afternoon at school. This seemed strange because there had never been band rehearsals during summer vacation before, and it was not her teacher, but a classmate calling to tell her this. Since we did not know the specifics of the situation, we decided to let Kathy go; but after she left, the more I thought about the situation, the more suspicious I became. About half an hour later, I decided to go to the school to see what was really going on. When I arrived, I saw the band room was dark, with no lights on. Only Kathy and another girl were sitting there, talking to each other. I knocked on the window, calling out, "Kathy!"

Kathy was surprised and quickly passed a slip of paper to the girl as the girl ran away.

After that, we chastised Kathy severely and enacted strict rules for her to follow. Every day, she had to come home promptly after school. If there were any extracurricular activities, competitions, or other events that would require her to stay after school, she had to let us know their time and location in advance. If she continued to deceive us, she would lose our trust; and if she needed to participate in any activities, she would have to show us a teacher's note as proof. After we made these rules clear to her, this problem was finally solved.

A Loving Family

As parents, we love our children and are responsible for them. However, we cannot spoil them and always give them what they want. We must encourage the development of good habits, understanding of others, and appreciation for the efforts of the people around them.

They must realize that they are only members, not the center, of the family. Additionally, they have their own responsibilities and duties to the family. It is important to let our children participate in family discussions, especially of their futures; the more involved they become, the more they will understand our practices and realize the importance of family unity. We believe that if children love and respect their family, they will be less vulnerable to negative influences.

Most American families pay their children an allowance in exchange for them doing housework. Their children are used to making money this way and feel that they have the right to negotiate payments with their parents. If both parties cannot come to an agreement, the children can simply refuse to help and find a job outside the house. The allowance system has some advantages: children learn the value of work and how to fight for their rights, protecting themselves through negotiation and compromise. However, there are disadvantages as well: this practice enforces a selfish mentality and equates family responsibilities with business transactions, diminishing the family's sense of warmth and kinship.

Some Chinese-American families take another approach and give their children money without asking them to do anything. Children raised this way often do not understand what it means to earn money and thus cannot understand the true worth of each dollar that they spend.

We approached this matter with a different mentality. Whenever our children helped around the house, sometimes we paid them, and sometimes we did not. If we did pay them, it was a symbolic gesture; relatively speaking, they did not receive much. However, our children did not complain about this because they knew that they were just doing their fair share of the work. The true value of a family lies in the ability of each person to help other members unconditionally. In our family, whenever our children run into difficulties, they first consult each other. If they cannot solve the problem amongst themselves, they then approach us. We have always encouraged this spirit of teamwork in our family, hoping this helpful, loving attitude toward each other would stay with them throughout their lives.

We have another tradition in our family: whenever someone returns from a trip, they always come back with gifts for everyone else. The gift is typically not very large or showy, but is a sign of the children's thoughtfulness. Each time Fanny and Kathy returned home from a summer camp or college, they would always bring Bill a small gift. Bill always counts down the days to their return, hoping to see his sisters as early as possible.

I remember once, when Bill came back from his summer camp, the first thing he did was carefully take out gifts, one for each of us. Feeling embarrassed, he admitted, "I only bought three mugs because I ran out of money for the fourth . . . I only have a lollipop. Can I use this as a gift?"

"Of course! That's no problem! Thank you for thinking of us," I answered. We knew gift shops were expensive, and I had only given him enough money to buy food, so I asked him where the money to buy the gifts had come from.

"Oh, I saved some money," he told me. When I checked his receipts, I saw that each day, he had only bought the cheapest food in order to save money for his gifts to us. On the way home from camp, he didn't even have enough money to buy his own lunch! Fortunately, his friend's father generously paid for his meal.

There is one memory about our children that we will never forget. In the winter of 1997, Fanny was seven, Kathy was five, and Bill was four. We took a family vacation to Las Vegas, and the three children had a wonderful time playing in an indoor theme park. After a Ferris wheel ride, Bill was trembling as he tried to step out of the passenger car. Fanny and Kathy, without hesitation, ran to him; and each of them took one of his small shaking hands and carefully helped him out. The expression of love and genuine innocence of the moment painted a very vivid, tender picture. Many parents watching this were moved and applauded their actions.

Our children's happy childhood

For many years, our family has worked together as a team. Whenever one member needed help, our whole family immediately mobilized. We used everyone's strengths and specialties to focus all of our efforts on to that one person in his or her pursuit of success. Sometimes, to benefit the team, individuals would voluntarily make sacrifices without regrets or hesitation.

In 2007, Fanny did well in the Rockland County Math League competition, becoming the top scorer in the region. Since Kathy was second place in their school, the two of them were supposed to represent Rockland County in the state competition. Each school could only send two students to participate, but the school's Math League advisor wanted Fanny's best friend to participate instead of Kathy. Relatively speaking, her friend was very strong in math; she and Fanny were the only two people that had advanced to the AIME competition at their school for at least six years. This math teacher, with two apparent math geniuses on his team, thought this would be the prime opportunity to showcase their talent. Since Fanny was the captain of the Math League team, he talked to her about this issue. It put Fanny in a difficult position: she had to choose between her best friend and her sister; all three of them could not compete. Finally, she decided to withdraw from the competition, ensuring that Kathy would have the chance to participate. To our surprise, in the end, Fanny's friend did not show up either! Only Kathy arrived that day to the competition, and so, in a twist of fate, the two math geniuses disappeared from the team. The two friends' consideration of each other's feelings resulted in this amusing incident. From another angle, we can see that the math teacher had good intentions and simply wanted to take advantage of an opportunity to increase the school's visibility. However, due to a simple lack of communication, he received the complete opposite of what he wanted! Later, we discussed this situation with our children, hoping they would realize the importance of communication.

When Kathy was in ninth grade, the school newspaper's club advisor sent her an invitation to join the club, so she and Fanny both began attending newspaper club meetings. However, since Fanny had many differences of opinion with the advisor that could not be resolved, Fanny left the club the following year. After this happened, Kathy approached John to discuss what to do. He analyzed the situation for her: if she stayed, she would have more opportunities to become the president of the club. On the other hand, she and Fanny had always acted as a team. If something had caused her teammate to leave, she had a reason to leave as well, in order to preserve their bond. However, he made it very clear that it did not matter whether she stayed or left; we would support her either way. In the end, Kathy chose to side with Fanny and left the club. She put her team above her own personal gain, rising above her own self-interest.

In 2008, both Fanny and Kathy took the U.S. National Chemistry Olympiad local exam. Fanny had become a national finalist the year before, and she was aware that each school could only have one qualifying student advance to the national exam. To ensure she that would not end up directly competing with her sister, Fanny purposely answered fewer questions correctly than was necessary to qualify to move on to the next level.

We have many more examples like these, where Fanny and Kathy's team spirit has played a very important role in their lives. Time and time again, it has helped them overcome many difficulties that could not be solved with the efforts of just one person. It is one of the most important aspects of our family values and a key factor in their successes.

CHAPTER 12

Social Development and Community Service

When one mentions community, many people think about the town or city they live in. While not wrong, I believe that, as humans, we are all part of an interconnected global community that grows closer every day with advances in technology. Time and space are no longer barriers to communication; the creation of the Internet, e-mail, and instant messaging makes it possible to talk to someone on the other side of the world almost instantly. This is the age of information, and whenever something happens in any part of the world, we can learn about it almost as soon as it occurs. Now, with all of these changes, we must learn to bear the social responsibility for a larger world, a world that we are all a part of. We must expect our children to love not only our family, but also our community. Love has no borders or nationality. Even if they are not rich, people can still be happy if they have a good heart, a grateful heart, a heart full of love.

If a child is self-centered, this selfishness will be reflected in his or her thinking, daily life, work, and interactions with other people. We have read some children's essays, but many of them were written only from the perspective of what they personally gained, without any consideration for how their experience affected their community. With such a narrow mind and nearsighted vision, even with outstanding materials, they could not create an impressive story. We believe that by fostering children's love and raising their awareness of their social responsibilities and obligations, we will make them into stronger people, improving their chances of becoming successful.

Sometimes, Asian immigrants struggle to become involved in mainstream America because of the culture difference. However, in their parenting, they only pay attention to academic development, disregarding their children's social skills and activities that could introduce them to mainstream American culture. They simply allow their children follow their footsteps and let history repeat itself. Why?

Breaking the Social Deadlock

Moving to New York from Utah was a turning point in our lives. Both the social and learning environments had changed, and we had to pay more attention to our children's feelings.

Many days after school, they were quiet. They rarely laughed and always seemed worried and unhappy. Sometimes, they seemed to have something to say to us, but the words could never leave their mouths. Finally, Kathy told us what was on both their minds. "Here, we have no friends! Everyone else has their own circle of friends already, and we can't join them. In class, nobody will work on group projects with us. During recess, we play by ourselves."

Or in Fanny's case, she simply buried herself in novels. How could we break this deadlock? Our whole family sat down together to talk it over and make a plan.

"Children love parties, so let's have a party!" I suggested.

"Let's try it!" Of course, the children were glad to have any reason to have a party.

"How can we ensure that the kids will come?" I asked next. Each of them was happy to make a suggestion.

"Candy, candy, we can't run out of candy," Bill responded first.

"I think they would like to have something exciting and fun. What about fireworks?" Fanny proposed.

"We can set up some games with prizes. Kids like prizes," Kathy added. The children were all getting excited for the party. Finally, we put the finishing touches on our plan: a piñata filled with candies and chocolates, bingo games, the volcano experiment, and small fireworks.

To attract our guests, we listed all of these activities on the invitations. As a result, all of the children who had been invited showed up to the party, and everyone had a great time. This was a successful start for our children. Whenever we had a party from then on, our house would always be packed.

A Vivid Lesson

The success of the first party laid the foundation to breaking the social barrier, but we realized that in order to successfully socialize with others, they also had to learn to rely on their own efforts. Thus, we encouraged them to look for opportunities to become involved in social activities. We recommended that they observe the environment closely and establish goals for themselves. Without goals, they could lose their way and their motivation.

Since 99 percent of the town was Caucasian, it was unlikely that the other children would approach our children first. Knowing this, we encouraged our children to take the initiative and approach the others. On many occasions, we discussed key points that could help them make more friends, such as:

- discuss topics that others may be interested in.
- be a listener. Let others talk first and wait for your chance to speak. Do not interrupt others.
- learn more about the topics that others were chatting about.
- help others if you can. Show that you care about others.
- do not criticize others or brag about yourself.

Kathy became good friends with a Spanish girl in her class. Maybe the same feeling of being a minority in the white-dominated environment brought them together. With the help of this girl, Kathy gradually expanded her social circle.

One time, in fourth grade, her friend's father took them to a carnival. They had a great time, and one particular incident demonstrated Kathy's insightful vision and incredible self-restraint. When they played a horse racing game, Kathy won a large prize, but her friend only won a small toy. Her friend looked at her toy in admiration. Upon seeing this, Kathy gave her toy to her friend. Kathy's action made her friend feel a little embarrassed. Her friend said, "You must like it, since you won it."

Kathy replied, "I don't care about this toy. Your friendship is much more valuable to me."

When she came home, she acted a little lost; after all, she was only a nine-year-old child. A stuffed animal toy was a big deal for her, no matter what she had said. I noticed that she was acting unusual, so I asked her what was going on. After I heard her story, I praised her, "You did great! That is a good way to make friends, and you have a friendly heart! Caring for your friend is the best way to make more friends."

John was also happy to see Kathy's generosity and the strong self-restraint capabilities. He said, "What Kathy did is extremely valuable. We should actively guide her in the future. Kathy will become a completely new person very soon."

As expected, Kathy soon made more friends. In this regard, Kathy taught us a vivid lesson.

Volunteering

Parents' behavior and ideologies can have a very strong impact on their children. When parents raise children, their moral values and obligations guide their children's behavior on a daily basis. If we cannot set a good example ourselves, our teachings will be unconvincing. Whenever the Parent-Teacher Association (PTA) had activities, I was always involved. When our children's schools celebrated Thanksgiving, we donated turkeys. If they and their friends needed a ride, we were always willing to lend a hand, and sometimes we drove several children a day. We also volunteered with our children to raise funds for nonprofit and charitable organizations.

The United States is a great country, but there are still people living below the poverty line. During the holiday season, a number of charitable organizations collect money and food for the poor. We would often encourage our children to make a contribution. When we went shopping in the supermarket, we would also buy extra canned foods to donate. We told our children, "One dollar is not a big deal, but for those who need it, it can be very important."

After we explained this to them, they were willing to make donations. Sometimes they even saved some of their lunch money so they could give it to charity.

One day, one of them asked, "If you do not have a lot of money, can you still help others?"

"Yes, you can!" I replied enthusiastically. We encouraged them to volunteer when they had the time, to help others and assume their social responsibilities and obligations. I often took our children to People-to-People, a popular nonprofit organization, to help fold clothes, organize canned foods, and communicate with donors. While making contributions to their community, they learned how to face reality, take care of others, and improve their interactions with other people. Their experiences also taught them that they should work hard so they could support themselves in the future.

Free Tutoring

When Fanny was thirteen years old and entering eighth grade, we considered sending her to do volunteer work by herself. She actively contacted several nonprofit organizations such as hospitals, the Red Cross, and People-to-People to explore her options. Unfortunately, these organizations all required volunteers to be at least fifteen years old to work there.

I asked, "Beside these nonprofit organizations, what else you can do that doesn't have age limits?"

We encouraged her to think creatively, and Kathy and Bill also offered suggestions. Everyone tried to find a solution, but without any success.

During an outing with our friends, we noticed some students tutoring others and were inspired. I asked Fanny, "How about doing free tutoring?"

"How can I attract students?" she replied hesitantly. To encourage her, we listed numerous reasons why she would be a good tutor. First, she was the math champion at her school and a top scorer in New York State math competition. Second, she had a nice personality and was very responsible. Third, many students had difficulties in learning, and she could think of creative ways to solve problems. Eventually, we convinced her to give it a try.

The next problem was how to make people aware of this new service. We worked together to design an advertisement and find various channels where we could send out the message.

"I can post the ads in the school hallways," Fanny offered.

Kathy interjected, "We can also post the ads on the bulletin boards in the community, supermarkets, and libraries so students in other schools can see them."

In addition, Fanny also talked to her school counselor, Mr. U, about spreading the news and keeping her in mind when students came to him to ask for help finding a tutor. It was a long shot, but later Mr. U did recommend several students to Fanny.

While advertising Fanny's free tutoring, we learned a small trick. One method of advertising is to create a poster with contact information in tear-off strips at the bottom. Before posting the advertisement, tearing off a few strips will help others overcome their initial psychological barriers and believe that other people are using the service as well, encouraging them to give it a try.

One student after another signed up and soon, Fanny's business was booming. Fanny's efforts inspired her classmates, and some of them also joined Fanny to do tutoring.

Although the free tutoring took a lot of time, Fanny also learned many things from it, such as how to organize her time, how to understand and explain problems from different perspectives, and how to use different strategies for students at different levels.

Additionally, the free tutoring also provided her with the opportunity to understand different people. For example, in eleventh grade, Fanny's class schedule was heavily loaded with Advanced Placement (AP) courses and college courses. She also needed to prepare for the PSAT and SAT standardized exams. However, when a girl approached Fanny asking for help in physics, Fanny devoted herself to helping the girl. The girl was very successful and received a perfect score on the midterm exam. Toward the end of the school year, Fanny needed to submit her community service sheet, so she asked the girl to sign the sheet as evidence that she had received services from Fanny. Unexpectedly, the girl delayed and delayed with no acceptable excuse. Finally, Fanny had to submit her community service sheet without this part.

This experience served as an important life lesson and was something we could not teach her at home.

Using this story as an example, we asked our children to consider why the girl may have acted in that way. By looking at the issue from another's perspective, they understood how they should behave and treat others. However, we were careful to explain that we could not give up our beliefs because of others' misconduct and that they should have an appreciative heart. Helping others is a beautiful thing to do, and if we hold on to this belief, we will be happier.

Study Group

Kathy's open and humorous personality, coupled with Fanny's experience, meant they both took to tutoring like ducks to water. Kathy's school counselor, Mr. U, told me a few times, "Your daughter Kathy is my best tutor!"

Many students asked their counselors to assign Kathy to help them. Before any major exam, our basement was always filled like a classroom. The students raised questions and explained solutions on the whiteboard that hung on the wall, tutoring and helping each other find the best way to solve their problems. Sometimes they were quiet, working on practice exams, and sometimes our basement was full of voices raised in lively discussion. These scenes were very warm and moving. Their friends all loved Chinese dumplings that I made, so whenever they were hungry, I would bring down fried Chinese dumplings and Italian pasta to support their efforts.

Community Service

When they each turned fifteen, Fanny and Kathy expanded their volunteer service efforts from just their school to the local community.

Every summer, they volunteered to work with young children at the local library, reading stories to them, encouraging them to read, doing projects with them, and organizing other activities. The most difficult part of this experience was learning how to deal with arguments between children and emergency situations such as a child crying for his or her mother. These skills are very beneficial to learn for the future and also played an important role in helping Kathy become a successful babysitter later.

Volunteering in the community also helped them understand their environment better and inspired them to think more creatively.

Through their interactions with their classmates and their volunteer experiences with several nonprofit and charitable organizations, they realized that many students were willing to make contributions to our society but did not know where to find the opportunities. On the other hand, many organizations needed volunteers but could not find them. To solve this problem, Fanny and Kathy formed a group of volunteers that helped out at whichever organization was short-staffed at the moment. With more helping hands, they could do larger and more significant projects.

They worked actively with the Association for Visually Impaired (AVI), a nonprofit organization that assisted visually impaired individuals. One such individual was an elderly lady, Mrs. J, who needed long-term assistance with her daily life. Fanny and Kathy accepted the task, dividing their group of volunteers in several smaller teams. Each week, at least two volunteers would visit Mrs. J and help her shop for groceries, arrange her pantry, and perform any other necessary tasks. Each visit from these children brought happiness to her life, and every Christmas, the volunteers received a Christmas card from Mrs. J with the message: "Thank you for making my life so easy and filling it with so much joy."

During the holiday season, other children in the group had to go on holiday vacations with their family and left the service with vacancies. Many times Fanny and Kathy asked us to rearrange or give up our family vacation plans so that they could fill up the vacancy. The girls said, "The holiday season is supposed to be a happy time, and if we left, she would feel even lonelier."

Their dedication and passion earned the trust of Mrs. J. She gradually let Fanny and Kathy help her review her credit card bills, bank statements, and other important personal documents. They became trusted friends. Each time when they met, they talked about their family, friends, and stories about their lives. After Fanny went to Harvard, she passed the torch on to Kathy. Kathy and the other volunteers continued to provide their services until Mrs. J's family made new arrangements for her.

Each year, Fanny, Kathy, Bill, and the other volunteers helped the AVI with fund-raising. In the days before a major holiday, they would set up a table at a local Barnes and Noble bookstore to wrap books and gifts and collect donations. During this activity, they witnessed a variety of human nature in the real world. Some people were very gentle and generous and donated without even asking for their service. Others were very stingy and asked the students to wrap their gifts but did not even donate a penny.

To be honest, we rarely noticed Asian faces in these kinds of volunteering activities. This lack of contact may be why mainstream America has a biased view of Asian-Americans. We kept encouraging our children to use their actions to speak for them and to remedy the stereotypical image that people generally have of the Chinese. We firmly believe that we are Americans, so we should act the same way as typical Americans by taking care of others as well as ourselves.

Rockland County is a place with beautiful mountains, clear lakes, and lush forests. However, some people do not appreciate the natural environment and leave garbage in the streams, lakes, and forests. On hiking trails or in campsites, we felt very bad seeing garbage everywhere, so we often quietly picked up the garbage left by people and threw it away. We were not doing it alone, though. Soon, our children found members of a nonprofit organization, Keep Rockland Beautiful (KRB), that were doing the same. Our children and their volunteer group joined KRB to help clean up our environment.

The volunteer work offered our children more opportunities to get in touch with their local community, to see real life, and to emphasize their responsibilities to our society. Each time they saw the work they had done, they felt a sense of accomplishment. Through our children's experiences, we felt that even though participating in community service decreased the time they devoted to their academic performance, it helped them relax and focus better on their studies.

Regardless of where we came from originally, we are now Americans. This land is our land, and this society is our society. It is our obligation to make our society better.

A Trip to China

Fanny and Kathy had never been to China before, so to them, China was a mysterious place. When they heard that we were going to take them to visit China, they became very excited and made plans to make the trip even more meaningful.

In June 2008, John took Fanny and Kathy to China to visit our relatives. While in China, they initiated and organized a cultural exchange project. For the project, they met with high school students to exchange information about the cultures of the two different countries and discuss questions they were all interested in. During their time there, they built close friendships with the students they met in China.

Fanny and Kathy in China

After coming back to the United States, they raised money to buy books to donate to the Chinese school to help them build an English library. Even now, they continue to collaborate and exchange information with the students. This memorable experience is reflected in an essay written by Kathy:

> *As a typical American teenager, I learned about and believed in the tenets of freedom, democracy, and the American Dream. I felt that everyone should discover them as well. So as the summer and my trip to China drew closer, I began formulating a plan to introduce these values to the students of China.*
>
> *Months before my expedition, I had already begun preparations: a proposal, a resume, lesson plans, and more. It seemed as if nothing could go wrong.*
>
> *After arriving in China, I immediately began contacting local schools, presenting them with my proposal. To my surprise, every school rejected my ideas. I was shocked—how could this be happening? I had already created and run several successful activities back home—the Volunteer Service Group, the Tai*

Chi Club, the school Chemistry Olympiad team—so it couldn't be a lack of experience.

Desperately trying to understand how I failed, I collected suggestions from relatives. Piecing together all the information I had gathered, I realized my mistake. The cultural differences between our two countries were huge, yet somehow, I had forgotten to factor this into my plans. In addition, I was in a rural area, which remained steadfast to its conservative beliefs. Maybe they were worried about my changing the status quo, encouraging revolution to overthrow the government, or something even more nefarious. To overcome these obstacles, I compiled a list of issues I needed to consider. With the help of my relatives, I carefully developed a new proposal to address these concerns. Even so, the principals' suspicions were still clearly evident, and the next schools I contacted all refused me . . . except one. That school granted me only one session, so I was more determined than ever to make it a success. Filled with excitement, I threw myself into my work once again, devising a more effective plan for the meeting. And the night of the meeting came . . .

A classroom full of students, staring expectantly up at me. Using the strategies I had prepared, I quickly got the students involved. They were truly interested, making insightful remarks and asking intelligent questions, such as:

"Can people actually criticize the government?"

"Do students really have the freedom to choose their classes?"

"How do you apply for American colleges?"

All too soon, the meeting drew to a close. Disappointed, the students and I tried to stay longer, entreating the teachers for a couple more minutes, and a couple more after that. When we finally had to leave, we parted reluctantly. I returned home, feeling regretful that I would not be able to meet the students again . . . or so it seemed.

A couple days later, the school invited me back for additional meetings. Thrilled, I eagerly jumped at their invitation and scheduled more sessions, as successful as the ones before. During the last meeting, emotions ran high. We all wanted to do something more, a collaborative effort to commemorate our time together and help the rural school, which suffered from a lack of resources. Finally, we decided to build an English library.

Returning to America, I immediately began working on this project. I held several fund-raising efforts to purchase books, shipping them back to the students in China. This fulfilling, gratifying experience clearly proved that cultural differences and political disparities do not have to be barriers to cooperation among willing minds.

Through this process, I realized that despite China's political repression, the students harbored the same inherent beliefs and values as I did. I speculated that this might hold true in other countries as well; everyone may believe in basic American ideals, but politics, religion, and other factors stymie their open expression. One small opportunity could spark a deluge of support for freedom. Perhaps the key lies in the unanswered question: how do we unlock these restrictions to let our truest thoughts flow free?

Many things cannot be measured by money. When people need help, it is not difficult to reach out to them with a warm hand. If we can dedicate ourselves to loving our community and shouldering our responsibilities and obligations, we can make the world a much better place!

CHAPTER 13

High School: Ready, Set, Go!

Selecting Courses

Selecting high school courses is a very important and strategic process with several factors to consider. Most high school student counselors are experienced in helping students decide which classes they should take, so parents should consult their children's counselors when selecting courses to ensure that their children are off to a good start every academic year. Pearl River High School, for example, distributes their *Program of Studies* booklet annually, which contains information that can help parents develop a long-term academic plan with their children. Typically, high schools will also provide a list of required courses with a suggested schedule of which classes to take each year of school. However, it is important to remember that parents know their children the best and that student counselors must help hundreds of students each year. It is always necessary for parents to look into the course catalog to find ways to help their children stand out.

Since Fanny was our first child, dealing with scheduling was uncharted territory, and we were unsure how to proceed. Initially, we simply chose to follow the school's suggestions. At the time, we had no idea how much we could influence her schedule! However, after learning from Fanny's experiences, we had a better grasp of what was going on when it was Kathy's turn to enter high school. With this, we helped Kathy develop a better plan to fully engage her potential while giving her a competitive advantage.

From our experiences, we knew our children's limitations. As long as they could handle it, we encouraged them to take the most rigorous courses possible in order to challenge themselves and allow themselves to grow.

An Assortment of Math Competitions

Fanny entered Pearl River High School as an eighth grader in September 2003. In the weeks leading up to this milestone, we worked together with her to try and find out as much information as possible about the U.S. high school system and seek out opportunities she could excel at. As a strong math student, she was immediately drawn toward the large number of math competitions at the high school level.

There is a surprising abundance of math competitions in the U.S. geared toward high school students, and Pearl River High School participated in a number of them: the American Mathematics Contest 10 (AMC 10), American Mathematics Contest 12 (AMC 12), New York State Math League, the American Scholastic Mathematics Association (ASMA) Annual Mathematics Contest, and the American Regional Mathematics League (ARML).

Here are a few interesting facts about these math competitions:

- The American Mathematics Contest (AMC) is organized by American Mathematics Association and consists of three levels of tests: the AMC 8, AMC 10, and AMC 12, each consisting of twenty-five multiple-choice questions taken in seventy-five minutes.
  - The AMC 8 is designed for students in eighth grade and below, the AMC 10 for students in tenth grade or below, and the AMC 12 for twelfth grade students or students under the age of nineteen and a half.
  - For the AMC 10, students who score higher than 120 points, or are among the top 2.5 percent of all participants, will advance to the American Invitational Mathematics Exam (AIME).
  - For the AMC 12, students who score higher than 100 points, or are among the top 5 percent of all participants, will advance to the AIME.

- o The AIME is a three-hour exam consisting of fifteen very challenging free-response questions. Each year, about two thousand students qualify for the AIME, and most of them can only solve two or three questions on average. The top scorers, based on a combination of both their AMC and AIME scores, are selected to participate in the U.S. Mathematical Olympiad (USAMO). In the last few years, Fanny and her best friend have been the only students to advance to the AIME at Pearl River High School.
- The New York State Math League is a national math competition administered by the Math League on a statewide level. Their results are announced and archived on their Web site: www. mathleague.com.
- The American Scholastic Mathematics Association (ASMA) offers another math contest with two divisions: a junior division for grades seven to nine and a high school division for grades nine to twelve. It is not as popular as the AMC or Math League, but Pearl River High School eighth and ninth grade students can participate in junior division of this contest.
- The Rockland County Math League, a subdivision of the American Regional Math League (ARML), is an interscholastic math competition. This monthly competition is hosted by a different local school each month from October to March. The highest-scoring students are invited to represent the Rockland County team at the annual New York State meet.

Motivated to continue excelling in math and science, Fanny joined the Math League Team at Pearl River High School, instantly accessing all of these opportunities. She thoroughly enjoyed these competitions and consistently performed well in all of them.

An Array of Club Activities

Pearl River High School is home to more than thirty activities: the Yearbook Club, Math League Team, Model United Nations (Model UN), Science Olympiad Team, Marine Science Club, Mock Trial Team, Chess Club, and a variety of sports teams, to name a few.

The sports teams, Model UN, and Marine Science Club have long been among the most popular student activities because they give members the opportunity to travel outside of school. For example, the Marine Science Club takes a few field trips each year to aquariums and beaches, where members can go whale watching, sleep over in Cape Cod, and explore marine life. It even owns tanks of marine animals, which students can observe and touch, creating a very interesting, interactive atmosphere.

On the other side of the spectrum, clubs like the Chess Club required more hard work and patience. The Chess Club, Math League, and Science Olympiad teams often intimidated students because of the level of effort and devotion the clubs seemed to demand.

Fanny after a parade with the Marching Band

Faced with so many enticing options, Fanny was both excited and confused, so she joined as many clubs as she could, including the Chess Club, Math League Team, Science Olympiad Team, Model UN, Yearbook Club, Ping-Pong Club, and the Marching Band. Her choices covered a wide range of interests; some were entertaining while others were intellectual in nature, but all of them enriched her life at school. Every afternoon, she would spend at least one or two hours after school participating in club activities, sometimes returning home very late because of club-related responsibilities. Occasionally, she had to travel on the weekends and during holidays with the different clubs and teams. However, as long as we were sure that she was doing the right thing and taking the proper safety precautions, we always encouraged her to participate in these diverse activities and find areas she would be interested in pursuing in the future.

The Right Attitude

We always believed that the first step, before even setting a goal, was to develop the right attitude toward life. Only by cultivating a proper mind-set can people truly understand themselves—their strengths, weaknesses, potential, and limits—and set feasible long-term goals. Whenever we could, we impressed this philosophy upon our children and found that it worked with considerable success.

An interesting policy at Pearl River High School is that students can change or drop their courses before the first Friday in December during the first semester or the first Friday of March during the second semester. This is meant to offer students a trial period for selecting their courses. However, this flexibility also has its shortcomings: some students assume that they can ignore their class performance during this trial period because they have the opportunity to drop the courses anyway. We always cautioned our children against this mentality, trying to imbue them with the right attitude toward always putting in their best effort in order to succeed. To ensure that they did not take advantage of this policy, we made sure that they always considered their course selection very carefully; once our children enrolled in a class, they never dropped it.

In addition, every student at Pearl River High School has to attend a physical education class at least every other day. Although Fanny was not particularly talented in sports, we still urged her to approach this class with the same positive attitude and to participate actively. Different people have different capabilities, but it is always important to think positively and stay in good spirits. People's attitudes affect their development, as well as others' perceptions of them. No matter what they do, a positive attitude will always help them do their best. Fanny took this to heart and tried her best in this class, always receiving reasonable scores and favorable comments from her physical education teachers. Children need to develop courage and an indomitable spirit, and we believed that, without a doubt, physical fitness training would help achieve this.

Unlike most American high schools, which start from ninth grade, Pearl River High School starts from eighth grade, which offered Fanny one extra year to freely explore the areas in which she was interested. Based on the advice of books and our friends' experiences, we believed that in order for Fanny to be successful during her high school years, she needed to set a long-term goal. In such a competitive environment, it would be impossible to perform outstandingly in every field she found interesting; she needed to focus on excelling in certain areas.

In eighth grade, Fanny proved to be on a promising path, continuing to be the leading scorer in the math competitions at school. She outperformed both her eighth-grade peers and ninth-grade upperclassmen in the ASMA math contest and was ranked among the top scorers in the nation. While doing this, she engaged in a few other interests as well. At the awards ceremony at the end of the school year, she received departmental awards in both math and music.

Around this time, we spoke to her about setting a long-term goal and narrowing her focus. She agreed and told us that mathematics and the sciences were the areas in which she wanted to concentrate her efforts since she had decided to become a scientist in the future.

Combined with Fanny's performance in eighth grade and the progress she had made in previous years, we believed that Fanny had the potential, ambition, and aspirations to compete for entrance into the most prestigious colleges. With our encouragement, she decided to aim for the nation's top universities as her ultimate long-term goal. However, we cautioned her that in order to reach this goal, she would have to work hard and strive to be the best.

The Planning Process

We have always believed that in order for our children to have a shot at a successful future, they must have a balanced development. We asked our children to be strong not only academically, but also socially, and to demonstrate dedication to their community. As a result, we paid a lot of attention to training and encouraging their creativity and leadership skills.

After Fanny started ninth grade, the first "official" year of high school, we realized that much of her confusion and rough starts in middle school had been due to a lack of information and preparation. Therefore, we started to explore and acquaint ourselves with the U.S. college admissions process, trying to prepare for the new territory we would soon be entering. We set our sights first on the most prestigious U.S. colleges, such as the Ivy League universities, Massachusetts Institute of Technology, and California Institute of Technology. Eagerly, we collected information from friends, books, and online sources. One day, we stumbled upon an extremely useful Web site, College Confidential (www.collegeconfidential.com), which provided us with almost all the information about the college admissions process that we could want.

In their ever-popular forum pages, students and parents asked questions and received very helpful replies from others in the same situation and from those with experience in the matter. From this Web site, we saw evidence of many Caucasian parents that had also dedicated themselves wholeheartedly to their child's education. It was a comfort to see that because until then, we had thought that only Asian-American parents put such a strong emphasis on their children's education. We were not alone.

After carefully studying the information that we had gathered and sorting out the requirements of each prestigious college that we were targeting, we were delighted to discover that we were heading in the right direction. In the last few decades, and even centuries, these renowned centers of learning have trained a large number of outstanding students who have made great contributions to the world. Their highly selective criteria have ensured that the best minds of a generation have the chance to collaborate and learn from each other as well as leaders in their fields. These findings made these schools even more desirable and greatly encouraged us to continue using our method of preparing our children.

In the last few years, some Chinese parents have questioned the way we have raised our children. Sometimes, we entertain ourselves by imagining ourselves as walking on a very fine line and trying to keep our balance as judgment rains down on both sides. On one hand, white people consider us to be a stereotypical Chinese family with a strict parenting style. On the other hand, many Chinese parents think we have lost touch with the much more unyielding Chinese tradition.

However, we stayed confident in our plans. To help Fanny and Kathy emerge at the top of their classes, both socially and academically, we carefully set long-term goals with them. Our plans could be divided into several categories: academic performance, creativity and leadership, extracurricular activities, community service, and research and competition.

Academic Performance

One particular experience really opened our eyes to the role that academic performance played in our children's future. We were attending a presentation given by a Columbia University admissions officer, and before the talk had even begun, the admissions officer was asked by a student, "Should I take the most aggressive courses or less aggressive courses which will ensure better grades?"

During the presentation, the admissions officer addressed the question, replying, "We want to see you taking the most rigorous courses . . . and excelling in them."

They wanted the best students, period!

As a result, we encouraged our children to take the most challenging courses provided, in the honors and AP tracks, and to do their best to stand out in their classes. We also urged them to use their own knowledge and expertise to explore and create opportunities to excel by themselves.

Creativity and Leadership

To further develop their creativity and leadership skills, we asked our children to pay attention to their environment and community and to use their strengths and skills to make meaningful contributions. We constantly asked them the question, "What can you do at home, at school, and in the larger community?"

Eventually, they answered this question in many ways, always considering their surroundings and doing their best to give back to the community. At home, they built a laboratory in our basement. At school, they created and led many clubs and activities. To better serve the community, they formed a volunteer service group.

Every child is different, with different interests and potentials, but regardless of what they wish to do, opportunities abound for all of them. Students who love politics can consider joining a candidate's campaign or conducting a social survey to understand what issues concern people the most. Science-oriented students should consider finding a mentor for a real research project to gain experience as well as an insider's view on the true life of a scientist. If students enjoy writing, there is always the option of writing an editorial and submitting it to a newspaper to offer a fresh young point of view. The list goes on and on and serves to show that people should never limit their minds and options; it is always better to view the scene with a broad perspective.

As long as children remain aware of their surroundings, they can always find something they can do to practice, train, and refine their creativity and leadership skills.

Extracurricular Activities

We were always happy to see our children joining school clubs and other extracurricular activities. At the same time, we encouraged them to not only participate passively, but also make contributions and achievements which would make them stand out. Joining a club or engaging in an activity is just like taking an academic class; simply being present is not enough. In order to obtain the maximum benefit from the experience, it should be treated as an opportunity to learn more and improve oneself. We suggested that our children only join the activities in which they were interested in gaining expertise. For any activity, only by demonstrating passion or devotion can people make a difference.

Community Service

Volunteering and doing community service not only help society, but also provide an enriching learning experience. They can help children develop a better understanding of the community, take responsibility, learn skills useful later in life, and broaden their horizons. Our children have actively participated in many volunteer activities since they were young. They started with free tutoring and helping at the local library. Upon entering high school, we asked them to take more responsibility for their community and become even more involved. We kept encouraging them to do their work in more productive and effective ways, and eventually, they created their own group of student volunteers to provide even better service to the community.

Research and Competition

Participating in scientific research had been Fanny's dream for a very long time. Unfortunately, Pearl River High School did not have the means to offer such an opportunity, so we encouraged Fanny and Kathy to utilize the resources available to them in order to excel in academic competitions.

Clearly, this was a very aggressive, challenging plan; but we strongly believed that Fanny and Kathy could achieve these goals. Thanks to their focused efforts and strong preparation, they performed well in nearly every competition they entered. Encouraged by this progress, they both gained the confidence to boldly accept the challenges that came their way. We were excited, as a family, to work together and reach for these lofty dreams.

Lost at the Starting Line, Again?

As we were entertaining our magnificent plans for Fanny and Kathy, we discovered that Fanny was already facing a major roadblock. Each year, Pearl River High School releases class rankings for its seniors, and this class ranking plays a very important role in the college admissions process. Although Fanny's scores in her classes were perfect or near perfect, she could still fall behind in her class ranking and, thus, lose at the starting line.

How was this possible? It turned out that their high school determined class ranking based on the students' weighted GPA. For instance, an AP course carried a weight of 1.1, a college course, 1.06, honors courses, 1.03, and regular courses, 1.00. This made sense because it rewarded the students who took more challenging courses and did well in them, but some parents already knew about this and took advantage of the system. They strategically had their children skip a year in math or another subject to allow their children to take an additional AP course, giving them a boost in the class ranking calculations. In Fanny's senior year, we found out that the competition in her class had been extremely intense: the average GPAs for the very top students were separated by mere fractions of a point on a 100-point scale.

Fanny was fighting an uphill battle; to even have a chance of being the top in her class, she would have to be perfect for the years to come.

AIME

By that time, the situation was clear: Fanny had to execute the plan perfectly in order to win. She understood this and was fully prepared and ready to launch her attack. Although she continued to participate in a variety of clubs, Fanny gradually focused more and more on math and science-related activities. Operating from this stronghold, she put in even more effort to ensure an outstanding performance.

From her results in previous years' math competitions, we believed that she had the potential to advance to the American Invitational Mathematics Examination (AIME), but it would be a challenge. In order to do so, Fanny would have to score extremely well on the AMC 10 exam, and it was slightly discouraging to learn that no tenth grader at Pearl River High School had qualified for the AIME in over a decade. However, we believed Fanny could be the one to break that streak.

During winter break, we purchased a set of previous exams from the AMC Web site and started Fanny on targeted training. The day of the contest came, and she was successful! She scored sufficiently high enough to advance to the AIME.

Fanny's qualification for the AIME was a very good start to gaining national recognition. However, she found herself at a crossroads as to what she should do next. Although she was very strong in math, she enjoyed science more. Should she continue pushing herself to excel in math, or should she instead explore the sciences? She was puzzled as to which path to take, and so were we.

To get a clearer picture of the situation, John analyzed the results from previous years' math competitions with Fanny and made a prediction. He believed that it would be extremely difficult for Fanny to advance to the USA Mathematics Olympiad (USAMO), one of the top national mathematics competitions. If she decided to pursue this goal, she would have to put all her efforts and energy into preparing . . . and even then, the outcome was unpredictable.

However, if Fanny devoted her efforts to the sciences—biology, chemistry, or physics—advancing to the finals in a national competition would not be as difficult. She would also have the time and energy to explore other areas. Furthermore, since Fanny liked science more than math, it made sense to focus on the area she enjoyed more and had a better chance of excelling at on a national level. Finally, we reached a unanimous agreement to abandon our pursuit of math and move on to a new science route.

At the AIME, she performed on par with most students, solving two questions.

In twelfth grade, Fanny took the AMC 12 exam and again advanced to the AIME, where she answered five questions correctly, a pretty good score.

No Time to Lose

In tenth grade, Fanny took AP World History, her first AP class in high school. This subject covers a wide range of material over a very extensive period, making it very difficult to master. To make matters worse, the AP World History teacher at the time was very irresponsible. She did not teach much in class, frequently expecting the students to study by themselves or in groups. This method made a lot of students and parents frustrated and angry, but because the teacher was protected as part of the teacher's union, no one could move against her. In the end, this course expected the students, most of whom were taking an AP class for the first time, to teach themselves in order to pass. Although Fanny did not particularly like world history, while taking this course, she spent two or three times more effort on it than on her other subjects, finally receiving a grade of 99 percent by the end of the year.

In order to do well in AP World History, Fanny worked not only harder, but also smarter, making the most efficient use of her time. By compiling all the important historical events in chronological order on a chart, she was able to organize her thoughts in a more streamlined fashion. For each event, she marked down important information: dates, causes, impacts, and the ensuing lessons we could learn from it.

Sometimes, she even borrowed relevant documentaries from the library to make the learning process less boring and allow her to gain a better understanding of the subject. It was not a very pleasant learning experience, and we could feel her pain every late night . . . but she had no choice. She understood that if she wanted to target the top colleges, she did not have a moment to waste.

Fighting from Your Stronghold

Math and science were Fanny's strongholds; they were the fields which she loved the most and which promised her the most success, thus motivating her to perform particularly well in these areas. Advancing to the AIME would help her a little, but she needed a more notable achievement in a scientific discipline in order to gain national distinction.

Her tenth-grade chemistry honors course opened a very promising door to her. When she was in elementary school, I would frequently set up simple chemical experiments that revealed phenomena that we saw in daily life and then explain the chemical principles behind them. This greatly increased her interest in studying chemistry from an early age. Her high school chemistry teacher, Mrs. M, was a very cheerful and open-minded individual; and in her classroom, students often found themselves infected by her positive mood.

Toward the end of the school year, we discussed taking the SAT Subject Test in Chemistry, but a problem emerged. Fanny told us that Mrs. M had informed the class that they were behind schedule and would not be able to cover all the required material before the SAT subject test date. This new development complicated the situation. If Fanny did not take the SAT Subject Test in Chemistry that year, she would have to wait until eleventh grade. However, eleventh grade is the most stressful year of high school. In addition to a heavier workload due to more advanced classes, students need to prepare for a number of serious standardized tests, including the PSAT, SAT Reasoning Test, SAT subject tests, and AP exams. We definitely did not want to wait and add excessive pressure to such a situation.

Understanding our concerns, Fanny decided to study the untaught materials at home. I encouraged her to learn as much as she could independently, but if she had any problems or questions, she could ask me for help. Each day, after she finished her schoolwork, she would spend one or two extra hours working on chemistry.

In order to give her additional preparation and practice for the SAT Subject Test in Chemistry, John bought several review books for her, including *The Official Study Guide for all SAT Subject Tests* (College Board), *SAT II Subject Test Chemistry* (the Princeton Review), *SAT II Subject Test Chemistry* (Kaplan), and *SAT II Subject Test Chemistry* (Barron's). These books contain a review of the material, diagnostic exams, and full-length practice tests. Although all of these books are structured similarly, each has its own unique characteristics. For example, since the SAT program is run by the College Board, the practice questions in their book are often the closest to the real SAT problems. However, the College Board book only provides answer keys to the practice problems. Without detailed explanations justifying the correct answers, it is difficult for students to understand what they did wrong and how to fix it. Fortunately, the other three books provide detailed explanations for their practice questions. Among these three, the Princeton Review's practice exams seem to be the most similar to the actual exam, followed by Kaplan, and then Barron's. In our opinion, the practice problems of Barron's books are often more difficult than those on the actual exam, but the review material in their books is more comprehensive.

Because she was short on time after she finished learning the extra material, Fanny only had time to complete the practice exams in the Princeton Review book before the SAT subject test. In the end, she took the exam on schedule and scored 790 out of 800.

On June 25, 2006, Fanny received a letter from Professor Allan S. Blaer of Columbia University when she was admitted to Columbia University's Science Honors Program (SHP):

Dear SHP Applicant:

I am pleased to announce that you have been selected by Columbia University to participate in the Science Honors

Program (SHP) during the 2006-2007 school year. The competition for admission to the SHP was very intense, with more than 1,900 students competing for 280 available positions. You are to be congratulated on the outstanding academic record that has earned you a place in Columbia's program.

[. . .]

Sincerely,
Allan S. Blaer
Professor of Physics and SHP Director

The SHP has been a prestigious science program for outstanding high school students in the New York metropolitan area for over forty-eight years. It is designed to offer an exciting, challenging opportunity for high school students to pursue their academic enrichment in a college environment. Not unlike college, admission to the program requires an application, a letter of recommendation from a teacher, a high school transcript, and a rigorous screening examination. Students who are accepted into the program have the opportunity to take courses at Columbia University on Saturday mornings during the academic year.

Once she was admitted to the SHP, Fanny elected to take a biology course. We had no objection because it was her choice, and we believed she should take a class she was truly interested in. So during that time when Fanny took her biology course at Columbia, John drove her to the campus every Saturday, rain or shine. Sometimes, they would hit traffic and not arrive home until after 2:00 PM, hungry. Although the commute was not convenient, we were delighted for Fanny. She was one of the few tenth-grade students at Pearl River High School to have ever been accepted to Columbia University's SHP. It was an honor not only for her, but also for the school.

The WordMasters Challenge

We often wondered how we could help Fanny further challenge herself and achieve national recognition with the very limited resources available. While we were struggling with this difficulty, an unexpected windfall appeared before us: the WordMasters Challenge.

Our efforts to improve Fanny's reading skills in middle school paid off in high school with the national WordMasters Challenge. The WordMasters Challenge is a competition that aims to develop the reading comprehension skills of students in ninth to twelfth grade and encourage the close reading of many different kinds of prose and poetry. Each contest provides a short story, essay, or poem accompanied by approximately ten difficult questions about the passage. Over six hundred schools in the U.S. participate in this competition every year.

In February 2006, Fanny was ranked 102nd in the nation in the tenth-grade division. The following year, she rose to eighty-seventh in the eleventh-grade division. It was a truly dazzling performance! Her unexpected achievements in the WordMasters Challenge made us even more confident in the way which we were raising our children. We were now certain that the most important thing was to set a long-term goal in order to lay a solid foundation and path for the future.

USNCO

As we have already described in the previous chapter, in order to participate in the U.S. National Chemistry Olympiad (USNCO), Fanny founded a Chemistry Olympiad team at Pearl River High School. As the competition loomed closer, we wondered how to ensure that she would stand out in the competition. After all, one should never walk into a battle unprepared!

To give herself a fighting chance, Fanny downloaded a set of exercises from the USNCO Web site. However, when she tried to do them, she realized that the material she had learned in her chemistry honors class was insufficient for even the preliminary round! Even if she made it past the preliminaries, there would still be another more difficult exam. It was a daunting prospect. However, Fanny was unintimidated by this challenge and asked herself, "Can I learn AP Chemistry by myself over the summer?"

We fully supported this idea, especially because there seemed to be no other solution. So the summer after tenth grade, Fanny launched an ambitious plan to teach herself AP Chemistry. That summer, Fanny was also very busy with many other activities: volunteering, visiting colleges, preparing for the SAT Reasoning Test and the SAT Subject

Test in Math, and experimenting in the basement lab. She was juggling so much—we thought she was a superwoman!

In eleventh grade, like the other top students in her high school, Fanny was heavily loaded with schoolwork. In order to stretch her limits, she deviated from the recommended course load and took AP Physics, largely considered the most difficult class for high school students. Additionally, every Saturday, she would spend half the day immersed in Columbia University's SHP.

As the date of the USNCO preliminary exam approached, Fanny became more stressed. Although we were aware that the local exam was scheduled on the first Saturday in March, there had been no time to prepare for it, except for when she had studied AP Chemistry over the summer. Fanny was very unhappy, exasperatedly asking, "I finally assembled a team for the competition, but I'm still not ready! How can I possibly do well in this situation?"

There is a popular saying, "When God closes a door, somewhere he opens a window." On February 27, 2007, just four days before the preliminary exam, it began to snow. In only a few hours, the streets and lawns were blanketed with layers of thick snow. The snow continued relentlessly through the night, and at around 6:00 AM, we awoke to the ringing of our phone. It was an automated message from the Pearl River School District: "For safety reasons, Pearl River High School will be closed for today."

What a relief! I jumped out of bed and excitedly called, "Fanny! Kathy! School is closed for today! Do you want to practice for the Chemistry Olympiad?"

"Yes!" Fanny and Kathy both called back enthusiastically. Bill was happy too, because it meant that he could sleep longer and play in the snow all day.

Before this day, I had spent considerable time and effort in organizing materials to prepare Fanny for the USNCO. To make our practices more efficient, I had also worked on and familiarized myself with many of the previous years' problems. Originally, I thought that these efforts would be in vain because Fanny seemed to have no time to practice at all. We had never expected that this snowstorm would come to rescue us, but thank goodness it had!

"Fanny is really lucky! It seems nothing can stop her!" John exclaimed. Due to the heavy snow, school remained closed for the rest of the week, giving us three precious days to prepare Fanny for the USNCO. During those three days, I trained Fanny intensively, using the method we had developed:

- Step 1: Practice an exam from a previous year in order to find the questions she had problems with or knowledge that she had not quite grasped.
- Step 2: For the problems Fanny did not understand, I would explain the question and show her how to solve it. If the problem was due to a lack of knowledge, I would help her learn the material.
- Step 3: After fully digesting the problems from Step 2, Fanny would try to solve the questions independently to make sure she had completely absorbed the explanations.

Fanny remained very serious and careful during this training process. For a single problem, she would ask many questions in order to thoroughly understand the concepts and the calculations. After three days of intensive training, she made impressive progress and was ready to compete. Before we took a deep breath, though, we realized that the snow that offered Fanny the opportunity to complete her USNCO training also posed the possibility of rescheduling the competition. Since the weather had caused many road closures, it seemed likely that the date of the competition would be changed. If the preliminary was postponed to the following week, it would conflict with Fanny's SAT exam, and she would have to give up on the USNCO. Every day, I kept hoping that the competition would proceed as scheduled.

On Saturday, March 3, John drove Fanny to the designated testing location. When I saw him returning alone, I was relieved to realize that the competition was still being held. Fanny and her Pearl River High School teammates all showed up and were able to take the exam that day.

On Saturday, March 17, in the very early hours of the morning, the USNCO New York District director Dr. G. called, looking to speak with Fanny. When John learned the call was from Dr.G, he gave me a thumbs-up and urged me to hurry and wake Fanny, whispering, "It must be good news!"

When Fanny picked up the phone, she was met with congratulations from Dr. G. for advancing to the next level as a national finalist before he informed her that the national exam would be held in late March. The moment she hung up the phone and delivered the news, we burst into celebration. Everyone exchanged high fives and celebrated this momentous accomplishment. It had seemed like such a long shot, filled with so many struggles, but finally, Fanny's efforts had paid off!

After learning that Fanny had advanced to the national exam, we analyzed the questions from the previous years' exams and tried to assess Fanny's desire to go to the next level and represent the U.S. on the USA International Chemistry Olympiad team.

The USNCO final exam is divided into three parts. The first part is a ninety-minute, sixty questions multiple-choice exam. The second part consists of 105 minutes for eight free-response questions testing students' in-depth knowledge of theories and models. The third part is a ninety-minute lab practical.

Based on my experience from training Fanny, I believed that Fanny was well-equipped with the appropriate level of knowledge and intelligence to prepare for the first two sections. However, for the laboratory section, she did not have enough experience in practical applications of complex concepts or equipment due to a lack of resources. We decided to let Fanny do what she could without much additional preparation.

Science Olympiad

By the end of 2007, Fanny had submitted all of her college applications, but she did not cease her efforts to excel. In her senior year, Fanny was elected captain of the Science Olympiad Team, and one of her favorite teachers, Mrs. M, was the club supervisor. After taking the post, Fanny took a number of measures to turn an ordinary team into a competitive team. In the regional competition, the Pearl River High School Science Olympiad team achieved an unprecedented success. That success was discussed in Fanny's supplementary letter to the Harvard admissions office:

February 10, 2008

Dear Admissions Officer,

I am writing to you with new information to add to my application materials. In December, I submitted my college application to Harvard. I am maintaining outstanding academic performance in the first half of my senior year, which can be seen on my Midyear Report. In addition, I am actively participating in and leading several school clubs and teams: Math League, Science Olympiad, Chemistry Olympiad, and Tai Chi Club.

For the past few years, the Science Olympiad Team has been very quiet, and only a handful of people have been involved. However, this year, as captain of the Science Olympiad, I was determined to turn this situation around. At the beginning of the school year, I worked hard to increase the visibility of the club and recruit as many people as I could. To boost the members' spirit, we decided to create a team T-shirt to further unify our club. Later on, I came up with the idea that each member of the club wears their T-shirts on the same, specified day, to show our pride in the growing club. I offered my suggestion to the club advisors, members, and the principal and received enthusiastic support. On that day, members, teachers, and the principal all wore our shirts, and many students were attracted by this event and joined our club. In this way, I finally built a strong team for our school. Last week, in the regional competition, the Pearl River Science Olympiad team performed exceptionally well and, for the first time in many years, we brought back many awards and medals. I believe this success will pave the road for the future success of this club.

Last year, I created a Chemistry Olympiad team and became a national finalist. My success inspired a large number of students to become involved in this competition. This year, our school will not only continue to participate, but also send two teams to compete. Next month, I will lead both teams to compete in the region. I'm very excited and looking forward to it.

If these accomplishments could be added as a note to my application, I would appreciate it. Please let me know if you need further information or have any questions.

Sincerely,

Fanny Wang

With our proposed plan, Fanny successfully moved forward step-by-step, fully displaying her competitiveness. In our plan, we ignored a factor most children are keen about: sports. According to statistics, about 60 percent of students accepted by elite colleges have some sort of sports background, but less than 10 percent are accepted simply for their athletic ability. If a child does not have strong athletic ability and there are many other more interesting and productive activities he or she can participate in, it doesn't make sense to pursue sports. Yes, they are a good way to promote teamwork and cooperation, but other activities can do the same thing. After all, "All roads lead to Rome."

The PSAT

The PSAT/NMSQT (Preliminary SAT/National Merit Scholarship Qualifying Test) is a standardized test designed for high school students mainly in eleventh grade. It is an abbreviated version of the SAT Reasoning Test and covers three subjects: critical reading, math, and writing. The exam is two hours and ten minutes long and consists of only multiple-choice questions, with a maximum score of 240 points or eighty per subject.

The PSAT is held in mid-October each year, though different school districts may have slightly varying exam schedules. The PSAT is especially important for eleventh graders because the results are used as a key criterion during the National Merit Scholarship selection process. In order to familiarize students with the PSAT, many high schools encourage students to take the PSAT in tenth grade as practice.

Each year, about sixteen thousand eleventh graders qualify as National Merit Scholarship semifinalists. The qualifying scores are state-specific and thus vary regionally. In addition to their SAT Reasoning Test scores and a recommendation letter from their high school principal, qualifying students must submit an application with an essay component to compete to be one of eight thousand National Merit Scholarship finalists. From the finalists, the Association of National Merit Scholarships honors 2,500 students as National Merit Scholars, and each receives a $2,500 grant in recognition of their outstanding achievement.

Often, National Merit Scholarship finalists are eligible to receive other college or corporation-sponsored scholarships. Some colleges even actively seek these students and provide them with very favorable terms of admission, including substantial financial aid or full scholarships!

One question that always emerges when talking about the PSAT is what score can qualify students as semifinalists. This question is difficult to fully address because each state has its own cutoff score, and that cutoff can vary from year to year. However, the following table can be used as a reference:

AL	AK	AZ	AR	CA	CO
209	212	210	202	216	213
CT	DC	DE	FL	GA	HI
220	221	217	214	215	215
ID	IL	IN	IA	KS	KY
206	214	210	210	214	219
LA	ME	MD	MA	MI	MN
208	214	221	221	210	213
MS	MO	MT	NE	NV	NH
202	211	207	204	207	214
NJ	NM	NY	NC	ND	OH
221	206	218	215	206	211
OK	OR	PA	RI	SC	SD
207	215	215	215	211	205
TN	TX	UT	VT	VA	WA
216	215	202	213	220	214
WV	WI	WY			
202	210	200			

From this table, we can see that a score of 218 can be used as an estimate of the score required for students in New York to become National Merit Scholarship semifinalists.

After Fanny took the PSAT in tenth grade, I eagerly asked her how she felt. Frustrated, she answered, "Very bad! I couldn't even understand some of the critical reading passages!"

Concerned, I turned to John and asked, "Should we try sending her to another tutorial school?"

"Calm down!" He saw my anxiety and tried to assuage my fears, reasoning, "Fanny is a perfectionist and cannot tolerate any mistakes. Let's wait to see the results and then make a decision."

He was right. After all, I remembered that a few years ago, Fanny took the SAT Reasoning Test with a friend in order to participate in Johns Hopkins University Center for Talented Youth summer camp. After that test, she had complained about not doing well, but her scores easily placed her above the threshold requirements. Thinking about this made me feel a bit better, but I still could not stop worrying about it.

"So . . . why didn't you understand those passages?" I asked, searching for an answer that would offer some sort of solution.

"I did not know a lot of the vocabulary," she replied, crestfallen. Too impatient to wait for the PSAT results, I bought her several vocabulary-building books, including *Wordly Wise 3000* (Hodkinson and Adams), *601 Words* (Bromberg and Liebb), *504 Absolutely Essential Words* (Barron's), *Word Smart* (the Princeton Review), *1100 Words You Need To Know* (Bromberg and Gordon), and *SAT Verbal Workbook* (Kaplan).

Fanny is a person with strong logical thinking skills, but with an aversion to memorization and recitation, which made learning this new vocabulary a painful ordeal. However, there was no way around it. Together, we set a target for Fanny to learn and memorize twenty new words a day; and each day, we would test her on the words she had learned. We also asked Kathy to do the same to begin building her vocabulary early. This gave her sufficient time to consolidate a much more expansive vocabulary.

In December 2005, we received Fanny's PSAT report. She had scored 228 points, ten points above the semifinalist reference line for New York. Finally, a weight was lifted off my shoulders, and I could breathe easier once more.

In mid-October of 2006, Fanny took the PSAT again as an eleventh grader. This result was even more crucial since it would be used to determine whether she would become a National Merit Scholarship semifinalist. We believed that with the additional year of experience and knowledge, she would naturally do better than she had the previous year, so she did not do any extra practice. This turned out to be a mistake. Although Fanny's eleventh grade PSAT score was still good enough to qualify her as a semifinalist, her scores showed no sign of the natural increase we had expected. This experience reiterated that we should never go into a battle without any preparation. This was a high-stakes game, and we could not take any risks if we wished to achieve our ultimate goal.

The SAT

During the summer of 2006, Fanny needed to prepare for the SAT Subject Test in Mathematics Level 1, as well as for the SAT Reasoning Test. Her schedule was also packed with independently studying AP Chemistry, doing volunteer service, and visiting colleges. Since her summer promised to be very busy, after taking a break for a week, she started the battle.

For the SAT Reasoning Test, we purchased four review books, which provided us with over thirty full-length practice tests. These review books were *11 Practice Tests for the SAT & PSAT* (the Princeton Review), *12 Practice Tests for the SAT* (Kaplan), *How to Prepare for the SAT* (Barron's), and *The Official Study Guide for the New SAT* (College Board).

To practice for the SAT Subject Test in Math I, she used *The Official Study Guide for all SAT Subject Tests* (College Board), *Cracking the SAT Subject Tests Math 1 & 2* (the Princeton Review), *SAT Subject Test: Mathematics Level 1* (Kaplan), and *How to Prepare for the SAT II: Math Level 1C* (Barron's).

Typically, we would use the College Board practice tests to measure the progress that was made during the practice. The Princeton Review and Kaplan books were mainly used for reviewing the material and practicing questions because of their more in-depth coverage of the material and detailed explanations of the answers. The practice problems in the Barron's book were significantly more difficult than the questions on the actual test, but because it provided even deeper coverage of the material, it was worth studying from as well.

While practicing over the summer, Fanny would first review the relevant concepts and finish the review questions following each chapter of the review books. Only after finishing that would she move on to the full-length practice exams. Most colleges allow students to take the SAT Reasoning Test up to three times and consider only the highest score in each subject. This gives a student a tactical advantage because they are not obliged to review and practice all three subjects at the same time. By approaching this strategically, he or she can achieve the best scores possible. Since we have already included detailed descriptions on how to prepare for the SAT Reasoning and Subject tests in the appendices of this book, we shall not repeat that here.

However, since Fanny was our first child going through this process, we were not aware of these tricks and strategies at the time. She simply had to learn the difficult way, by preparing for all three subjects at once. This held her back considerably from her independent study of AP Chemistry that summer.

The SAT Essay

Students are allotted only twenty-five minutes to write the SAT Reasoning Test essay, which poses a challenge to many students. We were worried about this section of the test and wondered how Fanny could learn to finish a high-quality essay in that limited amount of time.

In order to gain a general idea of the level of Fanny's SAT Reasoning Test essay writing skills, John asked her to write a practice essay within the time limit, and then he analyzed it to diagnose her problems. Unfortunately, her paper was composed poorly, and he estimated that it would have scored only a six to eight, out of a full score of twelve. This was worrisome because from John's experience, good writing skills were very important for successful scientists, who needed to write many papers, such as grant proposals and research papers.

We decided to reach out for help, seeking a professional tutor to work with Fanny for several sessions. However, the tutor never had any lesson plans prepared and did not institute any form of targeted training. After a few lessons, we still could not see any noticeable progress, so John decided to tutor Fanny himself. He would read each of Fanny's essays, making notes and comments on them. Through this, he discovered a common problem in her writing: whenever Fanny wrote about a story or an event, she spent too much time and space describing the example and not enough on analyzing it and using it to support her argument.

In order to fix this, she and John developed their own SAT Reasoning Test essay writing strategy, and Fanny repeatedly practiced this method. Their strategy was highly successful, and Fanny's essay became more clear and convincing. She took the SAT Reasoning Test twice, and each time, her essay received a perfect score of twelve. For your reference, in the appendices of this book, we have described our SAT Reasoning Test essay writing strategy.

The following is the essay that Fanny wrote on her first SAT Reasoning Test, for the topic: "Is it more valuable for people to fit in than to be unique and different?"

> *It is more valuable for people to be unique and different. Conformity is the bane of our existence—it is differences among people that gives each of us greater perspective and allows us to make better judgments. Throughout history and literature, numerous people have refused to "fit in," which allowed them to do many things they could not have if they chose to "fit in," such as Atticus Finch, Huckleberry Finn, and Copernicus and Galileo.*
>
> *In* To Kill a Mockingbird *by Harper Lee, Atticus Finch refuses to flow with society. When he is assigned to defend a black man accused of raping a white woman, he acts differently than most other lawyers would have. In a case of a white man's word against a black man's, the trial would only be a show because the black man would certainly have been indicted. However, Atticus is aware that the defendant is innocent and fights a losing battle to reveal the truth, which is what all lawyers should do. He is considerably different from most other men of his time, who would have realized the outcome was inevitable and would not have struggled against it. Thus, he is able to open the people's eyes to the truth, and although he does lose the case, he scores a moral victory. His refusal to go down without*

a fight marked him as different, but this difference opened the door for the truth, allowing the parochial townspeople to see a larger perspective, beyond their racial prejudices.

Huck Finn is also different, which allows him to see the truth and make better judgments. In The Adventures of Huckleberry Finn *by Mark Twain, Huck shuns "respectable" society, preferring his free, unchained life. This refusal to obey society's restrictions allows him to befriend a runaway slave, something that would be impossible in "respectable" society. His difference allows him to see the man as a person, not chattel to be sold at a whim. He begins to realize that slavery is wrong, that all men should be free. Therefore, when his new friend is captured, Huck decides to help him escape, going against all his society has taught him. He is described in glowing terms as a hero, simply because his differences allowed him a more encompassing view of his world, allowing him to make a very good decision.*

Copernicus and Galileo also refused to "fit in" with their society; when they discovered the true structure of the solar system, they went against standard views and aired their own. Many scorned them for their discoveries and ostracized them, trying to make them conform and manipulate their discoveries to support the older view of the universe. However, they persevered in spite of all the obstacles they faced and continued to promote their discoveries. They were unique—they created a new theory and published it during a time when difference was feared and struck out against. Eventually, their discoveries were verified, opening a new perspective and eventually leading to even more important discoveries. Their discovery changed people's perspectives of the world and led the people to become more open-minded, leading to the discovery of even more wonderful ideas.

These examples illustrate how nonconformity is an essential quality for mankind. The greatest thinkers were unique—they did not try to "fit in" and follow society; instead, they led it. Differences among people give each of us greater perspective and allow us to make better judgments, such as the decision to be different. With conformity, there cannot be change or progress, an essential process for the human race—uniqueness and differences allow us to prosper and flourish.

SAT Success

Fanny entered eleventh grade in September 2006. It was a year of hard work; in addition to college-level Spanish, she was taking three AP courses: biology, physics, and U.S. history. She also took the SAT Subject Test in Mathematics Level 1 and scored a perfect 800.

In December of that year, we gave up our traditional family vacation so Fanny could prepare for the SAT Subject Test in Mathematics Level 2, which she would take in January, and the SAT Reasoning Test, which she would take in March. As with before, she used several review books to prepare for the subject test: *The Official Study Guide for all SAT Subject Tests* (College Board), *Cracking the SAT Subject Tests Math 1 & 2* (the Princeton Review), *SAT Subject Test: Mathematics Level 2* (Kaplan), and *How to Prepare for the SAT II: Math Level 2C* (Barron's). In January 2007, Fanny took the SAT Subject Test in Mathematics Level 2 and received another perfect score.

Over the summer, although Fanny had continuously prepared for the SAT Reasoning Test, her practice scores remained consistently between 2250 and 2300; and it seemed it would be difficult for her to surpass the bottleneck score of 2300. To boost her score, John became involved, providing suggestions and supervision during the final weeks of preparation.

On March 10, 2007, Fanny took the SAT Reasoning Test. She surpassed the 2300 hurdle, reaching 2360, a score considered within the perfect range.

Fanny continued to work hard and took her AP exams in May, receiving perfect scores of 5 for the three subjects she had taken that year. In June 2007, she also received a perfect score of 800 on her SAT Subject Test in Physics.

Never Fight a War of Attrition

As we assisted Fanny and Kathy on their process through high school, we noticed a prevalent problem: parents and students unwittingly were inadvertently involved in a war of attrition, taking unnecessary, dangerous measures to seem more capable than their peers.

A common topic of conversation among eleventh graders was how late they had stayed up the night before. Instead of talking about how efficiently they had worked, they boasted, "Last night, I worked until two o'clock." And another would proudly chime in, "Yeah, I know what you mean. I was up until 3:00 AM!" They seemed to be under the false impression that working later meant that they were somehow working harder or better.

Parental anxiety was also major contributor to students' stress. Some parents even encouraged their children to burn the midnight oil, urging them to continue studying, reading, and staring at texts. What many of them did not seem to realize was that occasionally staying up late is okay, but over a long period of time, it creates many more problems. Students who do not sleep well at night end up dozing off during the day and taking frequent afternoon naps. Without a good night's sleep, they lack energy in school the next day. In this fog of fatigue, they cannot focus well during classes, which causes them to learn inefficiently, leading to further delays and struggles over their homework. This cycle simply continues as the students find themselves staying up even later at night to complete their assignments. Day after day, students decline in efficiency, trapped in a waking nightmare.

To prevent our children from falling into this vicious cycle, we asked Fanny to go to bed before 11:00 PM every night. In eleventh grade, the behavior and talk of her classmates began to impact her, and she worried about it. "But my classmates are all staying up and learning until two or three o'clock in the morning! I'm losing time and will be left behind!"

Anxiously, she tried to bargain with us to extend her study time into the early hours of the morning. However, our answer was simple and unyielding. "We want you to be efficient. You can get the same results by just going to bed earlier, and this will result in less time needed to study overall."

Despite her protests, we affirmed our rule: bedtime would remain unchanged at 11:00 PM. Occasionally, Fanny would truly be swamped with a large amount of work, forcing her to stay up later to finish. During those times, John would patiently sit on the couch in the next room over, waiting for her to finish. Once she was done, he would urge her to go to bed immediately, without staying up an extra minute.

Discussing efficiency and attrition reminds me of a story during Fanny's SAT Reasoning Test preparation. As mentioned before, Fanny prepared for this test during the summer and hit a ceiling around a score of 2300, so John decided to give her extra preparation, a last push, during winter break. However, his schedule for those ten days caused me considerable apprehension.

First, he arranged for a two-day visit to an indoor water park in Pennsylvania, in order to give Fanny a complete break. I was definitely okay with this, because this wasn't anything unusual. It was his plans for the next week that worried me; he asked Fanny to do practice problems for only two subjects each day. He intensively worked with Fanny every morning, making sure that Fanny completely understood the questions and the solutions; but in the afternoons, he insisted that Fanny do nothing: no SAT practice, no homework, nothing except relax!

Those first few days, I was lost in a fog of confusion and anxiety, wondering, *How do you want her to relax at night if she did not do any extra studying in the afternoon? How can this plan work?*

I could not find the words to properly express how apprehensive and fearful I was at that time.

Surprisingly, a few days later, Fanny's scores shot up to within the range of scores considered "perfect." It seemed like magic to me, and Fanny still had two more days to relax before school reopened. This was a vivid example of how efficiency can play a huge role in producing results.

When they are under a lot of stress, most children cannot manage their time efficiently and need their parents' guidance. Above all, parents need to be less stressed than their children during these critical moments because their children will look to them for cues on how to act.

Fight for Every Inch

As we mentioned earlier, since some of Fanny's classmates had an additional AP class advantage, so in order for her to have a chance of becoming the top student in her class, she had to pursue every reasonable opportunity.

In eleventh grade, Fanny wanted to test her limits and even asked us to allow her to give up her lunch period in order to take an extra AP course. While we appreciated her determination and willingness to push forward, we did not hesitate to reject this request. For a child at that age, her health was the most important consideration. Without proper nutrition and regular mealtimes, she would not be able to maintain her health; and without her health, everything else would fall apart. To ensure that she was staying healthy, we often barbecued a steak for her to snack on—even as late as ten o'clock in the evening—hoping to boost her energy and maintain her stamina during the difficult year of eleventh grade.

Eleventh grade was a struggle in so many other aspects as well. Before it had even started, we were already struggling with her course selection. She would take the most aggressive classes, without a doubt; but due to a scheduling conflict, she was forced to choose between AP Physics B and AP English Literature and Composition, even though she tried everything possible to take both.

Ms. S was the teacher for the AP English Literature and Composition class. She had been Fanny's tenth grade English teacher as well, and they shared many of the same characteristics: elegance, intelligence, responsibility, and classy mannerisms. Because of this, they both liked each other very much, and Fanny strongly wished to enroll in Ms. S's class.

When Ms. S first learned about the timing conflict, she expressed a certain degree of frustration and disappointment and attempted to persuade Fanny to take her class. Using her daughter as an example, she presented the case that acceptance into Ivy League colleges was not contingent upon taking AP Physics B in eleventh grade. We were, and still are, very grateful to her and appreciative of her passion for having Fanny as her student.

However, John could not understand why Fanny would not choose AP Physics B immediately, especially because Fanny had geared her future toward the sciences. Although AP Physics B was the hardest course in her high school, he was undeterred because he reasoned that Fanny had a solid mathematical foundation and the capability for rigorous, logic-based thinking, so she should do well. Furthermore, a girl excelling in physics, a largely male-dominated field, would surely stand out. He believed that the only way for Fanny to gain an edge and stand out among the other students was by taking this course.

In the end, Fanny ended up taking AP Physics B that year. Her teacher, Mr. Y, was a very amiable man who loved to tell jokes, which oftentimes elicited a mixture of good-natured groans and appreciative laughter. His students all enjoyed having him as a teacher and learning in the low-stress atmosphere of his classroom.

On some occasions, when Mr. Y made a mistake while teaching, Fanny would boldly point out the discrepancy and suggest a correction. Although Mr. Y approved of what Fanny did in his AP Physics B class, our traditional Chinese instincts made us alarmed. We did not know if Fanny correcting her teacher would cause tension between the student and the teacher, but unsure of the issue, we chose to neither stop nor encourage her behavior.

College Application Essays

College application essays provide another window through which admissions officers can see the applicants. It is also one of the few platforms a student can use to demonstrate his or her uniqueness and strengths, so students should spend plenty of time developing and editing their application essays in order to impress their readers. There are several books on the market that discuss how to write a successful college application essay, which may be worth looking at to obtain a basic idea of how others wrote theirs. Two such books are *Writing a Successful College Application Essay* (Barron's) and *50 Successful Harvard Application Essays* (Staff of the Harvard Crimson). From the examples, we noticed that in most of the essays, the tone was proactive and mature, the experience discussed had a deep impact on the writer, and the writer was mentally strong.

When she began to write her own college application essays, Fanny tried to apply this knowledge to her own writing:

> *Finally, after days of work, my proposal was finished. I had a concrete plan for creating a Tai Chi club.*
>
> *The next day, clutching my proposal, I walked into the principal's office and nervously began to present my ideas to Mr. F. I explained that I had been doing Tai Chi exercises at home and had found myself focusing better and thinking more clearly. As I talked about the potential benefits to the other students, he looked over my proposal, nodding and smiling. Finally, he told me that while he did not foresee any problems, he needed to look at my proposal more closely and get back to me.*

Anxiously, I waited for a final approval. To my surprise, when I was finally called into his office, it was not to hear good news. There had been a budget cut, and the school could not finance any new activities. I was devastated. For days, the encounter played and replayed itself in my mind, weighing me down. I could think of nothing but the club, the failure, the budget, the . . .

Refusing to give up, I shook off the gloom. I would make this work.

Over the next few days, I went to several club advisors, seeking their suggestions and searching for a new direction. I realized that the key issue was finding a teacher who would be the club sponsor, since that was a requirement for every club. I thought that if I could find a volunteer teacher, I might solve this problem. To try this out, I presented my proposal to several teachers and won support from one of them: Ms. D.

When I stepped back into Mr. F's office, he was surprised to see me. I carefully unfolded my plan, and I told him that I had found a volunteer teacher to sponsor the club. He smiled and gave me the final approval.

This turned out to be the first of many obstacles. I still had to find a practice area, obtain the equipment, and recruit members; but I managed to solve all these issues. The club has now been running for years.

During one of our early meetings, one of the members poked me. "Look, Mr. F is watching us!" I looked over and caught his eye. He gave a slight nod and a thumbs-up. We smiled at each other, satisfied.

Much to my surprise, the next year, several new clubs were created. Modeling themselves after the Tai Chi Club, they were able to form without consuming the school's budget. These successes encouraged me to form a Chemistry Olympiad team. During the competition, I did well and became a national finalist. However, I consider my work with the Tai Chi Club to be a greater accomplishment. For the first time, I took responsibility for a project and heralded it from idea to completion. By exploring new ideas and strategies every time I hit a roadblock, I was able to turn obstacles into opportunities; this has made all the difference. The leadership and social skills that I learned throughout this time are valuable assets that I will carry with me throughout my life.

Letters of Recommendation

Letters of recommendation play a very important role in the college admissions process. According to some statistics, about seventy percent of applications are rejected solely due to weaknesses in their recommendation letters.

Most colleges require letters of recommendation from two high school teachers and the student counselor. It is better to ask teachers who have taught the student in tenth or eleventh grade in a core academic subject for such letters. These teachers should ideally be aware of the student's aspirations and potential for development. Of course, it is also important to ask the teacher who knows the student best.

It is advisable to ask teachers for letters of recommendation as early as possible, giving them time to prepare and compose a quality recommendation. Both Fanny and Kathy approached their teachers at the end of eleventh grade.

Many students worry about which teachers can write a good letter for them, but a general rule is to find teachers who know the student well and have a good impression of the student. An observant student should usually have a pretty good intuition as to which teacher to ask.

However, for a long time, we were concerned about how Fanny would approach this issue, due to her quiet and relatively introverted nature. To her, all of her teachers were very nice, friendly people; and as a result, she did not know which teacher knew her best. When I tried to ask her, "Well, which teacher likes you the most?" She could only reply with, "I don't really know . . ."

We were unable to obtain a direct answer from Fanny, so we tried to find another solution. Eventually, we figured there were two ways to approach this dilemma: we could either read the teachers' comments from school reports to search for clues, or tell Fanny to ask her teachers if they could write her a strong recommendation letter. For the latter approach, if a teacher showed any sign of hesitation, he or she probably wouldn't be the best candidate.

While we continued worrying about how to find the best teachers to write letters for Fanny, Fanny brought us great news that assuaged all of our fears: Ms. S and Mr. Y had made the first move, expressing their willingness to write her a strong letter. We were surprised, especially because Fanny had corrected Mr. Y in AP Physics B and had not followed Ms. S's recommendation to take AP English Literature and Composition. However, we greatly appreciated the teachers' magnanimous gestures, a reflection of their kind, generous hearts.

Garland of Victory

In mid-December of 2007, when Yale admitted Fanny, we were all greatly relieved. To entertain ourselves, our family then proceeded to bet on whether Harvard would also accept Fanny. Each of us deposited five dollars into the pot. Because our children had long believed that their father was always right, Kathy and Bill trusted their father, betting "Yes" with him, confident that Fanny would be accepted. Fanny was more reserved, and I was not as sure of her chances; all the students at Harvard seemed to be geniuses capable of doing anything, and while definitely smart enough, Fanny had such a gentle soul. Fanny also joked that by betting against herself, she would win either way; she wouldn't care about losing five dollars if she was accepted, but if she was rejected, at least she would get some money out of it.

In December, Fanny sent applications to the following colleges: Harvard, MIT, Princeton, Columbia, University of Pennsylvania, Johns Hopkins, Caltech, Cornell, University of California—Berkeley, and NYU. In April 2008, Fanny was accepted into all of these colleges.

While we were all rejoicing, a bittersweet dilemma lay ahead: Where should Fanny go to college? Of all these prestigious colleges, which one would she choose? We knew that Fanny strongly favored Princeton because its learning environment and atmosphere were a close match with her own personality. However, we hoped she would choose Harvard; for Harvard held an insurmountable, absolute, lofty position in our minds. It is regarded as the top university in the nation, and its international recognition is almost beyond comparison. As the dream school of many capable young students, Harvard would give her the chance to interact with some of the best students in the world. Even though we did not make the decision for her, our opinions strongly influenced her choice.

During the rest of high school, with her usual sense of humility and desire for privacy, Fanny pursued her studies as usual, without telling the students or faculty about her many acceptances. Out of respect and gratitude, she told only the teachers who wrote her letters of recommendation and a few others with whom she interacted regularly.

People often asked her, "With so many offers from elite colleges, how can you be so calm?" They felt it was strange and seemed to half expect her to be trumpeting her success through the hallways, telling everyone she passed in the corridors. However, this was simply the way Fanny preferred to handle the situation. She was a dormant volcano, cool and collected on the exterior, with all the happy, excited emotions bubbling within.

As valedictorian of the Pearl River High School Class of 2008, Fanny delivered a speech at her graduation ceremony. Her heartfelt words expressed her sincerest thanks and profound appreciation to all the teachers for their help, to her fellow students who grew up and shared their lives with her, and to her parents for their guidance and her upbringing. She recalled those many times when she had been lost at the starting line, but time and time again, her perseverance and persistent efforts pulled her through. Fanny's speech, her story, and words of advice deeply impressed the audience.

Fanny's valedictorian speech

CHAPTER 14

Replicating Success

Jumping the Gun

During the 2006-2007 school year, Fanny was in eleventh grade, and Kathy was in ninth grade. At this time, we had a better understanding of Pearl River High School and the American educational system as a whole.

In eighth grade, Kathy had performed very well and still had energy to spare. Therefore, we encouraged her to challenge herself by taking honors chemistry in ninth grade, even though most students in Pearl River traditionally took chemistry in tenth grade, at the very earliest. However, when we asked the school if Kathy could take the course a year early, we encountered considerable resistance. First, they protested, honors chemistry required a level of math that Kathy had not yet learned. Second, there was no precedent for students taking honors chemistry in ninth grade, so we would need permission from the principal to register her for the class. Third, in order to graduate, students had to complete a set of required courses; not following the traditional scheduling could potentially prevent her from finishing all the requirements by graduation. Fourth, taking honors chemistry in ninth grade would mean she would be taking two honors science courses, and they were concerned that she would be overwhelmed by this course load.

In response to these concerns, we discussed the situation with Kathy and took a close look at Fanny's class notes from honors chemistry.

We discovered that the required math was relatively limited; the only new material involved basic logarithms, which we were confident that Kathy could learn by herself over the summer. We also devised an adjusted schedule that allowed Kathy to put off some of her required courses to later years and fulfill them all by graduation. In response to their concerns about Kathy's capability, we showed them Kathy's eighth grade transcript, where her grades were either 99 or 100, with perfect scores on the state Regents tests and reminded them that she had been the school champion in the American Scholastic Mathematics Association (ASMA) competition. When we were told that it was impossible to schedule all her classes without conflicts, Kathy talked to several of her friends to learn during which periods each of her classes were being offered, since most of them were taught several times a day to accommodate different schedules. Using this information, we compiled a schedule that included all her classes without any conflicts and submitted it to the school for review. Thanks to our efforts, the principal finally gave his permission. At the end of ninth grade, Kathy received a grade of 99 out of 100 in her honors chemistry class.

Smooth Sailing

Due to Fanny's pioneering experience, Kathy's path was much easier. Using the same strategies we had used for Fanny, Kathy succeeded in replicating Fanny's successes in academics and competitions. During Kathy's high school journey, everything went her way.

She was the school champion in the ASMA competition for two consecutive years. In the Rockland Math League, she was consistently ranked second place in her school, just behind Fanny.

In May 2008, at the school's awards ceremony, she received departmental awards from three of her AP classes: AP Chemistry, AP World History, and AP Environmental Sciences, as well as from several other classes. In addition, she received the Presidential Award for Community Service. We expected she would be happy that night. However, to our surprise, after she stepped down from the stage, there were tears in her eyes, and her mouth fought to keep from frowning. I asked her, "What's wrong?"

She replied, her voice shaking with disappointment, "Mom, I didn't get the English award!"

"Don't worry!" I reassured her. "Look at the larger scale!"

For a long time, we tried to broaden our children's vision, asking them to consider their accomplishments in the long run. After all, the competition was not limited to just their friends and classmates—it was on the national scale. Historically, we saw that elite universities admitted qualified students without school-specific quotas; they looked for outstanding students who distinguished themselves in some way. In order to reach that distant goal, we needed to challenge our children to set higher standards for themselves and consider everything with a wider perspective.

Of the three AP courses that Kathy took in tenth grade, only AP World History followed the typical schedule of Pearl River students. Why did she take these courses so aggressively? From our experience with Fanny, we realized that this method would give Kathy an advantage in the competition to become valedictorian and remove the necessity of taking too many high-level classes at once during the more stressful years of high school. By distributing her AP courses more evenly, she would have more time and energy to handle competitions, standardized tests, and the college application process.

In tenth grade, Kathy took AP Environmental Science because it had no prerequisites and did not require skipping any courses. The final project of her AP Environmental Science class was a solar cooker competition: each student had to build a solar cooker that used the sun's rays to heat water. On the final day of classes, they held a contest to determine whose design was the most effective and could heat water to the highest temperature in the shortest amount of time—the ultimate goal was to reach boiling. To incentivize the class to take this project seriously, their teacher announced that the winner would automatically receive a 100 on the final exam and would not have to even sit for the exam. Kathy excitedly seized this opportunity and proclaimed, "I want to do this! I want that 100!"

That evening, Kathy was busy searching the Internet for solar cooker designs. After comparing all the designs and descriptions, she decided to start by using an umbrella and aluminum foil. An empty can would serve as her water-holding vessel.

While it was all easy in theory, when she actually started the project, Kathy ran into practical problems. First, she had to find a way to apply the aluminum foil on to the umbrella without wrinkling the foil. The spokes of the umbrella, in particular, made this very difficult. If she did not stick the foil on smoothly, it would not be able to reflect the sun's rays efficiently. She also could not decide on an unobtrusive place to position the can.

"Would you be willing to spend more time and make a better solar cooker?" John asked. He reassured her that she was moving in the right direction, but offered her suggestions on how to make a more effective, parabolic solar cooker. In order to construct this, she had to adjust her approach and reconsider her choice in materials. To remedy the problem of the flimsiness of the umbrella's fabric, John suggested using poster board instead, which would also allow for easier, smoother application of the foil. After some more brainstorming, they went to Home Depot to buy aluminum tape, poster board, and wire. They cut the poster board into panels that could be easily shaped around a wire frame and after working for a few nights, finally crafted a solar cooker, its inside coated with reflective aluminum tape. With all the panels carefully placed, Kathy was anxious to attach the can and declare the project finished.

"Wait! Not yet!" John cautioned her. "Have you considered what the best location for the can is?"

She looked at her father curiously. "Hmm . . . but where would that be?"

"At the focal point! This solar cooker works like a parabolic mirror—there will be a certain focal point where all the heat is directed," John carefully explained. Since she had not taken physics yet, Kathy was unfamiliar with the principles of light, lenses, and mirrors; but now, understanding began to dawn on her face.

The next day, Kathy and John worked under the hot sun to find the focal point of her solar cooker. Kathy slowly moved her hand around the inside of the cooker until she exclaimed, "Oh! Dad! It's really hot right here!"

Happily, she fixed the can to that point. "There! It's done!"

"No! Not yet!" he warned again. "Is it really perfect?"

"Wait . . . but what else is missing?" Kathy asked, puzzled.

"If you want to be a champion, you need to account for everything. There is one more factor you haven't considered yet!"

"And what's that?"

"Do you know what color absorbs heat the most?"

"Obviously, it's black!"

"And what color is your can?"

Thus, she decided to paint the can black. John drove her to Home Depot once more to buy paint for the can. Finally, Kathy's solar cooker was finished. When we tested the solar cooker at home, we were surprised to see how quickly the water began to boil.

Kathy testing her solar cooker

On the day of the competition, Kathy took her creation to school and displayed it with everyone else's. Under the bright sun, they all filled their containers with water, and Mr. M started the timer. Everyone began to get comfortable as Mr. M called out the time, and the temperature on their thermometers slowly inched upward. One minute . . . two minutes . . .

Before the timer reached the three-minute mark, Kathy called out, "It's boiling!" Mr. M was amazed—the fastest record for reaching boiling in his class until then had been thirty minutes.

Her classmates stared at her solar cooker in disbelief. One boy, particularly skeptical, decided to stick his finger in the water to check. With a yelp of surprise and pain, he quickly withdrew his hand, howling, "OUCH! It hurts! It's really hot!"

Another one ran over with another thermometer and after a few tense seconds, shouted out, "It's true—one hundred degrees!"

After this exhibition finished, Mr. M asked Kathy if she could leave her solar cooker with him. To this day, he still has the solar cooker, keeping it as the record holder for the annual competition. Every year, when he introduces the final project, he displays Kathy's solar cooker to his students as the model to beat.

In 2007, our family gave up our winter break plans so Kathy could prepare for the U.S. National Chemistry Olympiad (USNCO). Since Kathy had taken honors chemistry in ninth grade, she had the basic knowledge needed to compete in the USNCO. Tenth grade was the optimal time to try to advance to the national exam because she did not have to face the daunting pressures of eleventh grade and had enough time and energy to thoroughly prepare. During our practices, we continued to use the method that had served Fanny well: alternating breaks with extensive training, balancing work and relaxation.

In March 2008, Fanny and Kathy both took the USNCO local exam, a preliminary exam used to select individuals to participate in the national exam. Fanny knew that each school could only send one student to the national exam, so if both of them received a qualifying score, only one of them would be able to advance—whichever had the higher score. Since she had already become a national finalist the previous year, Fanny deliberately answered fewer questions correctly than would qualify her to move on, ensuring that Kathy would attend the national exam if her score was high enough. When we asked Fanny about this, she replied, "We're a team, and Kathy needed this more than I did, so of course I would support her."

Thanks to Fanny's sacrifice, Kathy became a national finalist in the USNCO for the first time. In the following years, Kathy continued to participate in the USNCO and became a three-time national finalist.

The comprehensive critical reading skills that Kathy trained in middle school similarly proved to be invaluable. Combined with her personal ability and natural affinity for languages, Kathy performed very well in her tenth grade WordMasters competition, placing as one of the fifteen highest scorers in the nation in 2008, an achievement reported in *the Journal News* and other newspapers. In 2009 and 2010, Kathy continued to receive the highest honors in her division of the WordMasters competition and was again recognized by newspapers for these accomplishments.

In June 2008, Kathy received a congratulatory letter from the Columbia University Science Honors Program coordinator, Professor Allan S. Blaer. He commended her for being one of a handful of students, selected from nearly two thousand applicants, admitted to this prestigious program. Again, John drove to Columbia University and back every weekend so she could participate in this program.

Kathy at the Science Honors Program

While following Fanny's path, Kathy also used her unique talents and interests to open new doors and explore other possibilities. Twice, in 2008 and 2009, she was elected captain of the Pearl River High School Academic Team and led the team when they participated in the TV game show *The Challenge*.

She Is Not a Prodigy

Taking honors chemistry in ninth grade gave Kathy an additional opportunity to unleash her potential. In 2009 and 2010, she again became a national finalist in the U.S. National Chemistry Olympiad (USNCO), only the second person in the New York metropolitan area to have received this honor three times.

Kathy's success gained the media's attention. On April 29, 2010, *The Journal News* journalist Alex Taylor interviewed Kathy about her achievements. The newspaper devoted a whole page to cover this article, entitled "Chemistry Whiz Makes it to Nationals." After this report was published, Kathy received many congratulatory letters and cards from various people in the community.

During the interview, she thanked her parents for always encouraging her and her sister to explore and develop their interests in the sciences and other areas. Her chemistry teacher, Mrs. M, commented, "I always thought Fanny would be a hard act to follow. But Kathy is more than her own person in and out of the classroom."

Despite their successes, we never thought that our daughters were prodigies.

A vivid rebuttal of this idea occurred when Kathy tried to qualify for the American Invitational Mathematical Exam (AIME). Three times, she tried, and three times, she failed. Since Fanny had advanced to the AIME, this had become a natural target for Kathy. In tenth grade, when she took the AMC 10, her score was just barely short of qualifying; but we had not seriously prepared her for the exam, so we didn't think too much of it. In eleventh grade, though, we put a genuine effort into this endeavor because it was her last chance to qualify before she had to apply to colleges. If she could advance to the AIME, it would certainly strengthen her application, so John spent three weeks training her during the summer. For the first time, John told me that he was not confident that she would succeed.

I felt very strange. Kathy had done even better than Fanny had in the Math League competitions, so it didn't make sense that she couldn't at least qualify. John had always been confident in himself and the children, but this time, he wasn't. Why?

He explained to me, "Kathy did better than Fanny in the Math League because we learned from Fanny's mistakes, and Fanny also set a standard for Kathy to reach. However, Kathy's actual math ability is not as strong as Fanny's."

For many years, we had tried to promote Kathy's strengths to cover up this shortcoming, building an image that she would always succeed in her endeavors. This time, though, it seemed as if her weakness would be exposed. John knew that this would be an uphill battle, but they had no choice but to try their best.

Despite their efforts, Kathy failed again. During twelfth grade, Kathy tried for a third and final time and still was unable to qualify.

Generally speaking, becoming a national finalist in the USNCO is more difficult than qualifying for the AIME, but Kathy's three successes in chemistry were mirrored by her three failures in math. This was a clear example of why we needed to educate our children according to their own natural talents and abilities.

Joy in Writing

Since Kathy favored the humanities, we encouraged her to participate in more clubs and activities that reflected this interest, especially because she enjoyed debate so much and was a good listener. During lunch at school, she always engaged her friends in heated discussions about various controversial issues. For a more formal experience, she participated in Model UN and Mock Trial; each time she came back, she would talk for hours, entertaining us with stories about her experiences.

During debates, she always thought quickly and spoke with a ready wit and sharp tongue, particularly delighting in seeking out and attacking her opponent's weak arguments. Because of her skill in articulating her points clearly, all of her friends agreed that she would be a good candidate for a career in law.

Although it is good to have strong oratory skills, it is also necessary to be able to write well. We felt that most Chinese-American children turned too quickly to science and thus did not pay as much attention to societal issues. As a result, many Chinese-Americans remain unfamiliar with their own rights and legal power. In many instances, if they are treated unfairly, they do nothing because they are unaccustomed to using the law to defend themselves. In becoming a lawyer, Kathy would be able to bring awareness and knowledge of the legal system to defend these people; it was definitely something worth pursuing.

In order to practice and improve her writing skills, Kathy joined the school newspaper club and entered several essay-writing competitions. In December 2007, she participated in the New York Civil Liberties Union Essay Contest and was second place in the region. Currently, she is an editor on the editorial board of *The Harvard Crimson*, the university's undergraduate newspaper.

Kathy, editor of the Harvard Crimson

In February 2010, she began drafting an editorial piece entitled "Nuclear Power Must Go On," which she finished in early March. A few days after submitting her proposal for the article, a gigantic earthquake struck Japan on March 11, the fifth strongest earthquake in recent history. That earthquake caused a tsunami that washed away many villages, leaving thousands of people missing or declared dead. The damage was tremendous and devastating, but the most horrifying consequence was the massive nuclear meltdown caused by the tsunami.

As a result of this nuclear crisis, widely considered even worse than Chernobyl, the entire world began reconsidering the use of nuclear energy. On March 25, 2011, *The Harvard Crimson* published Kathy's article, attracting the attention of several different organizations and prompting them to invite her to participate in various discussions and debates surrounding the issue. Her story had coincidentally been written at the perfect time.

Living in Fanny's Shadow

For many years, Kathy had grown up in Fanny's shadow, which played a dual role in Kathy's life. On the one hand, it guided Kathy in moving forward, encouraging her to catch up to and surpass her sister. Since Fanny had been accepted to so many elite colleges, this encouraged Kathy to set similar goals to try to surpass her. However, Fanny's shadow had its negative effects too. Due to Fanny's outstanding performance, teachers and students all appreciated and remembered Fanny's achievements, setting a high bar for Kathy. This caused tremendous stress for Kathy, who constantly worried about whether she could do as well as her sister.

In addition, due to Fanny's shadow, Kathy was often ignored, forgotten, or mistaken for her sister. For example, when teachers talked about Kathy, they often referred to her as "Fanny's little sister." One time, in class, the teacher even addressed Kathy as "Fanny." This caused Kathy great sadness and frustration. More than once, Kathy joked, "Mr. Y always talks about Fanny like a goddess!"

In actuality, Fanny and Kathy are two completely independent individuals with their own distinctive characters and personalities. Fanny is quiet and a perfectionist, always chasing her ideals, an introvert with strong romantic tendencies. Kathy, however, is more of an extrovert, acting with great passion and making quick decisions with great insight. In addition, she enjoys social activities and being with groups of friends and other people. Sometimes we jokingly referred to her as the "cowgirl." In her interactions with others, she can quickly read the environment and grasp the subtle details of people and conversation; in this regard, Kathy's skills surpassed Fanny's.

Kathy with Governor Randell (PA)

Never Stop Playing

During the most stressful time of twelfth grade, Kathy was busy working on college applications when one of her friends invited her to a sleepover party. That day, when Kathy came home, she had tears in her eyes and announced that she did not want to attend the party. We immediately realized that this was not really the case. As the application deadlines approached, Kathy had not yet satisfactorily finished her college application essays, and she was very worried about what to do. On the other hand, though, she really wanted to go to the party; so she faced a dilemma, torn between enjoying time with friends and her greater responsibilities. When we decided to let her go, she looked at her father in disbelief.

"Yes," we affirmed, "you can go, but there's one condition. You must be back by eleven, have a good night's sleep, and be able to resume your normal schedule the next day."

"No problem!" she replied happily.

Children need friends in their lives, and such parties are important sources of bonding time. In most situations, we allowed our children to attend sleepover parties and other events, but our primary concern has always been their safety. I remember one time when one of her friends held her birthday party at a hotel. To be honest, I did not understand why the parents would choose to host a sleepover party in such a complicated environment. Since I was concerned, Kathy tried to assuage my doubts by explaining, "Having a party at a hotel is pretty normal. Other kids do it too."

However, another girl's mother called me to voice her concerns as well. Even though she had been raised in America, she also felt uneasy about this party. After discussing the situation over the phone, we came to the same decision, to allow our children to go to the party, but not sleep over.

A similar situation also happened once to Fanny. She had become friends with a girl in her Girl Scout camp and afterward, the girl invited Fanny to a sleepover party. Since we did not know the other girl's family very well, Fanny attended the party for the celebration, but did not sleep over.

Replicating Success

In the summer of 2009, Kathy began working on her college applications.

At the end of October that year, she submitted her Early Action application to Yale University.

The following weeks seemed to be the most nerve-racking, intolerable days of her life. She worried, day and night, about whether she would be accepted by Yale. Any e-mail, regular mail, or mention of Yale would make her jump. She eagerly tore open any letter with the Yale crest and checked for updates to her application every day; an air of anxiety followed her everywhere she went.

From time to time, John would try to talk to her to calm her and soothe her apprehensions. I also paid great attention to her, because I was afraid she would do something rash or impulsive. However, John was very confident in her application results.

On December 15, 2009, Kathy logged into her account on the Yale University Web site. The bulldog barked at us once more, "Woof, woof!" A familiar banner appeared: "Welcome to Yale!" Kathy had been admitted to Yale! Finally, she could breathe freely and smile once more.

Since Kathy was accepted to Yale under the Early Action program, she considered applying only to Harvard during the regular application cycle. I also agreed with this idea, but John suggested sending out all the applications that she had prepared to confirm that our method of educating and raising our children was correct. In the end, Kathy sent additional applications to Harvard, Princeton, Columbia, and Brown—four Ivy League colleges. In May 2010, she received offers of admission to all of them.

Kathy's success once again lent credibility to our way of educating our children, demonstrating that we were working in the right direction and that our methods were repeatable.

Fanny and Kathy with their parents at Harvard

The next year, another girl who received and followed our long-term consulting and planning advice was accepted by several notable universities and ultimately decided to attend Wellesley College. Distinguished alumni of Wellesley include famous names such as the first female secretary of state, Madeleine Albright, and the current secretary of state, Hillary Clinton. This girl's success further vindicated our model and its applicability.

One Step Further

With Fanny's experiences to guide her, Kathy's process of applying for college was much smoother. As a result, after finishing her college applications, Kathy still had energy to spare. Noticing this, John asked her, "Kathy, what do you think about applying for some scholarships now?"

Without any hesitation, she answered, "Yes! Let's do it!"

There are many types of scholarships available, but most of them require an essay or two as an important part of the application. However, writing was not a problem for Kathy at all; she actually enjoyed it.

When she was applying for scholarships, she attacked the task with great enthusiasm. The application for the Gates Millennium Scholar Program required writing seven full-length essays, but Kathy had no problem with this daunting task. Before starting, she discussed each essay with her father and then wrote several drafts, editing them again and again, sometimes even working until midnight. Yet through this all, she remained energetic and in high spirits.

In these seven essays, she described every aspect of her life: her joys and sorrows, triumphs and downfalls, and her dreams and efforts in pursuing them. Her hard work eventually paid off when she became a Gates Millennium Scholar.

On May 12, the largest Chinese newspaper in North America, the *World Journal*, reported that Kathy had received the Ronald McDonald House Charities (RMHC) scholarship. According to their article, "Kathy hails from upstate New York and, this fall, will be attending Harvard University [. . .] at the awards ceremony for the RMHC scholarship, she talked with us frankly about her experiences growing up in a predominantly white community and how she learned to accept and deal with the challenges she faced there."

The reporter also quoted my own sentiments. "As parents, we paid more attention to the development of our children's emotional quotient by encouraging them to give back to the community. It is important to for them to learn social skills and recognize that they have an obligation to help others. We believe this takes precedence over academic scores."

Kathy, a McDonalds Scholarship Winner

That same day, another major Chinese newspaper picked up the news. "Kathy Wang comes from a quiet town, Pearl River, in upstate New York. Do not look down upon this girl—her resume is impressive, full of awards and accomplishments: she has become a U.S. National Chemistry Olympiad National Finalist three times, worked with the Obama Presidential Campaign headquarters as a campaign intern, organized a student volunteer group [. . .] Even when visiting China, her efforts did not cease. There, she initiated and organized an information exchange program with Chinese students as well."

In June 2010, Kathy graduated from Pearl River High School as the class valedictorian and received departmental awards in math, physics, history, and Spanish, along with many scholarships including the National Merit Scholarship, Robert C. Bryd Honors Scholarship, Charles Cooper Award, Marilyn Reiner Memorial Scholarship, Superintendents Scholarship, PFIZER 2010 Science Education Award,

ELK Scholarship, Rotary Scholarship, New York State Education Department 2010 Scholarship for Academic Excellence, Pearl River Teachers' Association Scholarship, Pearl River High School PTA Scholarships, and Junior League of Westchester-on-Hudson. She approached the podium to receive her diploma, and the long list of honors they read as she walked across the stage took my breath away.

Kathy's valedictorian speech

CHAPTER 15

Conclusion

Throughout this book, we have repeatedly referred to the best of both Chinese and U.S. cultures. We have summarized their main aspects here:

- Chinese education emphasizes strict practice and hard work. It demands persistence and perfection, believing that hard work will produce successful results.
- The U.S. educational system focuses more on encouraging children and emphasizing their creativity, leadership, and team spirit. It trains children to become more considerate, contributing members of society.

In practice, we have tried to guide our children to develop a proper attitude toward both academics and social activities. When working on a project, they needed to really focus on it and approach it in a creative manner, infusing their own character and spirit inside. During the process, we asked them to stay open-minded, to look for and pursue new opportunities. We hoped that with every endeavor they undertook, they could reach a deeper understanding and view things from a broader perspective.

Before we conducted a project or set a target, we would first do a thorough evaluation of our children's abilities. We used their strengths to assist them in making the first breakthrough, which established their confidence and stimulated their self-motivation to drive onward. Each time they reached a target, we would sit together with them to discuss their experiences and the lessons they had learned. Again, we would review their capabilities and, with these in mind, help them establish the next reachable target, allowing them to move forward one step at a time.

In order to provide our children with a balanced development, we employed different policies at different ages. When they were very young, we spent a lot of time playing with them, building our relationships and a bond of mutual trust. We also watched them closely to understand their personalities and to help them establish a positive perspective of the world.

During their elementary school years, we emphasized the development of their own interests, encouraging them to spend time with others, make more friends, and become aware of the natural world. Through social activities and interactions with the environment, we started their learning processes.

When they entered middle school, we assisted them in discovering their potentials and exploring their future goals and interests. We helped them break through barriers and establish a solid foundation, building their confidence and self-motivation for the tough high school years ahead.

Once they began high school, we fully unleashed their potential, promoting their strengths and downplaying their weaknesses. We worked together with them to craft plans that fit their personalities, then carefully carried out these plans to let them shine.

Looking back on our journey in parenting Fanny and Kathy, we attribute their successes to the combination of Chinese and American educational philosophies. Our daughters' achievements are the products of two cultures meeting and integrating, and this experience has led us to more clearly realize the advantages of combining both in our parenting strategy.

Historically, this country has flourished on the shoulders and efforts of generations of immigrants. This tradition has allowed for the integration of new ideas, values, and interests into one society, building America into the world's most powerful nation. In integrating multiple cultures, there will be mutual misunderstandings and a certain resistance as each culture tries to maintain its own traditions. However, if we want to enjoy the benefits of an integrated, consolidated society, we should never give up our pursuit of the truth or our attempts to rectify these misunderstandings. People who try to take advantage of these misunderstandings, exaggerating them into prejudices for their own personal gains, should not be considered representative of any side.

During the process of integrating these two cultures in order to raise our children, our practices raised doubts from both American and Chinese perspectives. We frequently struggled with indecision, asking ourselves, "If this is the best way to educate our children, why are so many people against it?"

We published this book in the hopes that it can encourage more discussion, not only about parenting, but also about the meeting of very different cultures. Our story, we hope, offers a different perspective on how to educate children in a healthy environment, a strategy that draws inspiration from the diverse society we live in.

Methods for SAT Preparation

During our children's training, we developed various methods to help Fanny and Kathy prepare for their SAT exams. These methods worked very well for both of them, and here, we introduce them to our readers for their reference.

How to Practice the SAT Essay

Good essay-writing skills will benefit a student in many ways, not just on the SAT test. In the future, in order to gain access to more resources, they will always need to be able to express their ideas convincingly and concisely in written form. In this section, we will focus on how to write an effective essay for the SAT.

During the SAT Reasoning Test, students are required to write a two-page essay in twenty-five minutes. For many students, this is a difficult task. In twenty-five minutes, they need to brainstorm, outline, and then actually write the essay. Our method is to establish a fixed format that can be used for all essays and repeatedly practice writing essays with this structure.

The principle behind this is simple: students only need to write one essay during the actual test. Rather than spending time and energy devising different structures, repeatedly practicing with one structure is easier and far more efficient. Once students become accustomed to using this structure, they will save time during the test because their essay format will already be decided.

The type of structure depends on each individual student and what he or she is most comfortable with. Typically, an essay is divided into four or five paragraphs, and we have provided the structure we used as a reference:

- Start the first paragraph with a clear, strong statement of your argument. There is no correct answer to a typical SAT essay prompt, but a high-scoring essay usually chooses to either agree or disagree with the topic. Trying to write an essay to support both sides is more difficult. We have seen some excellent essays that addressed both perspectives and provided effective, balanced arguments, but these are extremely rare. Also, try to use some advanced vocabulary to impress the readers.

- For the next two or three paragraphs, use historical events, personal experiences, or literary examples to provide support for the stance in the first paragraph. Only utilize the portions of the stories that are directly relevant to the argument. Analyze the story to support the claim, but do not summarize the story or go off topic.

- In the last paragraph, summarize the examples and emphasize how they support the argument. Recall the claim that was made in the first paragraph, then try to end on an idealistic or philosophical level, raising the argument to a higher intellectual platform.

During practice, if there are several areas that need improvement, focus on fixing one at a time. For example, if the opening is not strong, the closing is confusing, and the argument drifts off topic, do not attempt to fix all three problems at once. Instead, first take a few days just to practice staying on topic, then establish a method to create a strong opening, and finally concentrate on writing an effective conclusion. This is much easier than attacking all three at the same time. For most students, editing the essay and improving their writing skills are painful processes. If parents expect perfection immediately, the experience will be much more difficult. Instead, they should work with their children to move forward strategically, step-by-step. Of course, every child is different; so in some cases, a different approach can be more worthwhile.

From our experience, a longer essay typically scores higher. During our children's practice, we asked them to write essays that were at least one and a half pages long; the ideal essay would leave only two or three lines blank on the second page.

How to Prepare for the SAT Subject Tests

There are several good practice books for the SAT subject tests from publishers, including the College Board, the Princeton Review, Kaplan, and Barron's. Because the College Board organizes and administers the SAT tests, the practice problems from their books are typically most similar to the problems on the actual tests. The next closest are the Princeton Review and Kaplan. The problems in Barron's are usually a little more difficult than those on the real test, but since Barron's books often cover the review material in more detail, there is still an advantage in purchasing them.

Whenever we did diagnostic or evaluative tests, we used a College Board practice exam to measure our children's progress. Before each practice test, we removed or covered the answer key and explanations. While many parents have confidence in their children, most students cannot resist taking a peek during the test. Often, they may be worried about disappointing their parents with lower-than-expected scores. If parents have time, they should watch their children during the practice exams, especially when the student takes a College Board test, since these are important for monitoring progress. For parents that work during the day, their children can take the tests in the evening and digest the problems the next day.

After calculating their scores, we recorded the results and saved their answer sheets in case we needed them for future reference. The detailed steps we asked our kids to follow are highlighted below:

- Step 1: Do a diagnostic exam using a practice test from the College Board. During this test, ask the student to mark all the questions that he or she is unsure of. This is a very important step in the process because it identifies problems that need to be reviewed. After the test, determine if there is any material that the student has not learned yet. If there is, the student needs to study this material independently. Usually, reviewing the material covered in the books from the publishers mentioned above is enough to make up for any gaps in knowledge. For the chapters that a student is unfamiliar with, he or she should do the relevant practice problems from all the review books.

- Step 2: Digest the material thoroughly. This involves fixing all the problems on the diagnostic test. For each question, it is necessary to not only know the right answer but also understand why the answer is correct. The Princeton Review, Kaplan, and Barron's books offer detailed explanations for each answer; and it is always important for students to read these explanations to ensure they really understand the underlying concepts.
- Step 3: Do a Princeton Review practice exam and mark any answers that were guessed. After this test, repeat step two to completely digest the incorrectly answered and guessed questions.
- Step 4: Do a few, or all, of the Kaplan practice exams and again mark any answers that were guessed, then repeat step 2. If there is time, also do one or two practices from Barron's and repeat step 2.
- Step 5: Do one more, or all of, the Princeton Review practice exams and repeat step 2. Now, compare these results with those of step 3 to see the extent of progress.
- Step 6: Do another College Board practice exam with the same procedure described above. Compare with the results from step 1. Any progress here can be considered the actual progress made from beginning to end.

After this process, their scores should show significant improvement of about 50-100 points. If there is no significant progress, this may be due to several reasons.

First, verify that the digestion process was complete. To do this, parents can sit with their children and ask them to answer the questions that they had previously done wrong or guessed on, to see how many of these questions they can now answer correctly. If more than 85 percent of the previous problems can be answered correctly, this means that the digestion process has been completed satisfactorily. After our children did multiple practice exams, they always fixed their problems at a rate of at least 95 percent.

If the digestion process is okay, this means that during the practices, the students may not have marked the questions that they guessed on, missing many problems. Another possibility is that the students may have seen the answer key during the practice test. Parents can check this by making their children repeat any test and then comparing the answer sheets from the same test. If their children answer questions correctly the first time and incorrectly the second time, and this happens more than once, then the process is compromised and the children must repeat all the steps again.

How to Prepare for the SAT Reasoning Test

There are many practice books available on the market for the SAT Reasoning Test. The four that we used most often offer a total of thirty-four full-length practice exams: *11 Practice Tests for the SAT & PSAT* (the Princeton Review), *12 Practice Tests for the SAT* (Kaplan), *How to Prepare for the SAT* (Barron's), and *The Official Study Guide for the New SAT* (College Board).

In addition to these books, these publishers also provide review books for each individual subject of the SAT: critical reading, math, and writing. Examples of such books include *Reading and Writing Workout for the New SAT* (the Princeton Review), *Kaplan SAT Verbal Workbook* (Kaplan), *Kaplan New SAT Critical Reading Workbook* (Kaplan), *Kaplan New SAT Math Workbook* (Kaplan), *Grammar Workbook for SAT, ACT . . . and More* (Barron's), *Barron's Critical Reading Workbook for the SAT* (Barron's), and *Barron's Writing Workbook for the SAT* (Barron's).

If students have sufficient time, they can first start with the review books from one publisher or in one subject; they do not have to finish all of them. As we mentioned above, the College Board's practice problems are closest to the actual test's, followed by the Princeton Review, Kaplan, and Barron's. Although the College Board's problems are most similar to those on the real tests, its practice books only offer a basic answer key without detailed explanations of the correct answers. This makes it difficult for students to digest the material by themselves. Therefore, the College Board exams are mainly used as a benchmark to monitor progress, while the Princeton Review and Kaplan practice tests are used for training.

Creating a practice schedule is also a strategic process. Since the SAT consists of three sections—critical reading, math, and writing—and students can take the test two or three times, the process of preparing for the SAT can be handled in different ways to maximize the score. One method is to simply prepare for all three sections at the same time. However, if a student has difficulty doing this, he or she can focus on two sections first and concentrate on the third section during the next round of testing. Each student is different, and parents should make this decision according to their children's capabilities.

Detailed Practicing Process

When beginning practice for the SAT, always start with a diagnostic exam. For each practice exam, record the results and scores and save the answer sheets. On the answer sheets, mark the date, incorrect answers, and scores of each section. This provides a source of information for future comparison and reference. While preparing our children for the SAT, we used the following schedule:

> *Day1*: In the morning, do a full-length College Board SAT practice exam. This is a diagnostic test, so strictly follow the time restrictions for each section. Students should mark down all the questions that they guessed on or are unsure of while taking the test.
>
> In the afternoon, students should take a good break. After that, they should begin digesting the problems that were answered incorrectly. Since the College Board does not offer a detailed answer key, questions that students cannot solve independently can be set aside temporarily. During the digestion process, students should take a ten- to fifteen-minute break every hour, which will improve the efficiency of their work.
>
> In the evening, continue digesting the problems. In order to have the energy to work the next day, students should not work past 11:00 PM. Since the diagnostic test includes all three sections, there may be a lot of questions to digest, and students may not finish all of them by the

end of the first day. However, this should not be a source of concern and can be postponed if they cannot finish.

Day 2: In the morning, do two subjects from a practice test from the Princeton Review, such as critical reading and math. Since this method of preparation involves very intensive training methods, doing three subjects a day is too much for most students and would decrease their efficiency.

In the afternoon, take a good break and then start the digestion process. In the evening, continue the digestion process for any problems that were not reviewed in the afternoon. Since this book offers detailed explanations for all of the questions, students should try to solve every problem by themselves.

If they finish digesting all the problems, they should take a break, even if there is plenty of time left in the day. In the beginning, most students will not have too much time to take a break; but after a few practices and improvement, they will have more time to rest.

Days 3 and 4: Each day, do two subjects from practice tests in the Kaplan book. If the student is preparing for all three sections of the exam, rotate which subjects are tested accordingly; otherwise, continue to work on the two subjects the student is focusing on.

Similar to Day 2, in the afternoon, first take a good break and then try to digest every problem. It is normal for the student's score to not change or even drop because typically, Kaplan tests are harder than the Princeton Review's, and the Princeton Review's problems are harder than those of the College Board.

Day 5: Do another Princeton Review exam in the same subjects as on Day 2. Compare these results with those from Day 2 to look for signs of progress. As always, continue the digestion process for any incorrectly answered questions.

Day 6: Do another College Board exam to check for progress. Again, only do two subjects. Digest any wrong answers after completing the test and compare the scores with those from Day 1 to see if any progress has been made in those specific subjects.

After the sixth day, students will have finished a complete cycle and can continue from day two in a similar procedure, starting again with one the Princeton Review exam, two or three Kaplan exams, one or two Princeton Review exams, and finally finishing with another College Board exam to measure their progress. This structure places the College Board and the Princeton Review exams at the beginning and at the end of each cycle to allow students to monitor their improvement most accurately.

Except for the diagnostic exam on Day 1, we normally do not add time constraints to the practice tests so the students can think more carefully without time pressure; speed will come with practice, and accuracy is more important. However, this also depends on each individual student; if he or she has serious time management problems, it may be beneficial to add time limits during the training. Since this is only practice, though, allotting each section a little extra time is fine. Before the real test, though, it is necessary to conduct a few formal practice tests following the time constraints so the students can familiarize themselves with the actual testing conditions.

In our experience, after practicing the same subject four to six times, there should be noticeable progress. After three cycles of training per subject, scores are typically raised by 50-100 points. Of course, this progress is relative; as a student's score rises, their improvement increases in smaller increments.

Additional Tips:

As with the SAT subject tests, before each practice test, remove or cover the answer keys and explanations. If no significant progress is made after two cycles of practice, parents should use the previous answer sheets to check the efficiency of the digestion process. If the students can answer more than 85 percent of previously wrong and guessed questions correctly, remind them to mark any problems they are unsure of during the test.

If students make tremendous progress too rapidly—most students will hit a plateau at the beginning and improve by ten or twenty points every couple of exams before hitting another plateau—parents should sit by them during a practice session to ensure that the test is being taken properly.

Specific Tips for the Writing Sections:

English is like any other language and contains certain rules and exceptions. Often, there is no choice but to memorize and become familiar with these. After our children finished a practice test, if they made a mistake related to a fixed structure, idiom, or specific rule, we suggested that they record the correction and review all of them before taking another practice test. This method has proved effective for other students as well.

Our children normally spent three to five weeks preparing for the SAT over the summer after tenth grade, and another week during winter break in eleventh grade, before taking the test for the first time the following spring. If they needed to take the test again, they prepared over the summer after eleventh grade and took the exam in October. The evening before the test, we always asked them to take a complete break and do absolutely nothing so that they could do their best the next day.